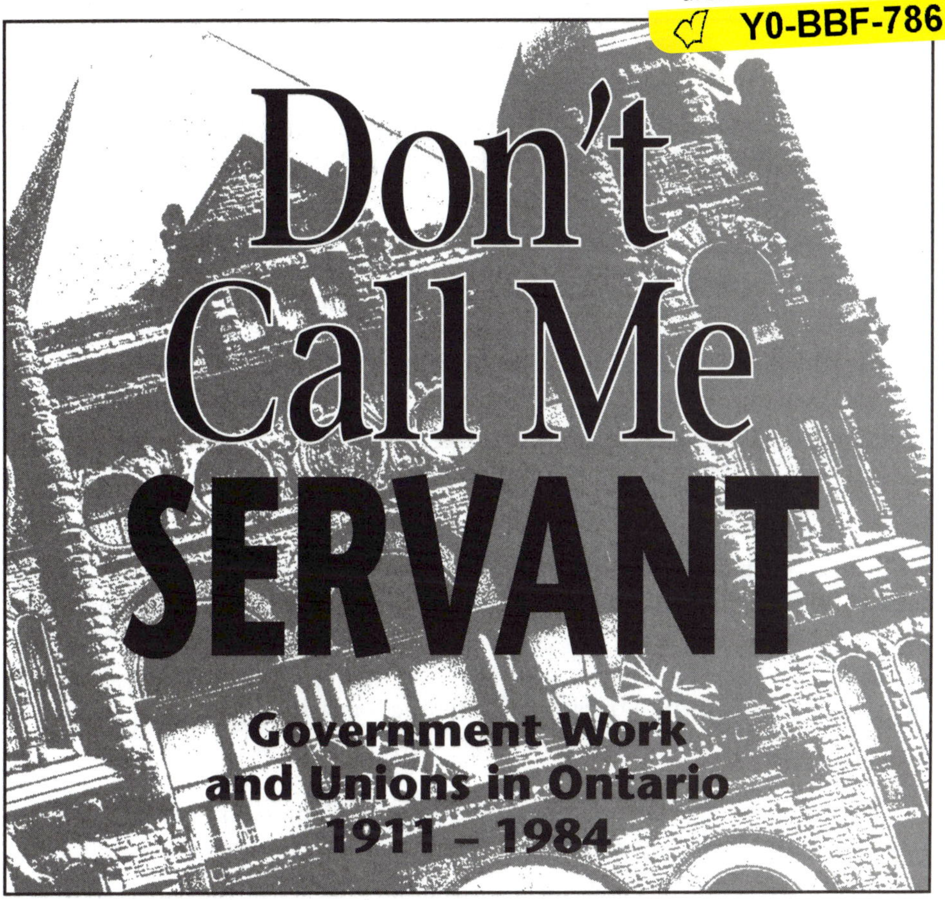

Don't Call Me SERVANT

Government Work and Unions in Ontario 1911 – 1984

WAYNE ROBERTS

Ontario Public Service Employees Union
Syndicat des employé-e-s de la fonction publique de l'Ontario

Copyright © 1994 Ontario Public Service Employees Union, 100 Lesmill Road, North York, Onario M3B 3P8

Copyright under the Berne Convention. All rights reserved. No part of this book may be used or reproduced in any manner whatsoever without permission of the Ontario Public Service Employees Union, except in the case of brief quotations embodied in critical articles and reviews.

Canadian Cataloguing in Publication Data

Roberts, Wayne, 1944 –
    Don't call me servant: government work and unions in Ontario 1911–1984

Includes bibliographical references and index.
ISBN 0-921089-30-9

1. Ontario Public Service Employees Union - History.
2. Trade unions - Government employees - Ontario - History.
I. Ontario Public Service Employees Union. II. Title.

HD8005.2.C23067 1994   331.88′11354713   C94-931080-8

Design and Typography: Steve Daynes
Set in 12 point Janson text.

Printed and bound by union labour in Ontario, Canada.

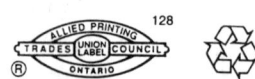

Contents

Chapter 1: Loyal She Remains   1

Women in the Civil Service: One in ten   3
Public Service by appointment   5
To serve, apolitically   7
A smoothly functioning machine   8
Tory paternalism   9
A customary sense of fairness   11
CSAO: Social togetherness   12
Whitleyism: The talkshop   16
"Proper supervision and control"   16
Pensions: Treating them too kindly   20
Job classifications as personnel control   21
Rule of thumb   23
In preference to excellence   27
CSAO incorporates   28
Just glad to have a job   30
Hepburn at the helm   32

Chapter 2: "Modern, Loyal, Efficient"   35

Wishful thinking   38
Simply doing what you're told   41
The cold war against the CSAO   44
The law in Killaloe   47
My door is always open   50
The best years of their lives   53
Oh happy days   58
The only difference is what we're paid   62
From the barber's chair   64
"Bargaining, not begging"   68
Trouble at the Don   73

Chapter 3: Accidental Unionism   78

    Union two-step   81
    Bowen in charge   83
    Outside agitation   87
    Little or nothing   90
    Conciliation   93
    Quiet revolution   96
    Caatacomb   100
    More for the mind   103
    The urge to regionalize   105
    Big government   106
    A thousand points of bureaucracy: the COGP   107
    Farewell to reform   112
    Death of a servant   116
    The Purple People Eater   120
    Faulty pillars   125
    A management bill of rights   130
    Keeping up with Jones   134
    Becoming politicized   137
    Four Horsemen of the Apocalypse   141

Chapter 4: Raging Bull   146

    Triumph of the will   148
    "Free the Servants"   152
    Close but no cigar   158
    Labour unrest   160
    The year of bargaining dangerously   165
    A new constitution   170
    Jake and the Kid   173
    Going the extra mile   177
    Bang bang Maxwell's silver hammer   181
    One out of three ain't bad   187
    Beep Beep   192

Organizing: hospitals and ambulance services	194
Good-time Charlie	199

Chapter 5: Desperately Seeking Union — 201

Playing post office	204
Let it bleed	208
Jailhouse rock	212
Union password	218
Fighting wage controls	220
Soul-searching	223
Taming of the screws	228
Tree hugger	232
Workers for social responsibility	235
Women's rights: Don't call me Lady	238
A generation of women activists	242
The Provincial Women's Committee	247
Sex in the office	251
Love's labour lost	256
CAAT on a hot tin roof	263

Preface

by Fred Upshaw
President, Ontario Public Service Employees Union

From the office or shop floor to the office of the president, a union's business never stops. Especially in hard times, employers act as though higher productivity and cost savings must be achieved at the expense of employee rights. The unions that represent those employees must work constantly to defend and extend their rights.

As a result, union members, activists, leaders and staff rarely have time to reflect on their history: the successes, the failures and the lessons to be gained from them. Too often, today's big and small events are consigned to the deep recesses of memory. As a result, unions can sometimes become complacent about victories they have won. The members of today take the gains of yesterday for granted.

This book goes a long way to correcting that problem. Here you will find stories and recollections of the early years of the Civil Service Association of Ontario. You will read how an association formed for self-help and social purposes was transformed into one of the largest and strongest unions in Ontario, slowly at first, and then with increasing speed.

Along the way, you will meet some of the people who made OPSEU what it is today: working women and men who believed in helping one another and in creating a better world, for themselves, for their children and, by example, for others. Without them, without their dedication, hard work and determination to struggle for better wages and working conditions, public sector workers in Ontario would be much worse off today.

This book is a tribute to those thousands of members. Their growth into unionism can be summed up in the words one of them spoke in 1974, as the CSAO was becoming OPSEU. I may be a civil servant, said Jim Fuller, but "I am seldom civil and I am a servant to no man."

Introduction

by Frank Rooney

History is full of irony and Ontario has certainly had its share. In 1993, a New Democratic Party government passed the most Draconian labour law in the province's history, the Social Contract Act. Barely six months later, the same government repealed the Crown Employees Collective Bargaining Act (CECBA) – which had been, until the Social Contract, the country's worst piece of labour legislation.

The NDP government was elected with massive support from workers, not least from members of the Ontario Public Service Employees Union. Finance minister Floyd Laughren and Economic Development minister Frances Lankin, members of the inner cabinet, were former OPSEU members, as was government house leader Brian Charlton. Lankin was a former OPSEU staffer. But without a hint of irony, Lankin rose in the legislature December 14, 1993 to recall her days as a jail guard, union activist and negotiator. Lankin echoed the union's rallying cry of almost two decades earlier, saying that the new law, which gave provincial public servants the right to strike, would "free the servants."

These were the same servants who were suffering, together with the rest of the public sector, a three-year wage freeze and important cuts in the level of services delivered to the people of Ontario.

In this book, Wayne Roberts shows that these contradictory actions are rooted in a basic feature of Ontario public life: the paternalism of a government convinced that it alone knows what is best for the province and for its own employees. Perhaps paternalism and arrogance are inevitable characteristics of governments, or at least of majority governments. They are, after all, elected to make decisions for the whole of society. But in old Tory Ontario, paternalism was a defining characteristic of government for a century.

Some of the worst practices withered away in the 1970s, after the explosion of government, the triumph of "scientific management" and massive reorganizations. No longer could problems be solved largely by personal appeals to deputy ministers. Rules and regulations reigned supreme. But the practical changes did not lead to a real change in attitude. The 1972 Crown Employees Collective Bargaining Act listed 18 non-negotiable management rights. Two decades later, the government said the social contract was to "encourage negotiations." In fact, the encouragement was at gunpoint.

CECBA was in many ways unsuccessful in assuring management's rights. Denying union members the right to strike or to bargain over issues like pensions, staffing and training did not dampen their energy or desire to see justice done: it simply re-routed it, away from the normal labour relations channel of collective bargaining, into a continuing search for other ways and means to achieve the same ends. On occasion, arbitration of collective agreements was successful. More often, the energy of union members turned up in grievances, court challenges and public campaigns that have made OPSEU well-known, and in some respects envied.

But campaigns, lobbying, grievances and court challenges, however successful, have a key failing: they lack the economic clout to force the boss to do something. They rely too heavily on a third party: an arbitrator, a judge, politicians or public opinion. They are the tools of the powerless. That is why OPSEU waged a 21-year campaign for CECBA reform.

OPSEU's use of other methods to fight for change is one way the union was shaped by the actions of its employer. Wayne Roberts shows how this also happened to the Civil Service Association of Ontario in the 1950s as it began to adopt a more union-like stance, and how the transformation of the CSAO into OPSEU responded to the growth of government in the 1960s and its reorganization in the 1970s. The democratic processes that mark OPSEU to this day are, in large measure, a reaction to the hierarchy of the civil service. The fact that some of the most trivial decisions are reserved to the union president is a reflection of that hierarchy.

OPSEU both reflects and reacts to the reality of bargaining under CECBA. Its lobbying, brief-writing and legal strengths are matched by a corresponding weakness: It lacks experience in developing a strategic approach based on the ability to strike. Under CECBA, OPSEU rarely had to take responsibility for its bargaining stance. Put bluntly, no union activist in the public service ever had to convince a member to give up wages on a picket line in order to achieve a bargaining objective. Staff, activists and members most often did not have to make hard choices. The final decisions were left to arbitrators.

This too has changed. For with power, including the power to strike, comes responsibility. A union's responsibility is first of all to its members. The union must ensure that it does not ask members to strike over insignificant issues, that its goals are realistic and achievable. And a union has a responsibility to the public: to use its power to achieve a greater good.

Many OPSEU locals in the broader public sector have had and used the right to strike over the past quarter century. Their experience, and their growing role in the union, provides a base for developing a new approach.

The ability of all public sector workers to develop clear goals and work to achieve them will be put to the test in the years ahead. Since the 1950s, there has been a kind of consensus in Ontario about the role of government, social programs and the rights of individual workers and their unions. Now, spurred on by the private sector, the government is eager to redefine its role. In Ontario, the Social Contract Act is the first step in this redefinition. Other provincial governments are taking a more radical approach; the federal government is considering how it will change.

The permanent restructuring of government will play an important part in political and social life in the next decade. It is an issue that must be faced by unions like OPSEU that represent employees in the public sector. As government considers whether and how it should deliver services, it will be up to unions to respond. It will take all their tools – lobbying, campaigns, grievances, court battles and strikes – to do it.

We could describe the years up to the mid-1950s as the gestation period of public service unionism in Ontario and the period from the late-1950s to 1972 as its childhood, followed by adolescence. That history is well documented by Wayne Roberts. Now, with the reform of CECBA, the right to strike, and negotiability of all issues, public service unionism is becoming an adult. That history has not yet been written. It is still being lived.

And it would be irony indeed if the union that reached its adulthood in the year of the Social Contract used its new power to play a critical role in redefining the role of government in Ontario.

Frank Rooney is an OPSEU Communications Officer.

Acknowledgements

OPSEU is a hard union to write about. There are few great clashes or heroic moments, the normal drama and benchmarks of labour history. Nor is it a place to look for a subject of a biography for any series on Lives of the Saints. But there's a lot to learn about what made this union so open to new ways of doing things, so effective at bargaining, and such a force for general social improvement. More than one person can master.

Shea Hoffmitz, probably the best private eye in the archival research business, combed the Provincial Archives of Ontario and endless haystacks of legislative publications looking for needles about the public servants who made government work. Susan Meurer interviewed many union members from the '60s and '70s. About a hundred union staffers and activists gave generously of their time and memory to offer the kinds of reminiscences that make a union history come alive. A number of people gave me essays they'd written on parts of civil service and OPSEU history and allowed me to use their research: Pat Bird, Lykke de la Cour, Shirley McVittie, Virgery Vanier, James Simeon. Ron Adams at McMaster University gave me the all-but-completed draft of a Ph.D. thesis on CSAO history by John Bursey. David Hawkins helped me edit my first draft. I couldn't have asked for a better editor than Lorraine Fairley, who knows labour and Ontario history as well as grammar and style.

Although the union provided funding for research, the committee assigned to review the first draft – which included Executive Board members Jack Armstrong, Joseph Bénard, Terry Connolly, Bill Kuehnbaum and Ron Martin, and staff members Ivor Oram, John Ward and Frank Rooney – never wavered from its commitment to grant me full freedom to write an unvarnished history of the union. I also owe the union the privilege of having served as assistant to president James Clancy from 1985 to 1988, during which time I came to appreciate some of the complexities of its traditions and the way union developments give a glimpse of the upstairs-downstairs realities of government operations.

Wayne Roberts
November 1993

Chapter One

"Loyal She Remains"

Premier James Whitney was bicycling to work at Queen's Park one day, when a man caught up to him and gasped that the sheriff of Manitoulin Island had just died. The man wanted to know if he could take the sheriff's place. "It's fine by me," the premier said, "but you'll have to ask the undertaker."

Whitney, premier of Ontario from 1905 to 1914, led a government with only nine million dollars revenue a year, about three dollars for every citizen. Big government was out of the question. Every penny was counted, down to the $66.25 Whitney had for personal expenses in 1911. Thrift counted for more than grandiose visions of what government could do to extend services. "Ontario does not think I am a great man," Whitney was fond of saying, "but it does think I am honest."

Queen's Park, a pink castle resplendent in its spacious grounds, surveyed a bustling downtown. Church spires dominated the view to the east, immigrant slums and factories to the west. The legislative building was massive and imposing, a big step up from its frontier-era address on Front Street, crawling with pubs, dives and squatters. Liberal premier Oliver Mowat moved government headquarters to the outskirts of the city in 1893, to a site formerly occupied by a lunatic asylum. But politicians had no delusions of grandeur. "You know, Charlie," Mowat confided to his messenger boy, Charlie Fitch, "I'm worried about that building. We'll never fill it in a hundred years!"

No one expected much from a provincial government then. The Fathers of Confederation kept the revenue-rich items of government in Ottawa, and unloaded the trouble-prone issues onto the provinces. Thus, the provinces got health, education, and charity. No one dreamed that they would become the meat and potatoes of government. Nor did constitutional planners think through giving the provinces control over mines and forests. Until pulp and paper and nickel came out of the wilderness at the turn of the century, they could not have been foreseen as revenue bonanzas that would turn provinces into economic powerhouses.

There were a few exceptions to the limited role expected of the province. Whitney won the 1905 election by backing the mass movement in favour of public hydro. His government paid for roads and rail lines to the north, hoping to tap the wealth of what was called "New Ontario." That experience didn't bode well for government mega-projects. The area north of Temagami's forests and rock had been opened for settlement with a world-wide campaign boosting its claybelt as the richest soil for wheat outside the Ukraine. It was only saved from disaster by the chance discovery of silver. "New Ontario" had to do with the private sector harvesting nature's wealth, not the government seeding a just social order.

In 1911, when Ontario civil servants organized their first association, there was just enough work to keep one thousand people on payroll. Factory and school inspectors, asylum attendants and jail guards carried out the responsibilities governments took on to protect and serve the population. Clerks kept tabs on the host of licence fees that paid for these services.

Legislators didn't generate much work for support staff. They met 44 days a year, in late winter when seeding, ploughing and harvesting wouldn't be interrupted. No secretaries recorded their speeches in Hansard until 1948. They asked few questions – no more than 16 in 1910

– that required researchers to scurry after answers. They planned no major projects that required an army of policy analysts. The premier and his ministers wrote all their own letters by hand. Welfare was handled by volunteers who followed a simple rule – he who gives quickly, gives twice – that required few regulations or field staff. Hospitals had only recently become places where people went to stay alive, rather than to die, and they were funded by philanthropists.

Policies for dealing with civil servants had been laid down in the Public Service Act of 1878. Workers were classed in one of two groups: a "special division" for professionals, and an "ordinary division" for the rest. On paper, they were all expected to pass a civil service exam, but this was never put into practice. New employees had to be bonded in case they ran away with the fees they collected, and had to swear an oath against taking bribes.

Salaries and working conditions were set from on high, by the Lieutenant Governor, the Queen's representative. Nor was there formal job security since all appointments were "during pleasure." Salaries increased with years of service, and long-serving staff were guaranteed first crack at promotions. There was no pay for overtime. Holidays lasted three weeks. Ministers handled discipline, and could fine workers up to $20 for misbehaviour, without appeal. There was no retirement age: a pension worth one month's salary per year was granted to oldtimers let go for ill-health, and to the widows of career officials. Those were all the rules that were considered necessary from the 1870s until the 1920s.

Women in the Civil Service: One in ten

It seemed unnecessary to formulate a policy on women workers, even though, in 1893, a Miss Bengough and a Miss Cowper took up non-traditional jobs at Lands and Forests (today's Ministry of Natural Resources), and became the government's first female clerks. Glass ceilings were in place by 1895, when typewriters came in and women's nimble fingers were deemed ideal to operate them. Men were still needed as supervisors, of course, and to place their firm hand on official documents.

Victorian prudishness gave a slight edge to a few women professionals. Since the major job of factory inspectors was to check up on workplace toilets, considered a threat to public health and female modesty, the door was opened to women inspectors. Margaret Carlyle joined the inspection branch in 1895 at half the salary paid her male counterparts.

Some professional women carved out a niche for themselves by virtue of reverse discrimination. Women were believed to be instinctively good at jobs based on painstaking details, self-sacrifice and caring for others. They made ideal nurses, librarians, dietitians and social workers. Mary Minty, for instance, was hired at the Mercer Reformatory in 1911, then went on to become Toronto's first policewoman. "She is tall and strong, and she looks business-like and systematic, and certainly appeals to one as being very well adapted to assume responsibility," the Toronto *Star* reported, "but at the same time she has a certain simplicity of manner, heightened by her Scotch accent, which makes her appear very sympathetic and kind."

By 1911, women filled one in ten civil service jobs. The government only hired single women, because married women already had someone "to look after them." Yet, in hospitals for the insane, tailors made $700, while seamstresses made $300. Male clerks made $300 a year more than secretaries, and messenger boys made $6 a week more than charwomen.

Laura McCarthy began working as a casual in the legislative library in 1906. She started with two strikes against her. She was Catholic and a woman in an Orangeman's world. In 1908, she wrote the provincial secretary (today's chair of Management Board) and complained that her manager was instigating co-workers to play constant pranks on her. They filled her inkwell with glue, accused her of being a lesbian, teased her for being bossy, joked about her befriending a "low-life" charwoman, then called her hysterical when she got upset. She confronted her supervisor, who became the first government manager to go on record to say he was only joking. "I leave the matter in your hands," McCarthy wrote the provincial secretary, "knowing that then, and only then, shall I get fair treatment."

The provincial secretary said this tension couldn't be tolerated. "It is very clear from the statements in your letter that it is impossible that your position in the department could be continued with comfort to yourself," he wrote back. "Every line in your letter reads discord," he claimed. "You have no doubt been zealous in your work, but this does not alter the fact that it would be impossible, under the conditions of matters disclosed, to extend the period of your engagement."

McCarthy then demanded a meeting with the provincial secretary, claiming "my friends, my family and myself are entitled to at least justice at the hands of the Government, and that we as clerks can scarcely claim some measure of protection against the insults, arrogance and calumnies of those in positions above us."

When she threatened to go public with her story, Miss McCarthy's file was closed. The minister "instructed me to acknowledge receipt of your letter of recent date," his assistant wrote her in February, 1909, "and to say that contents have been noted."

Public Service by appointment

The civil service of 1911 was a medley of different tunes and strains: populist and elitist, British and American, deep Tory and mild reform. None was overpowering, though deep Tory struck the most chords.

On the surface, everything seemed very properly British. This was the heyday of Imperialism, when streets, schools, chocolates and horse races were named after famous battles and heroes or just plain Queen or King.

Ontario's official seal, adopted in 1909, featured a bear, moose and deer with the Latin motto for "Loyal she began, so loyal she remains." Loyalty, no one had to be reminded, was to Britain.

British traditions showed in the province's parliamentary system, in the names of the major political parties, in the titles for cabinet ministers, in the oath taken to the monarch, in the office of Lieutenant Governor representing the Queen. The term "civil servant" was a British import, chosen over the plebeian American term "public servant."

The structure of Ontario's civil service was self-consciously anti-American. An 1895 Ontario commission on government appointments called the U.S. habit of electing sheriffs, judges and other public officials a sad sign "of an extreme democratic community" which "subordinates everything to popular control." In Ontario, cabinet appointed, in the name of the crown.

Not to put too fine a point on it, this spirited defence of British-style representative government as against Yankee-style direct democracy was sheer puffery. The commission set out to defend cabinet power over patronage. Government should be run like a business, the commission reported, and "no merchant could successfully conduct his business if his clerks, bookkeepers and porters were appointed and removable, not by himself, but by his customers."

Nevertheless Ontario was too much a land of pioneers for British practices to last. After the 1837 rebellion, Britain sent out civil service reformers, most notably "Radical Jack" Durham, who tried to modernize the colonies so they could pay their own way. In Britain, this generation of reformers championed the merit system to replace inexpert aristocratic appointees with members of the rising middle class. In Ontario, the only legacy of this generation of reformers was the title "deputy minister" granted to those who would be called "permanent secretaries" in the mother country.

When the cry for British-style civil service reform finally took hold in Ontario, it had a North American, not a British, ring to it.

To wield the influence they felt capable of, the educated middle class in the final quarter of the last century needed government jobs. But they felt thwarted by "boss politicians" who manipulated "the ignorant mob" with pork-barrel politics of corruption and patronage. In 1876, speaking as the voice of the reformers, the *Canadian Monthly Magazine* declared that "the price of a commission in the government service is the free exercise of a glib tongue, deftness in canvassing, unscrupulousness in everything." The original civil-service bashers, the middle-class reformers set a tone for those historians who, virtually to this day, have found their prejudices agreeable. Certainly patronage was a fact of life in government in Ontario before 1911. But it was rarely excessive or corrupt. According to the historian of patronage, S. J. R. Noel, Ontario's civil service came at high quality and low cost while Mowat held power through the late 1800s. There was no purge either, when James Whitney ended more than three decades of Liberal rule in 1905. Of 704 staff, only 31, all labourers and asylum attendants, were sacked. No one was fired at Queen's Park. A 1912 report found no evidence of political involvement among civil servants.

To serve, apolitically

The Garrow Resolution of 1897 is commonly seen as the high-water mark of civil service purification. To this day, Ontario politicians trace the prohibition against civil service political involvement to the revolt against corruption represented by this resolution. During the 1975 provincial election, when the Ontario Public Service Employees Union blamed premier Bill Davis for denying political rights to civil servants, Davis insisted he was only honouring an ancient Ontario tradition dating back to 1897, and demanded an apology from the union.

In fact, the Garrow Resolution cannot be blamed or credited for the province's rules against political involvement by civil servants.

Though it said civil servants "should not actively participate" in elections, it only had the status of a resolution, not a law. Staff were not required to sign an oath agreeing to it, or to any other limit on their free speech. Many saw it as a way to protect civil servants who wanted to abstain from politics, not crack down on civil servants who wanted to get involved. When the Liberal premier spoke in favour of the resolution, he stressed that he didn't oppose civil servants running for political office. Garrow himself said fears of civil service political involvement were overblown, and that he only wanted to prevent staff from being dragooned into election work.

Reformers from the professional middle class did not make much headway influencing government operations until about 1905. Their signature was firmly on new government bodies formed in that period, such as the Ontario Hydro-Electric Power Commission, the Toronto Transit Commission, the Workmen's Compensation Board and assorted municipal posts such as the commissioners of public works. Wherever the titles "board" or "commission," suggesting expertise and independence from partisan politics, were used, a new professional was to be found.

A smoothly functioning machine

The chief asset of the progressive reformers was expertise. They had the degrees to prove it. By defining merit in terms of degrees and tests, they turned it into an affirmative-action program for the educated middle class. They also redefined politics to highlight efficiency and administration, not choice or participation. Words that used to refer to politics in terms of the human body – the body politic, organs or arms or heads of government, for example – were replaced by words that described government as a machine – the smooth functioning machinery of state, wheels of government, etc. For every problem there was an institution, and for every institution there was an expert. To exercise their expertise without interruption, progressives promoted neutral and independent boards and commissions that let them plan on the basis of their technical mastery without fear or favour from politicians.

For the most part, however, their science was hokum. Under the spell of scientific miracle cures worked by surgeons, psychiatrists sponsored active treatments in mental hospitals. The London hospital removed women's clitorises and wired male penises to prevent masturbation, seen as the surest sign of insanity. Progressive reformer Dr. Helen MacMurchy, hired by the government to develop policy on the feeble-minded, led the battle to place all feeble-minded in institutions, lest they spread their seed and pollute Canada's gene pool.

Given these dark sides to scientific progress, it is not surprising that demands for wholesale application of scientific expertise to the government service lacked popular backing. However, middle class reform never had as much impact on the workings of the Ontario civil service proper, well-entrenched before the reform wave that started rolling around 1905, as did traditional Toryism. This Tory touch to Ontario's civil service is the key to understanding patterns of government organization and labour relations until well into the 1960s.

Tory paternalism

Old-style conservatives, often stereotyped as blue-blooded reactionaries from Britain, had deep roots in Ontario history. In the era of pioneer settlement, Loyalists fled the American Revolution to settle in Upper Canada under the protection and supervision of the British crown. Frontier society was cash-poor and had little to trade, so connections counted more than money in getting things done. Political scientist S.J.R. Noel calls the relations based on mutual back-scratching that developed in that society "dyadic clientelism." It was a society with a strong sense of "what we owe each other."

Wave after wave of immigrants breathed new life into this paternalistic Toryism, long after it might have died a natural death in an urban industrial society. Immigrants organized themselves into "friendly societies" like the Loyal Orange Lodge, the Masons, the Sons of England, and the Loyal Order of Foresters. These networks cut society vertically, along lines of religion, ethnicity or country of birth, more than horizontally, along lines of class. This paternalistic social order modified the impersonal labour market that normally arises with industrial capitalism. Claims of personal need and loyalty were honoured over anonymous standards of merit and academic qualification. Ontario's official seal emblazoned loyalty, not efficiency, as the cardinal virtue.

The government style that grew out of this series of social networks and values had little use for rules, the strong suit of bureaucracy. At the turn of the century, Queen's Park reporter Hector Charlesworth wrote of a moment when the Speaker was startled from his nap and automatically ruled an Opposition Liberal out of order. Asked for his rationale, he said: "I don't just know; but if you'll kindly repeat what you were saying I'll tell you."

In the same fashion, many government departments made up rules as they went along, with no manuals of procedure to weigh them down. Bureaucratic continuity was looked after in-house by old boys' networks. As just one example, Whitney picked his successor for the Conservative leadership by identifying him in his will. New government programs were delivered on a catch-as-catch-can basis. The Department of Agriculture picked up inspection of industrial workshops. Lands and Forests took over mine inspections.

Merit was not high on the list of Tory values. In 1912, the Liberals tried to ride the merit hobbyhorse, and moved that an efficient civil service be selected on the basis of impartial competitive exams. The Tories shamelessly passed a counter-motion that "success in a competitive examination is in no way a guarantee of pre-eminent or ordinary fitness for

Government service."

Despite many abuses, this system of human-scale paternalism operated as a force for employment equity – what some political organizers called "honest graft." Unions demanded government appointments for "those who enjoy the confidence of the toilers," namely themselves. Farm and women's groups did the same. To the extent they succeeded, they kept government offices staffed with people who came from and knew their communities. Indeed, Mowat and Whitney were patronage saints to many social reformers, most of whom bit the hand that fed them and lived to tell the tale.

A customary sense of fairness

Government annual reports were filled with passion. Factory inspector James Brown, later a president of the Civil Service Association of Ontario (CSAO), saw industrial accidents as the "butcher bill" of profit. J.J. Kelso crusaded against cruelty to animals and children. Clerk of forestry R.W. Phipps championed forest conservation and mobilized the public behind demands for more provincial parks. John Seath and Albert Leake championed manual and technical education. Dr. A.H. Beaton at the Orillia Hospital for Idiots called for training of the mentally retarded. Dr. Bruce Smith, inspector of prisons, denounced Toronto's jail as the worst on the continent and urged a grand jury to bring charges against the city. Wartime munitions inspector Laura Hughes scorned the war profiteers who exploited women.

Yet these outcries did not produce enforcement and prosecution. There were only 134 Factory Act prosecutions from 1900 to 1914, according to legal historian Eric Tucker. Of these, 31 were against parents for allowing underage children to work, 32 were against "Chinamen" for failing to separate lunch from work rooms, 11 were against women and children who worked too many hours, and most of the rest were petty. "Persuasion was not only the preferred technique, it was practically the exclusive technique" used by inspectors, he writes.

Civil servants caught in the web of these paternalistic relationships may not have liked favouritism and erratic methods. But cold impersonal rules that placed formal education over years of service weren't their cup of tea either. The ancient union call – "a fair day's wage for a fair day's work" – was not coined by efficiency experts, but by people with a customary sense of fairness and mutual obligation. "From each according to his abilities, to each according to his needs," the rallying cry of old-time socialists, did not lend itself to job measurement. By contrast, today's slogans such as "equal pay for work of equal value" challenge custom in favour of qualification and position. The change reflects different worlds of understanding, as much as different degrees of worker radicalism.

Civil servants couldn't decide what kind of labour organization they needed until they knew what kind of government they were working for. A government run by efficiency zealots leads to a union that is rule- and process-conscious. That's the language that bureaucrats understand. A government run by traditionalists leads to outbreaks of protest when obligations are betrayed, followed by inactivity when obligations are honoured. Until at least the late 1950s, Ontario civil servants were in that second mode, a reflection of both the dominance and adaptability of Tory paternalism since pioneer days.

CSAO: Social togetherness

In the spring of 1911, 200 government workers met at Queen's Park to discuss "the necessity of a Civil Service Association, pointing out its possibilities in the way of improving the Service, promoting social togetherness, urging healthy athletics and co-operating with one another in the purchasing of supplies." Women weren't invited to the meeting, though a newspaper reported "the young ladies of the Service were greatly interested in the movement and will be affiliated." The founding meeting was chaired by senior civil servant C. C. James, and the first president was Edward Bayly, a leading lawyer and King's counsel who later became attorney general. The meeting agreed to get the government's approval before going ahead.

By the standards of the 1990s, this was a mild-mannered organizing meeting. No mention of bargaining units, contracts, grievances, solidarity, taking on the employer. But turn-of-the-century unions put more emphasis on self-improvement, self-reliance and socializing than collective bargaining. There were important values and also a lot of savvy in the way these organizations expressed their aims. There's quite a bit of code between the lines, necessary in an age when unions only represented ten per cent of the workforce, enjoyed no legal protection, and when even the government's Bureau of Labour referred to unionism as "undoubtedly a good thing, but like strychnine it must be taken in small doses."

Self-improvement was a major obsession of that generation, part of the Christian's duty to strive. It was more about the need for inner growth than productivity or career advancement. Promoting social togetherness meant entertainment was not yet a commodity, rest and recreation were not yet centred in the home, work was part of community, and there was more binding people together than an anonymous pay cheque. "Healthy athletics" characterized a society still dominated by participants, not spectators. There was more to life than work, even if it had to be justified in the name of health, not fun. Like self-improvement and social togetherness, healthy athletics was "code" for the major labour demand of that era – shorter hours.

The civil service organizers knew their membership. By year's end, they enlisted 600 members. There are reports that the civil service association got into bulk purchasing of coal, clothes and food. But there were no qualms about moving onto straight employer-employee issues. In 1912, a group met Whitney to lobby for pensions. There was also pressure put on the government to start the shift to short summer hours in June rather than July.

Wages became an issue when the Great War of 1914-1918 heated up the economy and led to runaway inflation. Whatever could be bought for a dollar before the war cost $1.62 by the war's end and $1.90 in 1920. Purchasing power was cut in half at the same time as the horrors of war and the cynicism of the postwar settlement deflated respect for politicians. "Someone has said they took the Spring out of the world, and then expected the other seasons to behave as usual," said Dr. Martha Davidson, a wartime home economist with the Department of Agriculture.

In 1918, the CSAO demanded a $300 bonus to catch up with inflation. By 1919, members seemed to blame the CSAO as much as the politicians for the delay in getting a raise. A "sufferer" wrote the *Star* in February complaining of wages and staff shortages in institutions. The letter ended: "Is it not nearly time that an organization is formed to get a little redress?" In May, a Queen's Park reporter for the *Mail* sniffed mutiny in the corridors, and "a good deal of insurgent talk about forcing the resignation of the chief officers of the association, and substituting officers who will not hesitate to place the position of the service before the Government in a positive way."

CSAO president Grigg was considered too close to the government, the *Globe* reported. That was true. The official history of Lands and Forests says "Honest Albert Grigg" was appointed deputy in 1915 as a result of his business and political connections. In March, 1919, he fought against those in the CSAO who wanted to try out militant tactics, and argued for working through channels to get a major salary boost. His "channels" helped win a cost-of-living bonus. Married men got double the bonus that single men and women got. The lowest paid workers got a $360 bonus, while those making more than $3,000 got nothing.

But shortly after, on May 24, Grigg resigned, claiming it was time to give someone else a try. The same night, the CSAO executive called a mass meeting. While there's no report of the meeting, the CSAO went on to prepare a well-researched brief. Government wages had increased at half the rate of inflation, the brief said, and civil servants lagged far behind private sector workers. While government increases averaged 21 per cent, private sector workers had been getting anywhere from 33 per cent for charwomen to 44 per cent for elevator boys to 72 per cent for plumbers. The brief called for a $1,000 minimum wage for women, enough to live on without dipping into their savings.

Without a 30 per cent increase and regular annual increases thereafter, it was impossible for civil servants to meet their financial burdens "in a self-respecting way," the brief said.

It harped on the theme that a low wage "barely provides the necessities of life but not the comforts that tend to ensure efficiency in service." This made it clear that quality of work and loyalty, unlike simple obedience, had to be negotiated: with better and fairer pay, "this Government [could] rely upon the hearty service of a loyal, contented, and devoted Staff."

A month later, the government gave out bonuses ranging from $50 to $400 a year, with the biggest increases going to poorly paid workers and no increases to workers making more than $3,000 a year. The government granted another $300 cost of living bonus in 1920. According to CSAO president E.V. Donnelly, a senior official with the provincial secretary, cancellation of the bonus in 1921 left staff unable to concentrate on their work because of financial worries. He wrote the premier: "Even though we are civil servants, we are still men and women with a keen sense of what consideration is due us."

The struggle for wage increases after the war did not lead to restructuring of the CSAO or its relationship with the government. CSAO desires were expressed in letters to the cabinet and meetings with the premier, not formal negotiations. There was no notion of striking if the association didn't get what it wanted. At its annual meeting in 1920, the CSAO refused to join a nationwide civil service federation that looked too much like a union that might strike. The meeting did endorse links with civil service organizations to discuss "common problems" and "plans for improving the efficiency of the Service."

Whitleyism: The talkshop

This lack of structured employer-employee relationships was quite unlike Britain, where the civil service became the stronghold for "Whitleyism," which encouraged workers and employers in each industry to set minimum standards that kept cutthroat competitors at bay. That sort of company union system was never considered in Ontario.

A concern for minimum standards was the one element of Whitleyism that made the ocean crossing to Ontario. The CSAO toyed with this idea in its proposed minimum wage for women. The farmer-labour government elected after the war also applied the idea when it set up a Minimum Wage Board. "Old Man Ontario," the board report for 1922 said, "is determined that none of his daughters shall lack the necessities of life – even the insane and the criminals are to be fed, clothed and housed. And industry, which takes the life's efforts of thousands of working women, is commanded to do as much." This kind of protection was limited to women, who "for various economic reasons, are the most helpless class of workers," the report said. "No community can afford to stand aside and see them exploited."

This species of paternalism did not fit with company unionism, which required ongoing structures and machinery to resolve differences between employers and employees. The CSAO, like organizations of other workers in basic industry after the war, rose and fell with each struggle. It remained weak. It maintained a moderate tone. It included supervisors and deputies. But it was not a company union.

"Proper supervision and control"

During World War I, in the holy war against ruthless Prussian efficiency, Canada became a warfare state where the efficiency movement was born again. In all-out mobilization on the home front, Ontario rushed to feed and arm its allies while short 200,000 men in their prime who went off to fight. These were glory days for all those who believed workers had to be counted, controlled and commanded to win the domestic war against waste and sloth. Progressive reformers were able to wrap themselves in the flag, and gain powers that would never have been tolerated in peace time.

The state and statistics have a history of twinship. Yet to gain the information the experts needed required levels of government interference unthinkable without the crisis of war. Though conscription of men into the army produced bitter infighting between Quebec and English Canada, within Ontario the real story was conscription of the work force.

In 1914, "enemy aliens," as immigrants born in enemy-controlled eastern Europe were called, were ordered to report on their whereabouts to government officials who placed them under "proper supervision and control." In 1915, an Ontario commission wanted to make the unemployed register with bureaus run by "experts and authorities." In 1916, the province launched its first venture into labour market planning. Agencies took stock of unemployed workers' skills to "put the whole question of employment on a scientific basis," and make sure they were sent where they were needed. Conservative premier W.H. Hearst established an Organization of Resources Committee to promote "a high ideal of citizenship and a quickening of national efficiency."

Conscription of men and wealth became the slogan of the hour, especially among reformers. Volunteer recruiters, such as the Hamilton Recruiting League, became tired of haranguing idlers on the street, and petitioned the province to recognize that the war "calls for the most rigid economy of men and means." In 1918, Ottawa ordered all workers to give government agents information on their health and agricultural experience, and made idleness a crime, subject to six months at hard labour. Slackers were conscripted into the army the same year.

Civil service reformers got permission from politicians to turn government operations into models of expert-driven efficiency, precision and control. Competitive exams tested merit objectively with 1918's version of "Trivial Pursuit." After giving the names of the Roman general who conquered England and of Canada's first viceroy, and examples of reflexive, interrogative and relative pronouns, the applicant wrote an essay on desirable public amusements. In the same year, the federal civil service commission hired U.S. job classification experts, leading to charges from workers that "alien efficiency engineers have assumed control of Canadian Government offices."

At Queen's Park, it was J. M. McCutcheon who enlisted civil servants in the war against unscientific work practices. McCutcheon was a Doctor of Pedagogy, who taught in southwestern Ontario and wrote several textbooks on childhood education. He had no management experience until 1914, when he was appointed secretary of the Workmen's Compensation Board. Like most experts, he was full of himself and his qualifications. Whenever premier Drury, elected on a wave of farm and labour protest after the war, forgot to address him as "doctor," McCutcheon called the premier "Dr. Drury," and "this steered me back to the proper etiquette," Drury recalled in his memoirs.

In 1918, McCutcheon was appointed head of Ontario's new Civil Service Commission. On paper, this was a tall order. "No appointment can be made in a department without his certificate that the appointment is necessary, that the salary is not too large for the office, and that the person to be appointed is duly qualified for the position," his notice of appointment claimed. The Public Service Act gave him power to "recommend such action as will promote the co-ordination of work in the different departments, and the reduction or re-organization of the staff of any department with a view to greater economy and efficiency in administration."

Efficiency in government jobs required far-sighted management that recognized the importance of workers' loyalty and commitment, McCutcheon wrote in his 1920 annual report. "The growing demands of modern government, with its changing activities and enlarging functions, require a well-equipped and efficient body of employees who are prepared to invest themselves in the work of the state," he added in 1921. McCutcheon was attuned to the development of what labour historians call the "internal labour market," a hallmark of 1920s industrial change that historian Craig Heron calls "undoubtedly one of the most important and distinctive workplace changes of the twentieth century." The civil service best exemplified this shift.

Until the 1920s, most employers relied on an external labour market. Virtually the entire workforce was made up of "temps." Labourers lined up – toed the line, as it was called – to be hired by the day. Skilled workers were journeymen (from the French word for "day") who were such masters of their crafts that they could fulfil any role on a day's notice.

In the changes brought by mass production, factories and offices of the 1920s couldn't count on temps. Worksites increasingly had their own particulars that took some getting used to. Smart employers developed programs to reduce employee turnover and increase employee loyalty, and set out long-term plans for the smooth functioning of their operations. That's how scientific personnel management got its start. Many companies subsidized cafeterias and sports teams. The more sophisticated ones set up sickness and pension plans and offered career planning, ways of working up in the world without leaving the mother corporation. If these changes led workers to reject unions as disloyal to the company, so much the better.

Managers of the old school didn't always grasp the requirements of the new order. That cast many of the early personnel managers as reformers who took up the cause of employees, the better to marry them to new workplace needs. McCutcheon was of this school. Personnel administration, he wrote in his 1921 report, "is the direction and co-ordination of the human relations of any organization with the view of getting maximum production with a minimum of effort and friction and with proper regard for the well-being of the workers."

Pensions: Treating them too kindly

In his first report, McCutcheon championed "scientific retirement," which coupled pensions with compulsory retirement at 70. Pensions, he argued, were a "business proposition" that got value for the dollar. Without pensions, the government was stuck with oldtimers who were dead on their feet. In 1911, for instance, 30 per cent of government clerks were over 65. The government took pity on them, and the civil service degenerated "into a charitable institution, continuing employees in the Service long after they can efficiently fulfil their duties." This discouraged younger workers, who couldn't get promoted until their elders gave up the ghost.

Pensions were McCutcheon's first success. In June 1920, the Ontario government made retirement compulsory at 70, and paid half the costs of a pension plan that gave retirees a week's pay for every year of service. When the worker died, his widow was entitled to half the pension, "in recognition of the principle that, economically speaking, an employee's family is part of himself."

The cost of the plan wasn't high. In 1920, only two people in a hundred lived past 70: James Clancy, 76, was the first to cash out under the plan, and he didn't live out the year. In return, the government got to lock in their up-and-comers. "Employees who have many years to their credit for pension" the superannuation board reported in 1921, "and this is true of a very large percentage, will think twice before leaving the Service to accept positions elsewhere."

If pensions were a winner for civil service reformers, they weren't for the government that sponsored them. Premier Drury fought hard for the pension plan, hoping it would send a signal to urban voters that the United Farmers of Ontario was a broad people's party, not just the "Us For Ourselves" farmers' movement that Liberals and Conservatives made fun of. His approach didn't go down well among farm leaders, who denounced pensions as class legislation which they had to pay for but could never get themselves.

The air was thick at the UFO picnic where Drury unsuccessfully debated his position. On the drive back to Toronto, the UFO president told Drury that the last man who challenged him that way "went down on his back. You will go down on yours if you attempt to push such over on me, premier or no premier." The UFO never recovered from the split, and Drury's government was sent into retirement in 1923 and replaced by the Conservatives.

When the Conservatives lost again in 1934, Drury wrote the new premier urging him to learn from the UFO error of treating senior civil servants too kindly. "Part of your work during the next two years must be to shoot them to pieces so they cannot come back," he wrote. "They deserve no mercy and none should be shown." McCutcheon was one of the first to go.

Job classifications as personnel control

Efficiency experts became notorious through Charlie Chaplin's 1920s film classic *Modern Times*, which ridiculed piecework, stopwatches, and machine-control on assembly lines. Such ham-fisted methods didn't work in white collar and government operations. There, the job classification plan, not the stopwatch, was the thing to watch. Control, not brute speedup, was the name of the game.

This was McCutcheon's major project for the 1920s. Rating the output of government workers wasn't easy, he admitted in 1922, but it was worth the effort. "The value of recording in a systematic manner, the quantity and quality of the work of every employee in the government service is unquestioned as a principal factor in obtaining personnel control," he wrote.

In McCutcheon's view, classification rated the job, not the worker. It allowed managers to measure workers against "scientifically determined

21

standards by which to gauge efficiency." A job grid also encouraged workers to advance themselves. And it solved payroll problems by guaranteeing "equal pay for equal work and like responsibility." Once in place, the entire system would run like a clock, and "[would] naturally result in a more efficient Public Service," he promised.

McCutcheon's classification scheme took five years to complete. It was a list of job titles: clerk group 1 and 2, principal clerk, filing clerk group 1, senior clerk stenographer, clerk stenographer group 1, senior clerk messenger, clerk group 3, clerk stenographer group 2, filing clerk group 2, and on and on.

There was no definition of merit, no evaluation of required skills, and no consistency to the pay levels attached to different jobs. An attendant at the Ontario Hospital for the Insane got $900 a year, while attendants at the Guelph Reformatory got $1,150 and attendants at the School for the Blind got $600. When it came to male and female wages, blatant discrimination triumphed over objectivity. Caretakers made up to $1,125 while charwomen got $625. Laundrymen got $1,050, and laundresses $675. Tailors were paid $1,125 and seamstresses $900. Male clerks got $1,200, to female clerk-stenographers' $975.

McCutcheon did manage to enthrone pure merit in at least one case. Deputy ministers were to be paid $4,400, while his own more demanding job of civil service commissioner brought $5,000.

Despite the importance he attached to job descriptions, McCutcheon never rose to his own, laid out in the Public Service Act. The government's chief efficiency expert was wasting his time. The Conservative government elected in 1923 paid him no heed. A one-man operation with a budget of $15,000, he was really just a glorified record keeper until he was bounced by the Liberals in 1934.

Rule of thumb

McCutcheon's zeal for a scientific personnel system found few takers. Civil servants ridiculed his first questionnaire, circulated in 1919, and quickly dubbed a "McCutcheonnaire" for asking too many nosy questions about age, nationality, schooling (a tipoff to religion), marital status, and sick time claimed over the previous year. Charwomen enjoyed listing their degrees and military service. The press had a field day: "If there had been anything even weakly resembling a labour organization among the civil servants in the parliament building in Queen's Park Saturday, a strike would without doubt have occurred," the Tory-populist *World* reported. The Tory *Telegram* called the classification exercise "a joke" and fumed that the study had been sublet to U.S. consultants who "experted all right, but they knew little about conditions in Canada."

As for the politicians, they quickly tired of scientific management, and never allowed McCutcheon to be more than a figurehead commissioner. Unlike Ottawa's commission, Ontario's was never independent, and McCutcheon reported to the premier, not to the legislature. He never gained the power to appoint, to cross the power of ministers to hire their own people on their own say-so. He merely rubber-stamped appointments made by ministers and deputies. Merit tests started and stopped with typing tests.

The Ontario government just wasn't ready for the cold discipline of science in any area. In public policy, science couldn't hold a candle to wishful thinking. The year before McCutcheon was hired, when zeal for efficiency was at full tide, the Ontario government set up a farm colony for returned soldiers in the far north near Kapuskasing. Applicants weren't screened for farm or wilderness experience, and were given no training. Frost killed the first two crops. Crazed by mosquitoes, cold and loneliness, the settlers deserted the colony and demanded government compensation.

There was no foothold for the hard sciences. Lands and Forests did virtually no research on botany or biology. The department went along with ignorant stereotypes of the day and paid bounties for wolves and other "predator species," with no awareness of the functions they served in nature. Hired to bring the department up to speed after the war, professional forester Dr. Judson Clark denounced rule-of-thumb methods for setting policy, until his wrists were slapped for imposing strict standards on logging cuts, the department's official history recounts. A postwar inquiry into corrupt forest management practices, a showpiece for the new ethic of government, fell apart when the chief counsel for the inquiry was caught taking bribes from a major lumber company.

The social sciences fared no better. The Treasurer's office had no trained economists until after World War II. The first accountant was hired in 1927, mainly to catch the Opposition up on its mistakes.

Crackpot scientists got closest to doing their thing in schools, jails and asylums, traditional launching pads for scientific experimentation because of their dependent clients. Here, the scientific IQ test was the equivalent of the scientific manager's stopwatch and job classification plan. The tests were championed in 1917 by an Ontario commission on the feeble-minded, though Conservative premier Hearst, evidently not a science man, found the proposal to castrate low scorers "unsavoury." When compulsory education to age 16 was introduced in 1919, IQ tests were used to separate out the "subnormal," who would otherwise disturb the class. As might be expected, McCutcheon made common cause with these science experts. In 1930, he sat on a royal commission that promoted testing and castration of the feeble-minded to "lessen the amount of evil which is certainly promoted by unchecked sexual freedom of criminals or defectives who have a record of immorality." This was a classification and merit system with a vengeance.

Even here, however, scientists were checkmated. Doctors were critical of the IQ tests, and humanists also objected to them. The two groups limited the impact of the mental classification experts. Dr. S. B. Sinclair, government inspector of schools for the retarded during the 1920s, said the tests were counter-productive. "To have him run the gauntlet of half a dozen specialist examinations, label him with some opprobrious name, exaggerate his imperfection, and advertise him on the housetops as a menace to society, I not only unjustly stigmatize him for life and cause," he claimed, "but I also render all subsequent treatment doubly difficult."

The Ministry of Health was the exception that proved the rule about the low standing of science in government departments. Public health scientists pioneered in the field of workplace health and safety, and set sound standards for dealing with communicable disease. In both cases, the costs of neglect were higher than the costs of action, and unions and community groups actively enlisted scientific support. For the most part, however, the unbending rules of McCutcheon's scientific credo were dumped in favour of shrewd adaptations, practical give-and-take, and some warm milk of human kindness.

In the postwar dispute over cost-of-living allowances, for instance, McCutcheon opposed any raises based on the rate of inflation, rather than merit. He asked the government to delay any bonuses until he finished his classification system. Instead, the government awarded extra bonuses to those at the lower pay scales who were hardest hit by inflation.

The province backed off from the merit principle again in 1920, when it gave preference to veterans, especially those who were disabled by war wounds. Human obligations continued to take precedence over sheer qualifications. As late as 1941, Lands and Forests minister Peter Heenan, a former labour activist, was slow to hire university-trained foresters. That wouldn't be very fair to the men who'd spent years in the bush, he explained during an investigation of his department: "There would be little encouragement for a man to stay on his job, get interested in it and learn in the bush. I do not think they should be held back just because somebody else had an opportunity to attend school."

Decisions like these reflected the staying power of humane and flexible Tory paternalism. The Ontario government never moved to institute punch clocks, time-and-motion studies or piece rates, commonplace but demeaning features of triumphant industrial society.

As well, politicians were old-school, rather than progressive, in their management style. They were hands-on types. They could never wrap their heads around a system that ran itself, without them scurrying around. When Drury was premier, former premier Hearst burst into his office upset about a scandalous waste of public money. On his way to work, Hearst had passed 20 highway workers who were just standing around. An emergency call was put out to the deputy minister, who reported that the men had been waiting for a steam shovel but had been back at work for some time.

The politicians were sticklers for measures of working harder, not smarter. For that matter, so was the CSAO. In 1925, the CSAO asked for a raise. The premier said too many workers weren't punctual, and punctuality was the key to both promotions and pay increases. The CSAO dropped the unpleasant subject and wrote back that "it is unfortunate that the drones and those who do not appreciate the importance of punctuality and proper application to their work are, as it were, a millstone around the necks of those who are regular in attendance, faithful in their duties and give to the government a full measure of service." Later, S.L. Squire, an executive member and future CSAO president, said the CSAO must "impress the Service with the importance of punctuality, strict attention to duties, and willingness to serve the province, thereby insuring generous consideration by the government of all matters relating to the Service."

The province did not stack up well against large, often U.S.-based corporations, where professionalized and progressive labour relations were becoming standard practice during the 1920s. According to a survey of "factors in scientific management" in Ontario's 300 largest firms in 1929, "welfare capitalism" was much more advanced in the private sector.

Though the government matched or beat the paid holidays, sick days and hours of work offered by equivalent-sized corporations, it was left behind when it came to subtler forms of employee mind control or team-building. Unlike the progressive companies, the government offered no bonuses, no subsidized cafeterias, no company publications and no company unions. The CSAO had fewer rights than a company union to information and consultation. It also missed out on the internal grievance procedures granted most company unions. In 1928, the CSAO executive asked the premier to set up a formal grievance system, but this was "not enthusiastically received," according to the CSAO's *Civil Service Review*.

In preference to excellence

Neither McCutcheon nor the Tory paternalists seemed aware that they missed out on the opportunity of creating a British-style civil service. British civil servants traditionally shunned specialization and embraced generalist training, the better to serve wherever required. That kind of high-performance civil service had to be nurtured. It required pay systems based on knowledge and potential, not the particular job performed at any given time. It required long-term investment in staff training, not short-term recruitment from outside whenever new challenges arose.

McCutcheon's classification system, which he called a "merit system," destroyed the basis for that kind of excellence. It demanded that merit be shown at the point of entry, and that it be limited to the job at hand. That is a recipe for fitting in, not innovation. The merit principle ran contrary to training, which could explain why North America, where scientific management dominated organizational thinking, lags behind most of the world in training.

The narrow range of choices also doomed meaningful debate about how to make government more democratic, as distinct from cleaner and more businesslike. R.M. Dawson, Canada's dean of political science, wrote a book on the Canadian civil service in 1929, complaining about what he called the "phobia" with graft and corruption. It's one thing to be worried about robbery, he wrote, another to go around in an armoured car. Corruption "absorbed all attention to the virtual exclusion of everything else" about open and effective government. "The object of the new democracy must be to discover the best environment, the most suitable conditions of tenure in its broadest sense, the most adequate stimuli, which will produce the intense mental and volitional effort in the different officers of Government, while preserving in the last resort popular control over the whole," he wrote.

Ontario missed out on the chance to explore that challenge of the "new democracy," a tragic legacy of the passing obsession with scientific management.

CSAO incorporates

Throughout this period, the CSAO was always a haphazard affair. With membership fees set at a dollar a year, the organization never had more than $2,500. It had no office, and no full-time officers, which perhaps accounts for its leaders having been Queen's Park-based professionals or managers who could set their own schedules. Of 17 presidents between 1911 and 1938, three were deputies, two were doctors, one was a lawyer, five were chief clerks and four were supervisors. Women and workers in institutions were decidedly under-represented.

Yet, relatively speaking, the CSAO was a success story of employee organization. Unions did not crack the hold of many large corporations until the 1940s. Before then, they recruited almost exclusively among old-style independent workers who owed nothing to any one employer and who came and went according to the seasons and bumps in the business cycle. The CSAO's relative staying power came from presenting itself as a professional association. Professional associations were less confrontational than unions, but had more independence than company unions.

In 1926, the CSAO stopped sending out memos on government letterhead, and began publishing its own *Civil Service Review*. The front-page message from president Squire talked of the need to brush away cobwebs of misunderstanding, to bring branches closer together, and to win respect from the public and politicians. In 1927, with the government's permission, CSAO incorporated itself. On behalf of its 1,192 members, the CSAO corporate charter committed the organization to meet with government bodies to "improve the efficiency of the Civil Service and to promote the common interests of the members of the association."

Though unions refused to incorporate, and thereby create a legal entity that employers could sue, incorporation was standard with professional associations. The way the CSAO explained the move in 1927, there was no conscious design to imitate professionals rather than unionists. It was simply a matter of avoiding individual responsibility for any debts of the CSAO. According to the *Civil Service Review*, an "unincorporated society of individuals is merely a partnership and every member is jointly responsible for the debts and liabilities of the society. That is the great reason behind incorporation." This concern over debt load was probably related to the CSAO's extensive range of co-op services. The CSAO operated the government parking lot, ran the Queen's Park cafeteria, and sold gas at reduced prices.

The decision to incorporate had an extended impact on the CSAO, and even, eventually, on OPSEU. Thanks to the requirements of incorporation, the CSAO had a board of directors until 1975, while every other labour organization had an executive. The CSAO held annual general meetings, not conventions. And conventions continue to be annual events, at a time when most unions meet every two or three years.

Just glad to have a job

Like most workers who held onto a job through the 1930s Depression, civil servants kept their heads down and mouths shut. Cushioned from the mass layoffs and wage cuts that hit private sector workers, they probably counted themselves lucky. There were no moves to strengthen the CSAO until the good times returned with the outbreak of World War II.

As a public-spirited organization, the CSAO established a relief fund for the down-and-out in 1931. Arrangements were made to have donations deducted from pay cheques. When the checkoff was delayed, premier George Henry was asked for an explanation. Henry said he'd be happy to proceed with the checkoff "if those who contribute realize there is a possibility of a temporary deduction being made by the Government from the salaries of civil servants." He thought workers would like to know that an extra deduction for charity "would seem to be somewhat of a double collection." The salary cuts were on their way.

After dropping this bombshell, Henry agreed to meet the CSAO executive, and ended up accepting CSAO's suggestion that the cuts be imposed on a sliding scale. Those who made less than $1,000 a year suffered a five per cent loss, while those who made over $8,000 lost 35 per cent.

The civil servants did not resist. When the cuts were announced at CSAO's annual meeting, delegates expressed their "desire to assure the government of our cordial acquiescence in the plan proposed and that we shall in every way co-operate with them to maintain the credit, both financial and otherwise of the province of Ontario which the Government and the Public Service are jointly privileged to serve." When another round of wage cuts came in 1933, the *Civil Service Review* said such sacrifices "must be taken in a cheerful spirit as a measure of necessity," since cabinet ministers volunteered for an even bigger cut.

At that year's annual meeting, however, workers from outside Toronto complained they weren't involved in the decision to accept the cuts. They vetoed putting their case directly to the premier. A later protest from

CSAO president F. G. Beardall, chief clerk at the Ontario Hospital, was equally short-lived. Beardall wrote Henry to protest an increase in work hours. When Henry took offence, Beardall apologized for the "unpleasant experience" and offered to resign to absolve the board of any responsibility.

The absence of more militant tactics reflected the basic truth of class politics in the 1930s. There were two classes: the employed and the unemployed. Among the employed, civil servants had it best. The employed hung on for dear life. The unemployed waited for them to drop off.

As of 1933, the Depression's darkest year, union membership declined to 6.4 per cent of the Ontario work force. The highly-unionized building trades took wage cuts of 68 per cent. Wages in export industries dropped 50 per cent. Wages in tariff-protected home industries fell 37 per cent. The average pay cut across the province was 32.2 per cent. Unemployment, province-wide was 20 per cent.

Beside these figures, civil service concessions were piddling. In fact, they amounted to a raise in real wages since the cost of living tumbled 24.4 per cent in the four years after 1929. Layoffs never affected more than three per cent, despite efforts to hound out women. "There are cases in the Service where girls who have been married have failed to notify the Minister," McCutcheon wrote the premier, "and thus have been continued in their employment," contrary to the rules. As well, Depression-era civil servants enjoyed enviable fringe benefits. As of 1931, two-year employees got a month's paid sick pay, while those who'd stayed more than six years got three months. They had 18-day holidays each year. By 1933, they had disability insurance. CSAO self-help methods made the package even better. In 1930, it offered group life insurance rates, and in 1932, group car insurance. A group medical plan followed in 1938.

Beardall's retreat from his complaint about longer hours has to be put in context. Half of the 6,000-strong civil service had to work an extra hour and a half a week, for a total of 38 hours, still ten hours less than industrial workers.

DON'T CALL ME SERVANT

Hepburn at the helm

Job security appeared to end in 1934, when the rich and dull Conservative George Henry was turfed out by the flamboyant Liberal, Mitchell Hepburn. Hepburn promised "pep and ginger" when he took over the Liberal leadership in 1930. That had been his life. As a boy, he got in trouble for throwing firecrackers in the school stove, and for throwing an apple at the top hat of Sir Adam Beck, founder of Hydro. At a campaign rally with farmers, he hopped onto a manure spreader and said this was the first time he'd spoken from a Tory platform. A heckler yelled: "Throw her into high gear, Mitch, she's never had a bigger load on."

Hepburn posed as a champion of the common man in the 1934 election. Often accompanied by union activists, he'd say: "I swing well to the left, where even some Liberals will not follow me." He promised to go after the fat cats in government.

He came out of his first cabinet meeting promising to "rip out the deadwood, political appointees, hangers-on, those who draw big salaries for doing little." He denounced the Lieutenant Governor's palatial residence as "a haven for broken-down English aristocrats who should be paying for their rooms at the hotels." He refused to attend the Lieutenant Governor's state dinner welcoming the incoming government. He got back at Ontario Hydro for hiring a private detective to shadow him for evidence of sin and corruption. He set up a royal commission to uncover scandals at Hydro, and fired a senior commissioner he said got paid $3,000 a year to do nothing. "The man is still doing the same thing, but he is not getting paid for it," Hepburn gloated. He fired all civil servants hired after 1933, all game wardens and silent movie producers, 140 unemployment and relief inspectors, one historian, and 183 beekeepers, claiming there was "one for every bee." With 8,000 taxpayers cheering him on, Hepburn sold all the government's limousines for $34,000 at a Varsity Stadium auction. When told the auction lacked dignity, he said: "You can have too much dignity."

The pro-Conservative *Mail and Empire* called these moves a "slaughter" of the civil service, which "reminds us of the beheadings which took place during the reign of terror during the French Revolution." The newspaper was taken in by Hepburn's theatrics. According to the careful calculations by Hepburn's latest biographer, John Saywell, Hepburn fired 1,067 civil servants and shortly after rehired 839 of them. Most of those permanently fired got some sort of compensation. Once the stunts were over, Hepburn doubled provincial spending on schools, and started construction on a massive psychiatric hospital in his own riding of St. Thomas. A 1937 survey of psychiatric hospitals found doctors in too short supply, but more than enough nurses and attendants. No government spent more than Hepburn's until late in the prosperous 1950s.

Still, no one felt safe while Hepburn was around. McCutcheon, a Conservative appointee from the mists of time, rushed to Hepburn's service and offered to help cut the civil service in half. It would take a lot of unpaid overtime on his part, "but to assist the Government in its efforts to economise I will be glad to undertake it," McCutcheon wrote. Hepburn saved him the bother and fired him, replacing him with Charles Foster, a former aide to premier Henry. At Lands and Forests, deputy Frederick Noad prepared to fire all foresters and replace them with cheaper ones. Noad sent Hepburn his hit list. Hepburn crossed out all the names on the sheet and wrote in "Noad."

The CSAO didn't take any risks. When Hepburn was elected, CSAO president D. T. McManus, a senior staffer at the liquor board, told the board of directors that those who'd kept their noses clean of politics had nothing to fear. The CSAO did not protest any of Hepburn's firings.

The CSAO got its first formal audience with Hepburn in 1937, three years after his election. To prepare Hepburn, the *Civil Service Review* had made the case that the CSAO "is recognized by the succeeding governments as the official channel through which measures affecting the welfare of the Service shall be communicated to them." Hepburn told the delegation it was wasting his time. Then he raised civil service salaries back to pre-Depression levels.

A *Civil Service Review* editorial in 1937 read more like a plea for mercy than a call to arms. "If Ontario is to forge ahead in the years to come there must exist between the Government and the Service a sympathetic understanding one for the other, and a determination to work hand in hand come what may." In 1938, CSAO president H.C. Hudson told the annual meeting that most membership grievances were "petty in the extreme." Relations with the government were "as satisfactory as they could reasonably be expected to be," he wrote in the June, 1938 *Review*. Hudson was a superintendent at the Department of Labour. He took on the CSAO presidency at the urging of his minister, who said it would sharpen his conciliation skills.

The CSAO next met Hepburn in 1942, and asked him for a new classification system. Hepburn refused. Then shortly before resigning as Liberal leader, he granted a cost-of-living allowance to low-paid workers, followed by a five per cent raise across the board.

Chapter Two

"Modern, Loyal, Efficient"

If Mitchell Hepburn was the most boyish rascal Ontario ever had for premier, kids had more fun with George Drew, elected premier in 1943. The schoolyard nonsense song, "My dad knows George Drew. George Drew knows my dad," set to the tune of "Onward Christian Soldiers," was meant to puncture holes in the bag of wind that many adults called "Gorgeous George." More than any premier before him, Drew's personal style would be likely to radicalize the civil service. Leslie Frost, who picked up the Tory torch after Drew, had the opposite style. Kindly and fatherly, Frost calmed the troubled waters Drew had churned. Ironically, the administration he set up during the 1950s encouraged an irreversible trend toward unionism.

Sporting the red and blue tie of the artillery unit he led during World War I, the handsome and energetic Drew brought an air of military command to the premier's office.

With family roots traceable to Loyalist pioneers, a hero's record from the war, and a legal career that brought him to head the Ontario Securities Commission in the early 1930s, Drew fitted the stereotype of a High Tory. He was elected Ontario leader of the Conservative party in 1938, despite his public support for Hepburn's anti-union stand during the 1937 election.

Drew was slower than other Tories to see the political shift to the left when the economy picked up in the early years of the war and people lost their fears. Industry boomed during World War II, and as workers got their first taste of the good life, they were determined to secure it. Illegal sit-downs and wildcat strikes brought unions onto the shop floor. Polls put the socialistic CCF, forerunner of the NDP, in top place. Even Communists, supporters of Canada's wartime ally, got a hearing.

Within Drew's own party, an upstart group known as the "Drones," forerunners of the Big Blue Machine of the 1970s, tried to break the grip of the group they called "old stagers" and "reactionaries." Wartime labour unrest gave the Tory reform wing a golden opportunity to pass Hepburn on the left while gaining credit for slowing the drift to the CCF.

If voters are only given two stark choices between extreme capitalism and extreme socialism, "a general election means in effect a revolution," National Trust president J.M. Macdonnell told a Conservative conference in 1942. Tory labour strategist Fred Gardiner was of the same mind: "You cannot create satisfactory labour relations with bayonets and machine guns." Midway through the war, the Conservative party changed its name to Progressive Conservative, part of an effort to position the Tories as a reform option to the radical CCF.

In the 1943 provincial election, Drew unveiled a 22-point program, with some points so progressive they are still promised in elections today. He campaigned for publicly-owned stockyards, farm boards to keep up farm prices, advanced labour relations laws, public works to stimulate the economy, and provincial payment for half of local education costs. He promised to improve the civil service by increasing staff, eliminating political interference, and "giving to all civil servants a greater sense of security and pride in their work."

Even with this platform, Drew's 38 Conservatives barely outnumbered 34 elected for the CCF plus two for the Communist Party. The discredited Liberals elected 15.

In his first term, Drew worked at blocking a CCF-Liberal coalition by keeping to the left. New labour standards brought in the 48-hour week, paid vacations, improved workers' compensation benefits and expanded daycare. "The Ontario Civil Service will be assured of greatly improved conditions of employment, under a sound civil service system" reclassified on the basis of merit, his throne speech of February, 1944 promised. He kept his word on political impartiality. The 144 civil servants he fired for incompetence in his first 18 months as premier were only a fraction of the firings carried out by the Liberal Hepburn.

The Civil Service Association of Ontario had great expectations for Drew. The CSAO's paper, *Civil Service Review*, hailed Drew as a former civil servant – a reference to his stint at the Ontario Securities Commission – who championed civil service reform. Workers had "the strange feeling of hopeful excitement," the *Review* claimed.

Shortly after the election, the CSAO called for equal representation with government representatives on the Civil Service Commission. This was the CSAO's first request for a structured relationship based on equality. "We do not regard ourselves as mere machinery and our experience has led us to believe that no government can secure a truly loyal and contented civil service unless the civil servants themselves have representation with the administration in matters which concern them," the CSAO's brief claimed. Workers had to be treated "intelligently and equitably in the matter of appointments, promotions, and salaries."

Though bargaining over appointments, promotions and salaries went beyond what most unions of the day hoped for, the CSAO did not present itself as a union. On the contrary, it played on the government's fears of independent, militant unionism.

We are "trying to create a loyal and contented civil service. We are asking your help to this end," the CSAO brief said. "The temper of the times is such," it warned with very little subtlety, that if "we do not perform the duties which our members expect of us, some other...organization will be formed to do this most necessary liaison work, and we believe that any change of this nature would not be welcomed by either the government or the Association."

After the brief was presented, the *Civil Service Review* continued with its threats. The CSAO was "the link or bargaining agency" between workers and the government. But if the government failed to modernize the civil service, workers might form a trade union and get what they need "by some form of force."

Drew didn't call the CSAO's bluff. He said he was open to a new relationship and promised "to stabilize conditions in the service, to remove inequalities and remedy grievances whenever that can be done."

Wishful thinking

On May 18, 1944, Drew created a Joint Advisory Council (JAC), made up of government and civil service appointments. The council's job was "to study and consider," not negotiate. It was to look at "the general principles," not the particulars, of workaday issues such as hours, wages, holidays, discipline and promotion. It also had a mandate to explore long-term issues such as "methods for carrying on the public business," and "development of a career service." The agenda was far-reaching, well beyond what unions bargained for, but the status of CSAO, and the council itself, was purely advisory.

The JAC had more in common with the various premier's councils that sprouted up in Ontario during the 1980s, designed to develop consensus among workers and executives in the face of wrenching changes, than with the unionism of the 1940s.

Drew said the new system "would be an opportunity for members of the civil service to have their views considered, and the standing of the whole Service improved by their own direct contact with government." The Civil Service Commission likened the new system to Whitleyism, the labour-management talkshops that brought British workers and management closer together after the turmoil of World War I. The commission hoped the council would help provide a hero's welcome for returning veterans by guaranteeing them a sympathetic ear when they had problems adjusting to "civvie street."

Like the Whitley Councils, the JAC had a "staff side," made up of three CSAO members, and an "official side," three senior administrators picked by cabinet. Meetings were chaired by the civil service commissioner. While the JAC dealt with policy, a new Civil Service Appeal Board dealt with discipline. Chaired by the Minister of Labour, who had a representative from the CSAO and premier's office at his side, the Board heard appeals from workers who had been punished. There was no provision for routine features of a union-backed grievance system. There was no contract, and therefore no contract violations to grieve. To deal with workplace issues at the local level, Drew also set up departmental councils.

The CSAO raved about the changes. The JAC is "our bill of rights," the *Civil Service Review* claimed in June. President Beardall called it "the proper medium" for relationships, and said "the point of view of the employee is assured of proper attention."

JAC chair Charles Foster was under no such illusions, however. In June, he wrote privately to the treasurer to explain that salary levels would be decided by cabinet and sent to the council for approval.

The JAC never evolved into a place where senior administrators acted for management and the CSAO acted for workers. That was partly because CSAO wasn't recognized as a union, but mainly because the government wasn't willing to delegate its powers as a political employer to its own senior managers. Tories didn't recognize the political independence of either civil service management or workers. They continued to exercise hands-on political control of government administration.

The concept of an independent non-partisan realm for civil service administrators was therefore late in coming to Ontario. The idea of an independent civil service flourished in Ottawa during the war, where the fate of the nation was entrusted to mandarins, mainly professors and others with expertise in science, health, and social policy. "Dollar-a-year" men donated by large corporations provided executive talent, all under the direction of C. D. Howe, an engineer and booster of non-partisan "government by commission" from his early days. Howe was "minister of everything" during the war. In his effort to make Canada a major world player, he delegated the running of major operations to chosen experts. Ontario had no parallel experience or ambitions during the war. And Drew wanted none of it after. He sneered at the top Ottawa civil servants as a "brains trust," and "a small detached group of men without responsibility to anyone."

Nor did it cross Drew's mind to imitate the CCF in Saskatchewan. Elected in 1944, the CCF rushed to create a modern and expert civil service to mastermind its new health, social and economic programs. As a measure of its respect for an independent civil service, as well as its support for unions, the CCF became the first province to grant full bargaining rights to its civil servants.

The CCF had a profound commitment to government as an agency meeting crucial public needs. And it had a deep respect for the civil service as a group with a mind of its own that could pioneer top-notch programs defining the progressive political agenda for the country over the next 20 years. To keep tabs on his own boundless zeal for reform, premier Tommy Douglas imported George Cadbury, a brilliant executive who lost his rights to the Cadbury chocolate fortune when he declared himself a socialist, to organize relations between the cabinet and civil service. Cadbury set up an Economic and Planning Board to develop comprehensive planning systems free from the crisis management of politicians.

Ontario Tories didn't share the CCF enthusiasm for government as an agency of community development. Nor did they see the civil service as a brains trust one step removed from politicians. There was, therefore, no need to develop any structures to cope with the civil service as an independent force. To forbid civil service bargaining was to keep that independence from ever being asserted in the government's own backyard.

The Ontario government of Drew's era felt no need for the government experiments developed by Ottawa or Saskatchewan. In 1946, municipalities, with combined budgets of $231 million, outspent the province. Just half of Ontario's $183 million budget went to health, education and welfare, areas that required complex or independent planning. The rest went for roads and other capital projects that thrived on traditional patronage. Drew's bitter fight with Ottawa over the limits to federal power was an attempt to keep governments out of the health and welfare business and keep Ottawa out of the province's business in building roads and bridges.

The government's "manpower" programs were so far behind the times that Drew had to concoct an emergency airlift to bring in 10,000 skilled workers from Europe in 1948. According to John Porter, immigration was a substitute for educational reform. In those "good old days" of high educational standards, only 58 out of every hundred pupils reached high school. Only four went on to further education upon graduation. The misnamed Hope Commission report, which took up this scandalous state of affairs in 1950, was immediately shelved.

Simply doing what you're told

Growth, not planning, was the cure-all for post-war Ontario. Treasurer Leslie Frost's 1944 budget was based on a wish list, not a strategy. "We are planning for a greater population, for industrial expansion, for prosperous farms and for a happy and healthy people," he said. Government stimulated that growth with subsidies, roads and cheap electricity. There was no thought of directing that growth through complex fiscal policies or Keynesian pump-priming.

Government grew at the whim of politicians. The civil service had no planning function. It simply did what it was told. The workload was light enough for politicians to direct their own departments, and they felt no need to separate politics from administration. Ontario might not have the best laws, labour minister Charles Daly admitted in 1948, but it was an economic success story. Tories just hitched their wagon to the star of new-found prosperity brought on by massive U.S. investment.

If there was no pressure for new services and no need to plan, there was no reason to upgrade the civil service. Drew had gestured toward civil service reform in 1944, and launched what he called "the first step in a systematic program for applying the merit system for appointment to the Ontario civil service." He told the Civil Service Commission to begin hiring on the basis of merit. Deputies and supervisors had three months to approve the new employee, or ask for another. The commission, at last given permission to do what it was set up to do, hailed the decision as a milestone.

Drew quickly backtracked. By year's end, he told the commission to confine itself to typing tests for secretaries. The 1947 Public Service Act gave the commission no independence from government, and downgraded the title of its head from commissioner, which implied independence, to secretary. Ontario's commission was considered the weakest in the country.

Tories preferred giving face-to-face orders rather than providing impersonal rulebooks. The Civil Service Commission, which carried out the functions of a central personnel office, was kept tiny, with a staff of three and a budget of one-third of one percent of payroll. In 1947, it made an effort to classify employees with a questionnaire that asked nothing about education, equipment used, or experience required. A commission staffer explained that the pay system under the new classification was "Because I say so, chum." There were no training programs, just "learning by doing," according to one report in 1947.

Drew's 1944 experiment with a planning and development department was a repeat of the Civil Service Commission episode. Drew gave it no support, no mandate to co-ordinate programs. According to K. J. Rea's history of the Ontario economy, "It was soon apparent that the new department could not co-ordinate even its own varied functions."

The Ontario civil service lagged behind more dynamic governments. But management methods were about the same as in the private sector, save for the largest of corporations. In family-owned businesses, management was not yet a profession separate from ownership. Working harder, not smarter, was still the key to productivity in pre-automation offices and factories. Face-to-face bossing was still the order of the day, and personnel specialists who planned for long-term smooth functioning of an anonymous workforce were held up for ridicule.

The Toronto *Telegram*, a daily broadsheet of hands-on Toryism, published a definition of "personnel" that went the rounds of government offices. Personnel, it sputtered, "do not go, they proceed. They do not have, they are (or more often are not) in possession of. They do not ask, they make application for.... They cannot eat, they only consume.... Instead of homes they have places of residence in which, instead of living, they are domiciled. They are not cattle, they are not ciphers, they certainly are not human beings; they are personnel."

The advisory status of the JAC reflected the low standing and dependency of the civil service, not just the CSAO. The CSAO did not get bargaining rights as a union. Neither did it get the professional rights granted to another group of government-paid workers a month before the JAC was established. The Teaching Profession Act of 1944 made membership in teachers' organizations compulsory, just as it was for doctors and lawyers, the first groups to win automatic "union" membership and dues. This was never done for the CSAO. Teachers also got to set many of their own standards, just like doctors and lawyers. Their code of ethics was included as an appendix to the Teaching Profession Act. Seen as professionals, teachers were granted basic measures of independence. The contrast highlights the denial of independence, not just the denial of union bargaining rights, to civil servants.

The cold war against the CSAO

Drew won a landslide victory in 1945. Politics veered sharply to the right. Drew wanted the Navy sent along the Detroit River to quell Windsor autoworkers' fierce strike for the union shop. Business groups set out to vilify the CCF. One business paper featured ads from "Reliable Exterminators," specialists in getting rid of left-wing vermin. If Ontario did not go through a bout of U.S.-style cold war McCarthyism in the 1950s, it's mainly because witch-hunts did their work in the late 1940s.

The Public Service Act of 1947 was a sign of the times. The act had to be changed, it was said, to bring in compulsory retirement at 65. But a number of other changes were slipped in. This was the first act to refer to all direct government workers, not just officers and clerks, as civil servants. It was the first act to give deputies, as well as ministers, the right to fire workers.

It was the Public Service Act of 1947, not the Garrow Resolution of 1897, that introduced the oath of secrecy and prohibition against political involvement to the Ontario civil service. Without explanation, provincial secretary Roland Michener introduced changes to the compulsory oath taken by civil servants. The new oath made government workers swear they wouldn't disclose "to any person any information or document that comes to my knowledge or possession by reason of my being a civil servant." It was an echo of the U.S. oath introduced in the same year, at the launch of the red scare against "Communist" infiltrators, a campaign which propelled Richard Nixon on his political career.

One of the two Communist members of the legislature, Joe Salsberg, charged that civil servants who'd spoken out recently against low wages had been fired. He asked why the act gave no protection to civil servants who criticized the government. Attorney-General Leslie Blackwell came back in high form, and linked civil service dissent to Soviet spying. He would never hire a person who engaged in politics, Blackwell said. "It is a simple refusal to accept the practical necessity of that division which led to the necessity of spy trials at Ottawa," he said, a reference to Igor Gouzenko's revelations about spying by the Soviet embassy, an incident which involved no Ontario civil servant. No public servant, Blackwell said, has "the slightest right to go outside the service and advocate political views contrary to those of the administration." Salsberg then moved that the section of the act dealing with civil service salaries include a requirement to bargain collectively. That, Roland Michener replied, "would reduce the section to an absurdity."

The new Drew government felt no need to woo labour support. The JAC became a "talkshop" and met rarely. CSAO leaders were burned out; the president and three executive members resigned that year, leading the CSAO's paper to editorialize that the days of volunteer leadership were over. "This association must soon decide whether to employ full-time officers and pay them adequate salaries, or to disband the organization completely," the editorial said.

Members took the threat to heart. In 1946, the CSAO hired its first staffer, Cam Sebastian, and rented its first headquarters, a small room on Bay Street, paid out of three-dollar annual dues of 5,700 members. In another first, CSAO joined the Canadian Council of Provincial Employee Associations, though it was the only provincial section not to sign on with the craft union-based Trades and Labour Congress, one of two union centrals that later merged to form the Canadian Labour Congress. CSAO's increasing professionalism was linked to increasing complaints about low wages and long hours in the civil service, complaints which the new majority Drew government did little about.

In 1947, Ottawa lifted wartime wage and price controls, and inflation took off. The cost of living soared 16.7 points. Ontario civil servants, stuck with a small increase granted in 1946, demanded that wages be indexed to the cost of living. Instead, the province offered a 10 per cent hike in November, 1947.

In December, when the civil service glee club sponsored its annual Christmas carolling, the provincial secretary played Scrooge. Inflation protection would cost two and a half million dollars, he said. He made no promises, but asked the less than gleeful singers "for your confidence that we will meet the problem fairly and justly as we have attempted to do in all other matters which concern you." The de facto rejection led to a stormy annual general meeting, where the CSAO was denounced as a company union. It was time to join an outside union, many delegates said. Speeches were so hot, the preface to the minutes says, that names and arguments had to be altered to protect people from reprisals.

In July 1948, a CSAO brief complained that "no individual group has been forced to lower its standard of living as much as has the bulk of the civil servants." A month later, on election eve, the government gave a $15 a month cost-of-living bonus.

There was also conflict over hours of work. The CSAO wanted a five-day week. They claimed that, without reducing the hours of work, civil servants could cut their hour-long lunch break in half, and finish on Friday instead of Saturday afternoon. The Civil Service Commission supported the change. It was having trouble recruiting secretaries, since private-sector offices had a five-day week. Traditional summertime five-day weeks brought no complaints from the public, the commission argued. The JAC also endorsed the change.

But, in 1947, the government vetoed it, claiming that psychiatric hospitals needed full staffing on Saturday, and it wouldn't be fair to change hours just for office workers. Hours were not changed until 1951.

The government's veto made the JAC meaningless, and proved that cabinet wouldn't be swayed by its own appointees. "In this particular matter the government exercised its judgement with regard to the time at which the proposal would be acceptable to the general public," a government pamphlet later explained.

Political busybodies made for increased tension over workplace habits and practices. Drew and his provincial secretary exchanged frequent memos on the subject of civil servants who spent too long on coffee breaks. Drew wanted the CSAO, which ran the civil service cafeteria, to report all malingerers to their supervisors and even considered providing time cards to those entering the cafeteria. They tried closing the cafeteria except for meals and one 15-minute break period.

Top ministers also got into clockwatching. A new regulation forced workers to sign out at the end of the day. No one could leave early without written permission from a deputy minister.

Cabinet also cancelled office subscriptions to afternoon papers, claiming that workers read them on government time. The civil service manual for 1949 introduced fines for workers who used office phones for personal calls and government stamps on personal letters. Two can play at watching the clock, however, and the CSAO soon raised demands for overtime pay, formerly volunteered free-of-charge.

The cold war against the CSAO continued in 1948. Drew told the legislature he would never bargain with the CSAO. Government officials challenged automatic CSAO representation on department councils, and demanded that positions be open to all workers, not just CSAO members. In protest, the CSAO organized a vote to consider joining an outside union.

Then Drew called a snap election. The CSAO postponed its protest vote, lest it be accused of partisan activity. As soon as the election was over, the CSAO proposed changes to the Public Service Act "to deal with employer-employee relationships on an equitable basis." The government broke off all talks with the CSAO (which then represented 6,000 of 11,000 civil servants) until 1950.

The law in Killaloe

George Drew overplayed his political cards, and lost his own west-end Toronto seat in the 1948 election to the radical socialist and prohibitionist Bill Temple. The CCF regained its toehold in Toronto after being shut out in 1945, and the Communists kept their two seats. While the election wasn't a squeaker, it was certainly a rebuff to Drew's hard-line

Toryism. The Conservatives lost 13 seats.

Ontario Opposition members welcomed the new crew of milder Tory leaders. A.A. Macleod, the popular Communist known for his one-liners, dubbed the comparison between Drew and his successors as "arsenic and old lace." "Having suffered through four years of arsenic," Macleod hoped the new crew "[would] help to relieve the tensions which have existed here since 1944."

Leslie Frost, who won the Tory leadership in 1949, quickly established his reputation as "Old Man Ontario." Donald MacDonald, whose CCF caucus was reduced to such a rump that it was said to meet in a telephone booth, called him "the great tranquillizer." Rejecting Drew's High Tory railing against the welfare state, Frost led the party back to Tory paternalism and pragmatism.

Frost's views on labour relations were those of a fixer, not a fighter. While Drew and Hepburn led the war against allegedly Communist industrial unions, Frost stayed clear of ideology. In his maiden speech as a Member, after the 1937 election, Frost said workers could deal with Communists better than governments because "common sense will kill the radical element in any movement, whether it is the CIO, One Big Union or any other."

As Frost saw the late-1940s Ontario scene, people wanted to get on with their lives after 15 years of depression and war, and forget about protracted battles. For that reason – again in marked contrast to Drew – he ducked whenever the feds tried to start a constitutional war over provincial and federal powers. Frost claimed to stand above the political hurly-burly. In his legislative speeches, he referred to his wife as the leader of the Opposition, and gave her the credit for many of his humanitarian social policies.

During the 1959 election, he announced his creed: "More people, more industry, more jobs, more wages, more opportunity and from these, more productivity and revenues to do the job." He managed to keep a straight face when he told an Opposition critic that: "I must confess to you I haven't been too political in my outlook. I have been too busy looking after human betterment."

As premier, Frost got a kick out of the two Communists in the legislature, and used them to get the goat of his Liberal and CCF opponents. They were brighter than the rest of the Opposition put together, he'd say. "I'd listen to them. Often I'd just grab one of their ideas."

A Tory in touch with the grassroots, Frost showed his warmth when he met people. Shaking hands, he always said a few personal words before touching his new friend's arm. In contrast to Drew, who worried whenever workers deserted their desks, Frost always stopped to chat with civil servants when he bumped into them at Queen's Park. This was typical of Low Toryism, which opted instinctively for personal over bureaucratic relationships and exceptions over rules. When Frost entered the legislature to see CCFer MacDonald's desk piled high with research, Frost told him about a case in Killaloe, deep in the Ottawa Valley. When a city slicker lawyer came to court and started rolling out the legal precedents that favoured his client, the judge informed him that they were not the law in Killaloe. Thereafter, whenever Frost made an about-face turn in policy, the Opposition claimed he was following the law of Killaloe.

That's how premier Frost worked Ontario politics and relations with his own civil servants for 12 years. The towering Tory figures of the era were cut from the same cloth. Fred "Big Daddy" Gardiner, the first chair of Metro Toronto, cut red tape so he could cut ribbons at ever bigger openings. Allan Grossman, a political streetfighter elected from downtown Toronto's Jewish immigrant ghetto, was a success story of immigrant action-line Toryism in white Anglo-Saxon Protestant Ontario.

Grossman detested impersonal bureaucracies. He had no patience for the Toronto Transit Commission, left over from the days of government by all-knowing experts. He claimed these commissions were set up "to get the clammy hand of politicians" off certain matters but turned out to be answerable to nobody. "We transfer to them millions of dollars," he said, "but sometimes we don't even know how they're spending the money."

Political interference, not bureaucratic abstraction, was the only way outsiders could have a chance, Grossman believed. To defeat his Communist rival Salsberg, Grossman presented himself as the champion of Toronto's 260,000 recent immigrants. Within the Conservative Party, he lobbied hard for the province's first human rights legislation. To protect immigrants from exploitation, stronger minimum wage laws were a necessity, he argued. He defended patronage as another measure to help the disadvantaged. "It was better that these jobs should be controlled by nominees of a politician who had contacts in a community rather than by some bureaucrat who would dispense them without considering need and urgency," he said.

After a decade of political turmoil, the Frost government took on all comers with ease. And the style that worked so well with the voters was extended to the civil service with similar effect. The government's relations with the CSAO became another exercise in political pacification achieved through a combination of kind words, fatherly concern, and stick-to-your-ribs reforms.

My door is always open

Relations between Frost and the CSAO started with a cold snap. Frost didn't meet with CSAO leaders for two years. By that time, wages had slipped so low that the Civil Service Commission complained it couldn't recruit new staff.

In May, 1950, the CSAO executive sent Frost a file of 18 months' unanswered correspondence and asked for a meeting. Frost said he'd only meet with civil servants. The civil service "is by its very nature part of the government," and no outsiders – a reference to CSAO's paid staffer – were allowed.

The CSAO executive held its ground. They didn't want to negotiate, they said. That was the job of the JAC. They wanted to discuss the failure of the JAC, and the CSAO's executive secretary was the only person with the working knowledge to talk about that. The CSAO executive threatened to resign en masse if Frost refused to meet with their director.

Frost didn't bend, and the CSAO's entire board resigned in July, 1950. An emergency membership meeting organized a referendum that raised the question of joining the Trades and Labour Congress. On July 21, 2,816 members voted to join the TLC, with 1,473 against. Though only a minority of civil servants voted, Frost got the hint.

That's all the staged protest was. "It was a bluff. We wanted action and we were going to show the government that we were going to get the whole labour movement behind us," Harold Bowen, then a CSAO board member, later claimed.

By fall, Frost had killed both the CSAO and the JAC with kindness. The JAC met six times in two months. But the decisions were made in the premier's office. The 1944 law to depoliticize civil service labour relations became a dead letter. Ad hoc paternalism replaced a structured relationship and substituted for a code of rights.

In August, Frost signed a new wage schedule, and suggested that a cost-of-living bonus was coming soon. "A good Civil Service is essential to good Government and our objective is to make and keep our Civil Service the finest there is anywhere," he told the media.

For the Civil Service Commission, these helter-skelter increases were a nightmare. The commission wanted to keep wages in line with classifications, to prevent a wild ricochet from across-the-board increases. The commission warned the premier that, "unlike the problem which has faced atomic scientists, it is the easiest thing in the world to start a chain reaction in civil service pay rates."

In September, 1950, Frost told the JAC to launch the five-day week in the new year. The CSAO had no need to worry about delays from the JAC, Frost said. "If you can't settle your difficulties, come and see me. The door is always open." In October, Frost raised pension allowances. In December, he gave out Christmas presents: a $60 cost-of-living bonus, confirmation of the five-day week, 18 sick-day credits a year that could be cashed out on retirement, and four weeks' holidays for those with 25 years of service. He should be known as Santa Frost, said leaders of the Twenty-Five Year Club.

Frost started off the New Year with a $90 retroactive cost-of-living bonus and a $20 advance on 1951. He apologized for the delay, but explained that the government thought that inflation would be short-lived. That honest mistake was now being corrected.

In March, 1951, Frost asked the legislature to let CSAO members deduct their dues from their pay, the equivalent of a voluntary checkoff. Civil servants can't bargain collectively under the Labour Act, Frost explained, so government must "lean backwards" to deal with the association and ensure that civil servants get proper treatment. Frost called the CSAO "our civil service association." It was getting too big for volunteers to handle, he said, and offered to pay pension contributions and part of the salary of its executive director. The CSAO rejected this offer. But it did accept government funding for the typing and bookkeeping courses it sponsored.

While Frost's door was always open, his mind was shut on the question of union recognition. In 1951, amidst rumours that Teamsters were organizing liquor control board workers, Frost declared them civil servants "in the full sense of the term." Not to put too fine a point on it, it meant they couldn't form a union.

CSAO president R.C. Johnston understood full well that premier Frost could put CSAO out in the cold. Dealings with government, he told delegates to the 1951 annual meeting, are on a "take it or leave it" basis. "It is better to accept small blessings when offered than to press on still vigorously for more," Johnston said.

In March, 1951, CSAO bought a new headquarters, a ten-room house on Isabella Street. Premier Frost, a major donor to the building fund, cut the white ribbon at the opening. The CSAO's magazine was renamed *The Trillium* in 1951. Its logo was Ontario's official flower atop the CSAO's new motto: "Modern, Loyal, Efficient."

In 1952, CSAO paid $70,000 for a clubhouse on St. George Street. The three-story brick house featured a gracious library, five bathrooms, a dining room that seated 28, a banquet room that served 125, and a rose room, "a lovely sitting room for ladies." No gambling, boisterousness or unseemly language was allowed, the CSAO's brochure stressed. "This is your club. Keep it on a high plane." Yet there was a catastrophe waiting to happen. Three days after delegates to the 1952 annual meeting were told that CSAO was financially sound, officers admitted it was broke. The clubhouse and headquarters were sold at a loss. *The Trillium* suspended publication. Membership records were in a mess. The Toronto branch passed a motion of non-confidence in the executive and the entire executive and staff of three resigned.

The best years of their lives

The CSAO had set itself up with the trappings of a well-established organization, but what had been its organizational history? It took more than clever handling on Frost's part to keep the CSAO from becoming a bona fide union. There was sufficient union potential to force Frost to give just enough, just in time to take the edge off a sustained drive that might have demanded more. But mollycoddling wasn't the secret of Frost's success. Rather, the barriers to unionism lay in the nature of civil servants' work, and their relations with their immediate supervisors, clients and communities.

It helped that the 1950s were good times, when the money flowed into government coffers. If the premier wanted to attract good staff in those boom days, he had to keep up with the competition. Facing a recruitment problem in 1957, the province jacked up the wages of 70 per cent of its employees. Overall, average civil service salaries jumped from $2,250 a year in 1950 to $3,976 ten years later, when a dollar was a dollar and most prices were coming down. On top of that, promotions were commonplace. Every year, about one worker in ten moved further up the salary grid.

The civil service of Frost's day recruited mainly from the age bracket that knew the Depression and war first-hand. Frost's graceful concessions went down easier with a generation still grateful for three squares a day than it did with the youth of the 1960s who took good times for granted and wanted equality, opportunity and self-expression, not security.

For the survivors of the hard times, these were the best years of their lives. Many had grown up with grandparents in their home, a living arrangement made necessary by poverty, not close family ties. Until the 1950s, the pitifully low federal pension was only doled out to those who passed a humiliating means test. Working for the province, they knew they could count on a government pension, says Heather Murray, a clerk at the psychiatric hospital in North Bay. "That was the biggest thing for them, not to be dependent like their parents," she says.

Veterans came to the front of the hiring line at government offices as soon as the war was over. This preference wasn't viewed as discrimination, or violation of the merit principle. It was accepted as a spontaneous gesture toward employment equity, affirmative action on behalf of those who'd missed some career breaks while fighting for their country. In 1946, 80 per cent of new employees were vets. In 1947, 82 per cent were. As late as 1958, almost half the male civil servants were vets.

They had had enough excitement and instability for one life. It's no accident that most of the social reforms passed during the 1950s went by the name of "social security." They stuck to their jobs. Turnover in the civil service averaged about 15 per cent a year, well below the national pattern. Vets were also used to taking orders. "You did what you were told, when you were told," Roy Storey says of the vets he worked with as a lad on northern road crews.

Some vets were like Rusty Fawcett, a key CSAO activist in the 1960s and future OPSEU staffer. Recently awarded a medal by the post-Soviet Polish government for his role in a heroic rescue flight over Poland, he says he felt he'd fought for freedom in World War II, expected to taste it at work, and saw no reason to put up with guff from the "stand-back fusiliers" in management. But most vets, he says, kept their heads low, and didn't want to rock the boat.

Frost's management methods were also buttressed by work settings that went against the grain of traditional unionism. The workplaces, communities and clients of most civil servants didn't fit with standard union appeals. Indeed, the wonder with CSAO is that it was able to organize at all.

Until the 1940s, the standard-bearers of unionism were printers, shoemakers, carpenters, machinists and miners, masters of pre- and early-industrial crafts who shared a fierce occupational pride. In the 1950s, steel, auto and textile unions still celebrated union breakthroughs into anonymous mass-production factories, commonly in one-industry towns where an entire community was pitted against an elite of outsiders.

In the 1950s, unionism made little headway among white-collar and service-sector workers. They had more complex and open-ended relations with their supervisors, and they worked with people, not machines, for the most part. Appeals to worker solidarity can fall on deaf ears in small country towns, where workers mingle with their "superiors" at church and at the local rink. Most government institutions were built in towns like that. Sociologists say that straight-up worker solidarity doesn't wear well in anonymous metropolises, either. Cities are cosmopolitan, a good place for radical intellectuals to gather. But for workers, they usually spell strict separation of work, family and neighbourhood, the trinity of social supports that old-style unions relied on. All government head offices were located in Toronto, the quintessential metropolis and stony ground for those organizing a meeting, let alone a union. Ministries were still called "departments" in those days, and civil servants were departmentalized in their daily lives and thinking. For most civil servants, this was a blessing. Though civil servants had few rights by virtue of a union contract, many enjoyed independence and self-esteem grounded in informal working methods and distance from management control. Benign neglect wasn't far from workers' self-management.

Especially in the north and northwest, back when there were no "faxes" to "improve communications" from the centre, locals liked the long-distance feeling from Toronto head office. Cec Morancy joined the Department of Labour in 1960, counselling apprentices from Sault Ste. Marie west to Manitoba. "I was absolutely completely without supervision. I think my boss was up here three times in five years," he says. He had "free rein," and bent the rules to help people qualify for their trade papers, perhaps by helping out francophones who couldn't pass written exams in English.

Jack Armstrong was a fire ranger in Kirkland Lake. Relations with management were excellent, he says. That was easy for him to say: he communicated with management by radio. "The working people then had a lot more input into the direction the government should be taking" with resource management, he says. "I really enjoyed going to work because you did your job. There was no interference; there was no bureaucracy."

The characters and companionship that flourished in remote areas made Highways and Lands and Forests work gangs a breed apart. Workers from these departments became the power brokers of the CSAO, and dominated its board of directors throughout the 1950s. At Quetico Park in the deep northwest, legendary rangers like "Terrible Ted" and Bob Wells listened for the call of the wild, not the call from Toronto. They knew their way around the bush. There was no road to the park until 1954. From 1927, says park interpreter Shirley Peruniak, they spent each winter deep in the woods, watching out for illegal trappers. They adjusted rules to meet the circumstances, let poor families caught poaching get away with a warning, and turned a blind eye to their own traplines as well. They didn't call in a supervisor if a new crew member was slow getting out of bed. "Terrible Ted" threw a wolf into one lazy partner's cabin. It saved chewing him out personally. Park superintendent Ross Williams was an ex-military man who barked "very much like a sergeant major" but "ran a very tight ship" and was "fair and square," oldtimers said.

Management wasn't overcome by professionalism in the 1950s, and even when managers were closer at hand, they did not always put workers under their thumb. Neil Lang started with Lands and Forests as a tree planter in 1956. He was 17, and this was a nice way to make some spending money during off-seasons, when he wasn't needed on his family's subsistence farm near Parry Sound. Lang describes the management style of the time as "creative neglect." Oldtime chief rangers were "cut from the same cloth (as the workers), great lads. They came up the hard way." Whenever his chief ranger, who'd worked in the bush since the age of 12, came to the work site, and "you wanted a rest, just bring up the subject of hunting." It was the workers who looked after slackers. If someone wasn't carrying his share of the load, "he would run into a doorknob or something," Lang says.

The staff moved around and pitched in according to the demands of the season. "We were never married to one thing," says Lang, who rotated from fires to fish to wildlife to planting. "That's what made Lands and Forests such a good place to work for. You had a feeling of helping, of being part of the organization." Workers weren't given orders, he says. "You were saddled with the job and you did it to the best of your ability." There were regular staff meetings to talk about problems. "You were always part of it," he says.

Since most managers came up from the ranks, they already had training in the essentials of bending rules to meet reality. Mel Vezina, who started in maintenance at Thunder Bay's psychiatric hospital in the 1950s, was called in for an emergency repair one New Year's Eve. The nurse was asleep at her station, following a party. Vezina met her again years later, when she was head nurse and he was chief steward defending a worker caught napping on the night shift. "I seem to remember one night at two o'clock in the morning…" Vezina started. "Okay, we'll settle it," she said.

Many managers encouraged workers to get involved in CSAO, and gave them a wide berth in local CSAO activities. Lang's senior manager, 75 miles away in Parry Sound, asked him to be a CSAO rep and help out with the curling bonspiels. Lang became local president in 1958, a post he held for the better part of 30 years. If there were problems, he'd meet with the manager, but there was "nothing too hard set," he says. If the budget allowed it, something would be done. "They wanted good cooperation." Lang's district forester used to tell him: "I wouldn't mind if you put a grievance in." Managers liked having the CSAO, Lang says. "It could work both ways when their hands were tied."

Oh happy days

Sometimes, these local coping mechanisms brought people to CSAO who weren't normally attracted to unions. Jim Peden, a timber scaler based in Thunder Bay, worked with CSAO during the 1940s to bring the first health-care scheme to the area. He got active in CSAO, eventually became branch president and provincial board member, as a way "to get out and help people." But he didn't want a union. If workers didn't like the pay or conditions, they should have the gumption to quit and see if they could do better, he says. "I always worked for both the CSAO and the government," he says.

Over at the Department of Highways, work gangs knew about camaraderie, if not union solidarity. Road gangs were happy campers, says Fred Nice, who worked on his first highway in 1959. The crew set up camp a mile from Kapuskasing, and "the companionship was just out of this world." Workers turned hard times into fun: a freezing day was perfect for hiding a fellow's boots in the snow. After work, there was boxing, cards, carousing, heading off to town to beat up on some locals who snubbed a crew member. "Whatever we did would draw us all together," Nice says. But togetherness didn't exclude the boss. "The boss was one of us," says Nice. "If we got into muskeg, he got into muskeg. He paid his dues."

Working for the government in those days was being a somebody. As soon as Lang got on permanent, he went to a bank for a car loan. His government job was all the security he needed, this at a time when banks almost automatically turned all workers down, forcing them to build up credit unions. Uniforms, standard in Lands and Forests and institutions, weren't seen as a denial of individuality but a mark of worth. "They were kinda neat," says Lang of the forest green pants, shirts and police-style brim hats he sported. He was proud when the public singled him out and asked his advice on any matter looked after by the department. He took it as a sign of prestige, not subordination, that civil servants were told not to hang out in low-life bars where people might recognize them.

When Nice settled in Timmins, a civil servant was ranked "one notch below a bank manager," he says. He was welcomed into the local Lions, Kinsmen, Kiwanis and Masons. The jokes about DOH – department of holidays – and MTO – more time off – didn't come until later. In the 1950s, workers took fierce pride in the fact that Ontario, despite its demanding climate and distances, built the best roads in North America.

Government workers in jails, psychiatric hospitals, and institutions for the retarded had their ways of making the best of a bad situation. Conditions in Ontario institutions were stock scandals and standing jokes, regularly described as "archaic" and "shameful" in the media. Ron Haggart, a top investigative reporter, wrote that "nothing symbolized the administration of Leslie Frost more than the fact that the disgraceful, crowded and smelly hospital for retarded children at Orillia, subject to pleas for help for years, could be reached by the most modern and expensive four-lane boulevard expressway." After describing the overcrowded conditions at Orillia, Pierre Berton likened the see-no-evil attitude of Ontario's citizens to the Germans who said they didn't know what went on in concentration camps. "Well, you have been told about Orillia," Berton wrote.

Though most of these exposés told it like it was, there were complexities and softer edges that crusaders on the outside didn't always see. Some of these complexities relate to the way workers coped with their dismal situations and conducted themselves on and off the job.

DON'T CALL ME SERVANT

Ontario's many century-old psychiatric hospitals were chronically underfunded. The province paid $1.06 a day for each patient's upkeep, about a quarter the amount paid for each patient in psychiatric wings of regular hospitals. The North Bay hospital housed 993 inmates in quarters built for 400. When Heather Murray came to work Monday mornings, she noticed many patients had bruises and black eyes, some inflicted by other patients, some inflicted by staff. The attendants were "all Masons, Conservatives, and big, big, big," she says, but untrained to deal with the frustrations of patients sent to hospitals for lifetime sentences. They herded patients into the showers like cattle, she says. "It was absolutely inhumane."

Yet Murray doesn't look back in horror. She's seen worse as a result of half-hearted efforts at reform since. At least the meals were good and there was plenty to keep people occupied back in the 1950s, she says. Hospitals worked at being self-reliant in food, partly to save money and partly to keep patients busy, and patients joined staff working the 15-acre garden and farm. The head doctor knew everyone by name, and always had time to talk with staff and inmates when he strolled down the halls. Non-professional staff stood at attention whenever doctors or nurses entered the room. They weren't so quick to stand up for themselves.

The CSAO looked after workers' social needs. All employees donated 50 cents every pay day to the CSAO. That paid for a weekly Saturday night dance at the Empire Hotel, a graduating party for nurses, a yearly cruise on Lake Nipissing, a summer picnic, a Christmas party, and two formal dances. "Poverty drew them together, like a big happy family," she says.

There were no clear lines between work time and free time. North Bay workers took patients home for weekends, took them out shopping on days off, came with their families to see movies on Sunday nights. "It wasn't like going to work. It was like a small city all of its own," Murray says. "You never minded staying late. Everybody got along. There wasn't any of this 'I'm the boss and you'll do what I tell you,'" she says. "Payday wasn't the biggest day in the world, because it was so damn small. You really felt you were accomplishing something, you were contributing something."

Mel Vezina says the same about Thunder Bay. "The whole crew worked together," he says. "It was like a family. There was none of the bureaucracy that's moved into the hospital. We were a team." Job satisfaction, he says, came from working relations that were "much freer." Workers felt appreciated. The pleasure of making a contribution, of being part of a tight group, made up for a lot. This explanation of the relative weakness of unionism among civil servants during the 1950s flies in the face of 1990s stereotypes of passive government employees.

Cynics may say that solid patronage had a lot more to do with cementing loyalty and debt to the government than sentiments about a job well done. Fred Nice got his highways job after helping pull the vote for a cabinet member from Kemptville. In those days, the powerful Tories could promise "my way *and* the highway." On northern road crews, "we were all Conservatives," Nice says. "They put three squares on the table, and they paid for the roof over the house." He thought he owed the government loyalty. "They put up with me and I put up with them," he says.

But patronage and political debts don't build loyalty. They just build the desire for more favours. That's been known since Machiavelli: "The nature of man is such as to take as much pleasure in having obliged another as in being obliged himself."

It's this – in all likelihood unplanned – reverse psychology of the civil service workforce that made rank-and-file unionism difficult to achieve during the 1950s. As long as workers felt needed and part of something, as long as their bosses gave them leeway to do their job, they were prepared to put up with a lot.

DON'T CALL ME SERVANT

The only difference is what we're paid

Women were the likeliest candidates to see their problems in terms of denied rights that required formal changes to policy. There were only 900 women in the civil service in 1950, a mere nine per cent of the workforce. About 80 per cent of the women were single. Married women were only hired as temps, unless they could prove that no single woman or man could handle the job. "This policy appears to be sound and cannot logically be criticized," Civil Service Commission secretary Charles Foster wrote the provincial secretary in May, 1950. Sometimes, however, married women had to be hired as nurses, nurse's aides or typists. "These are jobs that men cannot fill and for which sufficient single girls are not at present available," Foster explained. No married women got pension benefits.

Like other labour organizations of the time, CSAO went along with this discrimination against married women. Their desire for pin money shouldn't take a job away from a breadwinner, the saying went. An editorial in the CSAO magazine claimed in 1951 that men should be paid enough so they didn't have to send their wives out to work.

Women made less than men throughout the civil service. The average male salary in 1950 was $2,722 a year. The average female salary was $1,885. This did not disturb the Civil Service Commission, supposedly in charge of classifying pay according to the job, not the person. There's only one case on record where civil service commissioner Foster went to bat for an underpaid woman. A Miss E. M. Sanderson started work as a secretary and acting administrative assistant to the Minister of Education in 1908. In 1927, when classification was introduced, she made $2,000. At that time, male head clerks with considerably less responsibility made $3,600. In 1950, Sanderson made $3,300. Male executive assistants were paid $4,600. Foster proposed what he called a compromise (presumably with Miss Sanderson's request for equal pay). He said she should get a raise on the basis of her long years of service.

In 1956, the commission stopped discriminating against married women. According to the commission's annual report, that meant women now enjoyed "full and equal privileges" with men. Two years later, almost half the women working for the Ontario government were married.

This was the group to watch. As permanent workers, women were relatively new to the civil service. They had fewer reference points in the past, in the Depression of the 1930s or the war of the 1940s. They were concentrated in a small number of jobs. Usually, they formed an overwhelming majority of any occupation they worked at. That gave them opportunities to run their own locals and demand action from the CSAO.

In institutions, for instance, the segregation of male and female wards meant that women worked entirely on their own, and developed their own leadership. The participation of women in rank-and-file CSAO activities was greater than in most unions, and perhaps accounts for CSAO's early raising of equal-pay demands.

The CSAO's *Trillium* of March, 1956, was turned into a music sheet for the country's first "rap" song.

"Male Attendant" and "Nurse Aide"
Two classifications the Government made.
What is the difference? May we ask?
We are all assigned the self-same tasks.
On nurse aide or male attendant
Patients for their care are dependent.
We both work a week of forty-four hours;
There are as many on their wards as on ours.
Bathing and dressing you cannot shirk
Whether patients are wearing pants or skirt.
All are entitled to eat three meals
Be they men or mere females.
Beds must be made and no dirt found
For the same supervisor will be around.
On the men for stretchers we depend,
We help with medications, treatments and such;

> But are the nurse aides paid nearly as much?
> "Male Attendant" or "Nurse Aide"
> The only difference is what we're paid.
> Do men get their groceries at a dearer store?
> When they buy a car, do they have to pay more?
> Our registered nurses have the self-same beef,
> For three years' training they get only grief.
> In grandma's day the suffragette
> Worked and fought equal rights to get.
> But still at the end of '55
> We wait for wages to equalize.
> Our goal before '56 shall end
> Is that equal cheques to us they'll send.
> Equal pay is a government law,
> But law unenforced sticks in our craw.
> Women!! Up and Shout!! and have your say,
> For equal work we want equal pay!!
>   – "An Interested Nurse Aide"

From the barber's chair

Leslie Frost always claimed to look at Ontario politics "from the standpoint of the barber's chair in Lindsay," his home constituency. His view was government as "the people's business. Good government therefore, is a matter of common sense." But as Frost settled into the barber's chair, the province became an urban industrial giant and the provincial government a major actor in the economy and society. Within government, anonymous methods of handling workers began to creep in without Frost or anyone else being aware.

The economic boom in the 1950s changed the face of the province.

Two-thirds of new jobs were in the service sector. There was a 65 per cent increase in professionals. The number of farmers and industrial workers was declining. As the lines between social classes became finer, the old-time "pyramid of class" was turned into "more of a beehive shape," John Porter wrote in *The Vertical Mosaic*. But the new job openings didn't make the province less elitist or more democratic. On the contrary, the new demand for degrees and paper credentials broke down the traditional ladders of promotion that let people work their way up from the bottom.

As the economy changed and became more complex, so did government. When Frost began, the province was a regulator and law enforcer that dabbled on the side as builder. Ten years later when Frost retired, the government had the outlines of a full-fledged social service state. Since the turn of the century, the Civil Service Commission noted in 1954, "the concept of the state has changed radically. The mainsprings today are communal well-being and social justice and towards this end the state now employs scientific and technical personnel whose services were not even contemplated half a century ago."

Frost broke through the barriers of limited government. In 1956, the province's first fiscal budget was tabled. It was drawn up to stimulate and direct the economy, not just count money in and money out. In 1957, the budget matched the Depression all-time-high spending record, five per cent of gross provincial product. In 1959, it hit nine per cent.

The new state cost more. Permanent staff increased from 12,869 in 1949 to 27,360 in 1958. Real government spending jumped from $466 million in 1950 to $1,081 million in 1961. To meet these costs, Frost hiked the corporate tax rate to 11 per cent in 1957. The next year, he brought in a three per cent provincial sales tax, quickly dubbed the "frost-bite."

As government grew complex and took on more of a life of its own, labour relations started to become institutionalized and professionalized. Methods that got by with last-minute political fixing couldn't deal with the new situation.

In 1955, government personnel officers began meeting to exchange notes with colleagues in other jurisdictions. In 1958, a director of personnel was appointed. In 1959, the Joint Advisory Council got its first permanent secretary, an indication that bargaining was more than the premier and a few part-timers could handle. A personnel council launched an eight-day training program for 60 officers. A formal grievance procedure replaced the old review board that only heard appeals on dismissals. In 1960, the government started a pay research bureau to match rates of other employers. A classification rating committee heard complaints about improper job descriptions. In 1961, under pressure from CSAO and academics, a fledgling Department of the Civil Service was created.

Frost's Tories took their cues in labour relations from Jacob Finkelman, about the only labour law expert who supported them. Since the 1930s, Finkelman had championed independent and expert boards as the way to handle disputes. He believed that their flexibility and adaptiveness best met the new realities of industrial relations. Judges were too biased against workers to be fair, and too hamstrung by criminal procedures. Blind justice didn't see the need for shrewd and fine-tuned solutions to problems that went beyond simple innocence or guilt, he wrote in a series of pioneering studies in labour law.

Finkelman was the major mover and shaker in setting up Ontario's 1943 labour code, and chaired the board which administered it. He had a falling-out with Drew, and was replaced by a businessman who soon created havoc with his one-sided and arbitrary decisions. Frost pleaded with Finkelman to resume the chair in 1953, a position he held until 1967. According to the leading labour lawyer and arbitrator Harry Arthurs, the Tories may not have appreciated Finkelman's support for collective bargaining, but they were politically smart enough to know that "so long as they kept the labour movement tolerably happy, the CCF would not be the beneficiary" of militancy.

Finkelman knew how to make the Tories look good at little cost. In one instance, unions and business were deadlocked in a do-or-die battle over voting procedures in organizing drives. Business insisted that non-voters be added to the tally of anti-union voters. Unions insisted that non-voters, as in all other elections, not be counted at all. After calm and dispassionate study, Finkelman found that the legal difference rarely affected the outcome of organizing drives, and advised the labour minister to come down on the side of labour. If "you want to give the unions something, let us show, make a show, of giving something, but not really giving them anything, if this is what you want. If it's the window dressing, here's the story," he said.

Finkelman more than paid for his keep with shrewd advice like this that helped stabilize labour relations. This was no small matter in a decade when, according to a 1956 Gallup poll, 69 per cent of the population favoured unions, and 71 per cent of white collar workers thought unions had been a good thing for the country.

Finkelman had as hard a time as anyone understanding where civil servants fitted into the labour relations scene. "Public servants are peculiar people," he said. They are generally well-educated, "and a lot of them are accustomed to spending countless hours looking at documents and construing them. And the result is, they come up with some rather weird ideas as to what their rights are," he told one researcher.

It's likely that the Tories' top labour advisor shaped, or at least reinforced, Frost's approach to civil service labour relations. Expert boards suited a paternalistic regime that was concerned with appearing fair-minded but worried about being bound by rules. The rash of hearings, boards, experts, specialists and hard-nosed comparative studies bear the signature of Finkelman's private-sector style.

The government was also spurred on to change by a 1956 auditor's report, which said it was time to look into the size and purpose of government and its agencies. In 1958, Frost appointed Walter Gordon to head a commission to come up with some answers.

Best remembered as a courageous economic nationalist, Gordon's claim to fame in the 1940s and '50s was his prestigious accounting and consulting firm. In 1946, he chaired a royal commission for Ottawa on public service classifications, and pinpointed organizational defects in classic scientific management jargon. In his view, senior managers were overwhelmed with trivia, incapable of delegating, and unable to exercise overall control. As a result of an outmoded merit system, classifications were too rigid, and the road to promotions was "bestrewn with a vast number of closely spaced blocks."

Gordon's 1959 report on the Ontario government, and its "growing pains" in the midst of expansion, urged that senior managers be freed up from trivia, experts be given freer rein, amateurs pushed aside, and policy makers placed in command. That meant upgrading the Civil Service Commission and personnel branch. Gordon lambasted the senior managers who resisted personnel planning and who had defied directives to set up personnel branches in half the government's departments.

In 1960, a select committee heartily endorsed Gordon's report and called for personnel departments and other modern approaches so that government could conduct itself with the efficiency of business. Two future premiers, John Robarts and Bill Davis, were leading members of this committee.

In his directive to Walter Gordon, Frost took pains to remind him that government of, for, and by the people must not be overshadowed by the efficiency of business methods. Sound advice from the barber's chair. Frost retired in 1961. When he paid a visit to Queen's Park a few years later, he told CCF leader Donald MacDonald: "I don't feel at home. Things have so changed."

❊

"Bargaining, not begging"

Changes in the way the province dealt with civil service labour relations didn't only come from on high or from the inner workings of bureaucratization and modernization. A rejuvenated CSAO was also pushing for change from below. "I used to swear by Harold Bowen, then I used to swear at him," says Fred Nice, a CSAO director in the late 1950s, later a member of OPSEU's executive board in the mid-1980s.

There's little doubt that Harold Bowen rescued CSAO from financial and moral collapse in 1952 and turned it into a force capable, by the end of the decade, of winning major gains. Though he got sworn at for staying on as leader for too many encores, he was the mastermind of CSAO's evolution toward unionism throughout the 1950s and most of the '60s. A former Lands and Forests clerk and branch president, he combined the rugged face and huge hands of a labourer with the horn-rimmed glasses and impeccable suits of a labour official dressed for success.

Bowen led a slate that took over CSAO in 1952, "under conditions which would have bankrupted any commercial business concern," he said. Despite those reservations, he nurtured it back to health as an independent labour organization.

By 1954, CSAO had recruited 85 per cent of civil servants to its ranks and put its finances on a sound footing by doubling dues to six dollars a month. In 1955, Bowen forced the JAC to grant CSAO official standing as "the recognized organization representing Ontario Civil Servants." The CSAO board explored taking that recognition one step further by applying for formal union certification under the Labour Relations Act, but pulled back on the advice of lawyers. They warned that if the Act were made to apply to the civil service, then any union could set up shop as a competing union. The board decided to let sleeping dogs lie.

The format for labour relations remained that of a government and its employees. Thus CSAO continued to present its requests in briefs to the premier, rather than table demands with managers designated to act for the employer. The CSAO's 1956 brief raised 26 requests, small and large. CSAO wanted payday every two weeks, rather than once a month. It also wanted a measure of sexual equality: the right of spouses of civil servants to apply for government jobs. Frost granted most of CSAO's demands, and took pains to give CSAO full credit for the changes when he announced them to the legislature. He even let CSAO trumpet its victory – and his generosity – in a press conference preceding his announcement.

But the nuances of a government-worker relationship escaped notice in the context of Bowen's concerted drive for a formal bargaining relationship. Beginning in 1956, when CSAO had 20,000 members and seven staff, Bowen set out to raise the sights of civil servants to the point where they felt comfortable dealing with the massive Ontario government as an equal in hard-edged bargaining.

He spurned standard CSAO activities as "collective begging," beneath the dignity of an employee organization. He didn't want too much attention paid to self-help activities such as discount volume purchases. He winced at executive member George Gemmell's way of taking advantage in bargaining. Whenever Gemmell headed off to an important meeting, he took off his artificial leg and put on his peg leg so he could gain sympathy when he entered the room.

Bowen tried to break out of the confines of a civil service bargaining mentality. Traditionally, CSAO had asked the Ontario government to match the wages of the federal civil service. Those wages, geared to rates in many poorer regions of the country, lagged behind the standards set by private sector workers in Ontario. Bowen wanted a piece of that larger action, and bargained accordingly.

"The horizon of the Association is widening, and our sights must be raised," he told the 1956 annual meeting in his presidential address. "We cannot make a policy and then sit on it. Our policies must change with changing conditions."

The meeting amended CSAO's 1927 charter to spell out a full range of union functions: "to represent the employees of the Government... in all matters governing appointment, promotion, remuneration, vacation, hours of work, superannuation, transfer, discipline, including suspension, demotion and dismissal, and in all matters relevant to conditions of work."

The board established a grievance committee that year, a gain Bowen pushed hard for in 1957, when he became the CSAO's full-time general manager. CSAO had to focus on changing general policies, not fixing isolated problems, he stressed. Many individual problems conceal a principle, he said, in a swipe at paternal shows of mercy in particular situations. CSAO must build structured relationships "policed as actively as the policies and regulations themselves."

For the same reason, Bowen preferred bargaining to arbitration. He didn't want to short-circuit the need for direct and mature relations. A loss at arbitration was lost for a long time, he argued, while ongoing bargaining could continue to build pressure for change.

In December 1958, CSAO's brief demanded formal bargaining. In this case, Bowen supported neutral arbitration rather than strikes or lockouts in the event bargaining broke down. The Tories didn't see that as a concession. Independent arbitration spelled an end to the politicians' monopoly over decisions affecting government workers.

Frost didn't respond. On March 22, 1959, in Toronto, three thousand civil servants filled the Odeon Theatre to the rafters, while an overflow crowd filled the Westbury Hotel. Theatre walls were draped with banners and placards proclaiming "Bargaining is not disloyal," and "bargaining, not begging." Bowen said further talks with government were "a waste of time, money and effort." Other speakers denounced the government's refusal to pay time-and-a-half for overtime. A unanimous vote supported an all-out push for bargaining rights, a grievance system and higher pay. One old-guard director resigned rather than obey an additional motion ordering the board to fight for bargaining rights.

"No longer mouse-like, the civil servant is talking union," a Toronto *Star* editorial noted two days later. The right to strike was out of the question, the *Star* said: "A civil service strike is essentially a revolutionary policy; if the strike is protracted, government is overthrown and succeeded by anarchy." But that didn't justify denying collective bargaining with arbitration, it concluded.

Frost continued to play cat and mouse with CSAO and refused to meet. But with each month of delay, CSAO raised the stakes. The demand for bargaining rights came from a new assertive, even adventurous, spirit within the civil service. In the March *Trillium* the CSAO announced: "We seek opportunity, not protection; a future, not security; merit, not patronage; action, not promises; realistic attitudes, not outworn platitudes."

A decade of dallying had frayed the blanket of Tory paternalism. "More and more our members are being forced to acceptance of the unpleasant conclusion that the apparent good will of the Government toward the Association as their acknowledged representative, is no more than a mask for indifference and high disregard for any representation, however well justified," the *Trillium* said in April. "It is clear," it noted a month later, "that the next step can only be introduction into the present system of negotiation of a form of bargaining which will result in a memorandum of agreement, signed by representatives of both parties, and binding upon both."

The CSAO was beginning to distinguish the government's role as government from its role as employer. Once the sovereign, all-powerful overlay of government was peeled off, civil service relations could be seen for what they were – labour-management relations, pure and simple, with no additional burden of privilege or obligation that justified denial of workers' rights. And changes in that relationship could be registered in a standard labour contract, not a set of legal or regulatory changes that required umpteen delays.

Bowen threatened a strike unless there was progress in wage talks. In the fall, CSAO staged its version of a sit-in. The board of directors held a marathon session, and refused to return to work until Frost agreed to meet. Frost's door re-opened. He agreed to raise wages, to assign a cabinet member to handle civil service problems, and to set up a Public Service Grievance Board to hear workers' appeals of all management decisions. This was a marked improvement over Drew's board, which only heard appeals from workers who were fired. Although the CSAO did not enjoy standard union rights to appoint its own nominee to the board, one board member was a known CSAO supporter.

These reforms were not enough to prop up the old system. On the contrary, they put the spotlight on the basic problem of the JAC. Although the JAC included CSAO and government appointees, it had no power to implement its decisions. For instance, it had supported a grievance board since 1958, but Frost only acted when he was good and ready, or when his hand was forced.

Trouble at the Don

As often happens, the old order was brought tumbling down by a show of farce. An incident in Toronto's Don Jail brought out the true colours of Tory paternalism, and held the government up to contempt and ridicule.

The Don had been in the public eye in the mid-1950s, when Edwin Alonzo Boyd of the notorious Boyd Gang twice escaped. Prison bars made from cheap iron bend easily, he told the media after his first escape. For an encore, he took the imprint of a key while shaking a guard's hand. Inmates sang "Down By The Old Mill Stream" to cover up the sound of Boyd's filing, and he bust loose with his cell-made key. "I hope we proved something about the Don Jail," he told his eventual captors.

Throughout the 1950s, jails were run by municipalities and counties, which ran them on the cheap, as holding tanks, not reform institutions. Colonel J. Hedley Basher, the deputy minister in charge of reform institutions, apparently lived up to his name. CCF leader Donald MacDonald regularly exposed brutality in Ontario jails. In 1956, he broke the story of a 12-year-old Native girl who attempted suicide after 92 days in isolation. Her custodians said they needed to break her spirit.

A prisoners' riot at Guelph in 1952 pressured the government to appoint a commission which called for modernizing jails and handing them over to the province. The commission also recommended organizing guards under the CSAO. In 1961, the province took over most local lockups. But it refused to recognize CSAO in its dealings with guards, and refused to override military-style discipline of employees by extending new civil service grievance rights to the jail guards.

The issue was brought to a head at the Don Jail in December, 1961, when guards and inmates poked fun at guard T. Brendan Keatinge when he permed and dyed his hair. "Wolf calls greet beauty salon jail guards," the *Star* reported on December 16. Keatinge was charged with creating disorder and suspended for ten days. In January, Don guard Tony Simonson was fired for breaking his oath of secrecy and snitching to the media. CSAO local president Jim Keatings was fired for refusing to answer questions about the incident. His refusal was branded illegal and unacceptable for a guard. Both were refused a hearing.

In January, Frank Tumpane, a popular columnist with the *Telegram*, asked why men did not have the same right to dye their hair as women. In March, NDPer Ken Bryden needled the Tories in the legislature, and asked why the men were denied an appeal. The minister of reform institutions, Irwin Haskett, said the jails were full of "troublesome agitators" and dangerous criminals, and "nothing in the nature of subversive activity on the part of the staff can be tolerated." Nevertheless, as a matter of grace, he allowed that the men could appeal to him, and he might decide to hear their case. The CSAO publicly rejected this offer and demanded that the guards be granted standard grievance rights.

The government refused to budge. That guaranteed full play for the incident on the front pages for the better part of two months. Keatings got a new job working for the CSAO. In April, the CSAO broke off all talks with the JAC. It refused to meet again until full-fledged bargaining was in place.

In May, after heated debate, the CSAO board decided against future discount bulk purchases. The historic co-op function of CSAO had to give way to bargaining campaigns. Membership participation was stepped up with a series of regular "activity reports," newsletters that kept people up to date with CSAO's "determined stand."

A September, 1962 report criticized cabinet for refusing to meet with CSAO leaders. It's likely that CSAO still saw politicians as the people to deal with. This cast the shadow of government sovereignty over straight bargaining disputes. In October, for instance, the board favoured making all matters negotiable, "subject to the overriding authority of the legislature."

By then, the Tories were open to depoliticizing labour relations. A hands-off approach was in keeping with the wisdom of modern management. It also got rid of some hot potatoes. Once a source of political credit, direct responsibility for civil service matters increasingly brought public discredit on the government. Once a source of political strength, direct responsibility increasingly made politicians vulnerable to political pressure.

Impartial civil servants

In November 1962, the CSAO board met as usual at the Westbury Hotel, watering hole and home away from home for many top politicians. The penthouse door was always open for CSAO leaders who wanted to play poker with rising star John Robarts and his cronies. "I took a trimming there on numerous occasions," says Fred Nice.

Bowen was addressing the board, when a knock was heard at the door. A bellboy hand-delivered a letter, carried with great ceremony in his white gloves. The Tories had put their gloves back on. The letter said the Public Service Act was being changed. The JAC would be replaced by an Ontario Joint Council made up of four government appointees and four CSAO appointees. The joint council "should negotiate such matters as were put on its agenda." If council appointees couldn't agree, an arbitration board made up of a government and a CSAO appointee and a neutral chosen by them, would decide.

"Negotiations, do we know how to spell it?" a board member asked. "All 26 of us didn't know sheepshit from tar" about collective bargaining, says Nice. "We thought it had something to do with Jimmy Hoffa and baseball bats. We thought we were going to have to be bad guys like that."

The board members were as unschooled in politics as in bargaining. Another section of the new Act spelled out, for the first time, prohibitions on political activity by civil servants. The Conservatives had been thinking about this for some time. The preamble to the 1962 Act referred to a new civil servant, who "must be well equipped with the arts, skills and knowledge of a complex society to do his or her job effectively." Civil servants must be impartial and efficient, and "because of our type of government, necessarily must remain silent in matters of public policy."

When the draft bill delivered to the CSAO board became law in February 1963, it was presented as "model legislation for a progressive democratic state." It claimed to update the old 1890s Garrow Resolution, with its "outright prohibitions against political activity." "In the days of positive government, it is necessary that we have the minimum of restrictions on the persons of high qualifications who work for the province," the preamble to the bill claimed.

This was hogwash. Seventy years before, the Garrow Resolution had set no limits on taking part in municipal politics, no limits on free speech, no limits on small-scale as distinct from "active" participation in provincial and federal elections. Aside from that, the Resolution had no force, since it was a resolution, not a law.

The new Act laid down the law on political rights. It ordered all deputies to stay clear of all politics. It stopped civil servants from running for school board or city elections if party affiliation was involved. Any civil servant standing as a candidate had to take a leave of absence. No civil servant could canvass or speak on political matters during an election. Unless on leave, no civil servant could "at any time speak in public or express views in writing for distribution to the public on any matter that forms part of the platform of a provincial or federal political party." Given the range of views held by Canadian political parties, this amounted to a virtual ban on big-P and small-p political free speech – a ban that remained unchanged for 30 years.

Liberal leader John Wintermeyer came close to the mark when he said the new act recognized the civil service as a distinct branch of government. This was the measure of the changes brought about in Frost's era. In this shift, the civil service was removed from hands-on political control and put under bureaucratic control. That made the new Tory politicians more comfortable with the idea of granting bargaining rights. However, to make sure that the civil service retained the neutrality that warranted bargaining rights, civil servants as individuals became politically neutered.

It is a mark of the CSAO, the union movement, opposition parties, civil libertarians, and social critics of the time that no one noticed or complained. The invisibility of the change no doubt reflected the domination of the technocratic ideal that swept across North America in the 1950s and '60s, and was said to mark "the end of ideology." As the power behind that ideal worked its way through the civil service of the 1960s, the spanking new Joint Council became as unstable and unsatisfactory as Drew's Joint Advisory Council.

Chapter Three

Accidental Unionism

Times were good in 1966, and school was a drag. So Art Lane quit school at 18, and went job hunting. His first morning out, he left his name at three factories and the Brockville Psychiatric Hospital, a major employer in that arch-Conservative town. The hospital called him back that afternoon. He started the next morning. The days of seeing a job as a favour were over. "I figured I did them a favour by working for them," Lane says.

A personnel officer told Lane there'd be no unemployment insurance deducted from his pay cheque. If he kept his nose clean, he'd be there the rest of his life. He'd get fringe benefits like hospital insurance after nine months. "That's because it takes nine months to have a baby," the man whispered: The government wasn't going to pay for something he did before he started work. But it did supply his attendant's uniform: grey trousers with a black stripe, blue shirt, black bow tie, grey tunic. The clip-on bow tie, the last word in safety equipment, was designed so patients couldn't use it to wring attendants' necks. There was no excuse for not wearing it, and he'd be disciplined if he took it off.

There were 16 wards in the hospital, all locked, with 140 patients in each ward, beds jammed beside each other. Troublemakers were locked in solitary. The patient known as "Mike the Russian" never saw the light of day for 11 years. It was always easier to get admitted to a psychiatric hospital than to get out. One nine-year inmate from nearby Cornwall had been put in for whistling at a priest while drunk. A 1964 medical entry claimed he "has difficulty understanding questions put to him – certified as mentally ill." That was his last professional visit for five years, until someone discovered he didn't speak English. "Society wanted these people off the streets, and this is where they put them," Lane says.

The women's wards were run by nurses, but the men's wards were run by less-schooled male attendants. A doctor dropped by to see patients once a month, asked them what day it was, marked down "disoriented" if they got it wrong, then scribbled "seclude whenever necessary" at the top of each chart. The rest of the month, attendants ran the show, cleaning, feeding, handing out pills, supervising inmates when they did their chores, making five cents an hour at shovelling snow, cutting grass, baking, milking cows or tilling gardens on the hospital farm. Once a week, on bath day, 70 naked men lined up, and Art Lane was given one razor to shave them. On visitors' day, he kept an eye out for anyone passing weapons. Keeping order meant being a bouncer, making sure big patients didn't steal food too often from weaker patients, helping other attendants when they were attacked.

The job had its perks. Free meals at the cafeteria. Free institutional tobacco, one grade up from sawdust. But Lane's buddies who took factory jobs were all driving cars and buying homes. He walked, and rented a small apartment.

As a new "hire," Lane got the CSAO's welcoming brochure. Collective bargaining was a way of solving problems as a group rather than individually, "an orderly way of doing things," the brochure explained. Management also mailed out a brochure, encouraging workers to join the CSAO, the official bargaining agent for government employees.

After nine months on the job, Lane went to his first CSAO meeting. For the first time, a proposed wage agreement was put to a membership vote. Lane's parents were both factory workers and active unionists, so he stood up and said it was time to get moving on wages. From the back of the room, someone yelled: "Where were you in '42?" Lane thought to himself: "Christ, I wasn't even born then." Then he caught on. This was a veteran speaking, a man who had stood up when it counted. He wasn't going to let anyone forget it, and wasn't about to let anyone forget who hired the vets after the war, looked after them and turned a blind eye to their foibles. It was an open secret that many vets drank too much. One of the jobs of new attendants was to take home the ones who were too far gone to stagger on their own. "Vietnam wasn't the first war to leave a generation of walking wounded," Lane says.

In Lane's day, 20-year employees who could stand proud when asked "Where were you in '42?" made up less than ten per cent of the government work force. Almost half the civil service had been with the government for less than five years. About one in six were just like Lane, hadn't been born in '42, hadn't known the Depression, had buddies with cars and homes.

When George Kerhanovich finished school in Sault Ste. Marie, he took one look at the inside of the steel mill and decided it wasn't for him. He decided to break the invisible barrier – Ukrainians were supposed to stick to steel and leave the civil service to Anglos – and take a job at the Department of Highways in 1963. The military style was still in fashion. Supplies were picked up at the quartermaster's store. Oldtimers still muttered to supervisors who got too nasty: "I shot better men than you during the war." And they didn't take to newcomers with Beatles-style hair.

The 1960s were when civil servants like Kerhanovich let their hair down. Youth were the dynamic new force that joined the swelling public service. They worked at jobs that were ripe for unionization. Labour relations experts say the following conditions breed unionism: standard rates for each classification, several layers of management between workers and the big boss, some form of group identity, confused methods for granting wage increases. That's another way of describing the Ontario civil service in the 1960s. Those conditions turned CSAO into a baby boomers' union.

Union two-step

The CSAO of the early 1960s didn't look, sound, feel, walk or talk like a union. It changed the name of its paper from *The Trillium* to the *CSAO News*. But little else changed when it moved toward collective bargaining in 1963. It still called itself an association, not a union. The association was organized into branches, like the Legion and the Lions, not into locals like unions. It was run by a board of directors, not an executive, and members met for annual general meetings, not conventions. Staffers were called "regional representatives," not "staff reps" or "business agents." Members called themselves colleagues, not brothers and sisters.

Their employers, ministers and premiers, were invited to speak at annual general meetings. Greetings were read from the Civil Service Commission, personnel office for the employer, shortly after the toast to the Queen. Managers, even deputies, could join. And alongside bargaining, CSAO hustled deep discounts with retailers of furs, cars, auto insurance and charter flights, above all to Britain.

Still, employers sensed what the CSAO was about. When the CSAO applied to join the Toronto Board of Trade in the early 1960s, it got turned down. The board doesn't accept employee organizations, it explained. CSAO's names, titles and practices, taken from outside the labour movement, weren't just examples of an organization with its head in the clouds. Sometimes there was a shrewd organizing or bargaining rationale behind what was said and unsaid.

Take the willingness of CSAO to accept deputy ministers in its ranks, for example. That's not much different from what printers and building tradesmen do when they take in foremen, or teachers do when they include principals. It can be a way of boosting bargaining power. Indeed, it was the politicians who insisted that senior managers be excluded from CSAO in 1963. Some "non-union" practices were good for keeping in touch with members. A union that can deliver the benefits of collective action in everyday purchasing power has more links with its members than a union that brings back new contracts every two years, for instance.

A union that sponsors recreation gets remembered for good times, not just problems people want to forget.

And, sometimes, the CSAO didn't follow strict union procedures because it had its own methods that worked just as well. Take grievances, for example, often seen as the high point of workers' rights, the right to disagree with the boss and get a fair hearing from an independent arbitrator. The reality is not so pleasant. Arbitrators making $1,500 a day aren't exactly peers, and getting a ruling based on a strict and legalistic reading of the contract isn't always justice.

Civil servants didn't resort much to arbitration in the 1960s. In 1964, for instance, CSAO members only filed 42 grievances. To some extent, this showed workers were afraid to defy their managers or didn't know their rights. "It was a real snap to be president of a local then," says Jack Armstrong, former president of the Kirkland Lake branch. "There wasn't all that much doing because the members didn't really know what the CSAO was about or what their rights were."

But the lack of formal avenues for complaints was often made up for by back channels that gave workers influence. John Offler was a steward in the Windsor revenue office. A Tory stalwart, a leading volunteer in the Moose Lodge, Lions Club, Red Feather charity and local boys' club, he rubbed shoulders with managers and politicians as an equal. When he needed wrestling mats for his youth club, he phoned Syl Apps, the former hockey star and originator of the slap shot. As Minister of Reform Institutions, Apps could get his hands on plenty of mats, and was happy to spare some to keep young boys out of mischief. When one of his members got in trouble with his boss, Offler called Apps for another favour, to move through the bureaucracy to get the manager straightened out. "You had to have a little grease to get it done," Offler says. It was only when the system lost its grease, after top brass set up a tight bureaucratic regime in the late 1960s, that workers pressed for a more formal system. It didn't always give them more rights or power. It was just more union.

Even that grievance system, according to former Thunder Bay rep Cec Morancy, wasn't very stately. "Coax, beg, plead, convince, argue" was what he did. It was people talking to people, not lawyers, he says. If a worker got fired, Morancy went through the number of kids the worker had, and made the case for giving another chance. Professor Ross Presgrave, chair of the old Public Service Staff Relations Board, umpired these cases and called Morancy "the greatest violin player of all time, all hearts and flowers." Morancy fiddled with the jurisprudence and often convinced Presgrave with common sense and compassion. That was no longer possible in the 1970s, Morancy says, and "we spent all our time reading law books."

Bowen in charge

Ultimately, the confusions and contradictions of CSAO were footprints of Harold Bowen. The dominant figure in its history for 20 years, he was Mr. CSAO. As president from 1953 to 1957, he brought it back from the brink of ruin. As executive secretary, general manager and chief negotiator from 1958 to 1972, he brought it to the brink of unionism.

Bowen looked every inch the textbook corporate executive, curly hair tightly groomed, horn-rimmed glasses over eyes that looked straight ahead, a firm jaw and mouth that gave only the slightest hint of ever smiling, strong hands and firm shoulders draped by dark, quiet business suits. He spoke quietly, properly, sure of his command. Most staff called him Mr. Bowen. Close friends called him Taffy, a nickname for Welshmen. No one thought to call him Hal. "He was the king, the boss, the father image," says Jim Keatings, who worked under him for most of the 1960s and was fired by him in 1970. "He was perfect for CSAO at the time."

Bowen ran the show, just like the top staff in British unions, or in most professional and business organizations, or in government itself. CSAO president Wilf Foster, a Department of Highways employee who had a heart condition that barely allowed him to function, disagreed with Bowen once, in 1966. Bowen forced a showdown, and Foster had to resign. After Foster came George Gemmell, another highways man, mainly remembered for the leg he lost during the Allied invasion of Italy. His hollow leg got credit for his prowess in downing rye with the boys when touring locals. Staff remember the towering pile of members' letters that were never answered. "He controlled the board through his bonhomie," says Don Brown, the Toronto lawyer who advised CSAO in the 1960s. But there was no doubt that Bowen controlled Gemmell.

"Bowen had a dream, as long as you didn't use the word 'union,'" says Keatings, who got fired for using the word. Only press demands that can be justified, he told delegates to the 1966 general meeting, or arbitrators in future would "look with suspicion on any demands and rule accordingly." In itself, this was the discipline of a negotiator in for the long haul, trying to establish a no-nonsense reputation. But it was also the mark of a leader who censored tough talk, who looked to building respect for his skills, not the membership's resolve. To meet the government with some strength, he tried to consolidate power in his office, says Brown, who notes that CSAO was the only union to come to a management firm like his.

Grenville Jones, a CSAO staffer long viewed as Bowen's heir apparent, got sacked along with Keatings for challenging Bowen's lack of militancy. "But in all fairness to him, maybe he felt there was a certain level of effectiveness that could be achieved," Jones says, if Bowen "didn't allow the pot to boil." In British Columbia, the government workers' union got burnt when it confronted the government head-on. The B.C. union didn't get the checkoff that Bowen got in Ontario, and was almost pushed into bankruptcy. Bowen's sense of CSAO's relative weakness and the government's absolute strength was not to be lightly dismissed.

Kevin Burkett, a researcher hired by Bowen in 1968 and later a respected arbitrator, says Bowen hasn't been outdone. At a time when unions were getting nowhere in the white collar and service sectors, the CSAO was winning the automatic dues checkoff, getting settlements, bringing them back for the members to vote on. "Who was in charge when it happened, and what did he have to start with?" Burkett asks, "Who has done him better by winning the right to strike? Where have these people who were so critical of Bowen taken the organization since? If they were begging then, they're begging now," he says.

No matter what Bowen didn't do, CSAO did move toward union-style bargaining and organizing during the 1960s. David Lewis, a respected labour lawyer as well as fiery leader of the NDP, was featured speaker at the 1964 CSAO convention, and handled CSAO wage talks in 1965. He got CSAO to hire staff who could prepare for a full-scale bargaining relationship. That year, CSAO doubled its dues to pay for researchers, educators and grievance officers. CSAO pushed for a $1,000 annual wage increase, unheard of in those times, for institutional workers.

The pressure for tougher bargaining dashed the government's earlier hopes that face-to-face meetings at the Joint Council could solve problems within the government family, without recourse to outside arbitrators. As the two sides grew further apart, the government all but junked the council after 1966. It became a "post office," which received ceremonial briefs from each side before they headed off to arbitration.

Though Bowen had autocratic powers within CSAO, increasing numbers demanded that CSAO act like a union. If Bowen didn't, they did. In 1963, highway truck inspectors in the Toronto-Hamilton area got less from the arbitrator than the government had offered of its own free will. In co-operation with the Teamsters, they started working to rule. If government paymasters wanted to play by the book, they had their own rules to follow. A proper inspection of all tires and equipment took hours. As trucks lined up for inspection, traffic on the country's busiest expressways was snarled for miles. The OPP did nothing to hurry the inspectors. After three days, the inspectors jammed the government into a four per cent wage increase.

In 1966, road crews in northwestern Ontario organized protest meetings to demand a show of force in wage bargaining, which president Gemmell denounced as the "storm of a few agitators." Larger groups of workers in major population centres were not so easy to dismiss, especially when other unions were ready to leap into the breach if CSAO failed to act. Institutional workers were hepped up for big changes in 1966. The men, threatened by government moves to demand nursing degrees for attendants, were in a panic about losing their jobs. They also wanted major raises. In September, Bowen warned the provincial treasurer that he would face an epidemic of "blue flu"– a contagious disease that results in workers booking off sick when they're dissatisfied with bargaining – and warned that "we have reached the point where we will lose control of the situation."

To step up the pressure, Bowen proposed rotating demonstrations at Queen's Park. To make sure no patients were harmed, he wanted to limit picket lines to 50 people, drawn from across the province on workers' days off. This wasn't good enough for Heather Murray, newly-elected branch president at North Bay's psychiatric hospital. She came down to a board meeting to press for North Bay's plan of direct action at the workplace. People should work to rule and book off sick, she said. If the action had to be at Queen's Park, there should at least be a march with a rally demanding a response from the politicians in charge. That, Bowen replied, would look bad in the press.

Bowen did launch a series of media ads pointing out the plight of institutional care workers. That won the *Globe's* editorial sympathy for "victims of an antiquated approach to hospital work, which for too long in our society has been viewed as charitable work, with most of the charity being provided by underpaid workers." On December 7, hospital workers marched on Queen's Park. "Recruiting problem? No wonder!" a prominent placard declared. Another, turning Marilyn Monroe against health minister Matthew Dymond, said: "Dymonds aren't a girl's best friend." It looked good in the media.

Without much help from CSAO, women hospital workers carried on their battle for equal pay and the right to work in integrated wards. Men didn't take to female staff being allowed in male wards. They knew this spelled doom for their chances at promotion, since they didn't have degrees as the nurses did. The men booked off sick. They also played pranks on the women to make life difficult. In an age of sexual modesty, they made sure women got assigned to shower duty on the male wards.

The women hung in because jobs on the male wards paid more. In North Bay, says Murray, a big, strong woman went to the front of a staff meeting and confronted her male antagonists. "I'll take any of you on, I'll kill you, but I'm as good as you are and I'm going to get paid as good as you are," she said.

In 1967, the North Bay local took the case of nurses paid less than male attendants to the Ontario Human Rights Commission, the first time the code was used to press for equal pay. The judge upheld higher wages for men, since their work was not "absolutely identical" to women's. The men lifted heavier patients and had to use their strength to hold down violent patients, the ruling said. That gave women a special incentive to get strong, and from then on, women militants refused to call men for help with difficult patients.

Outside agitation

Neither Bowen nor the CSAO rose to unionism of their own free will. They also had unionism thrust upon them.

Far and away the biggest pressure on CSAO was the fear of losing members to other unions. As the government expanded its range of services, it increasingly set up agencies one step removed from the direct civil service. Once workers were transferred to these agencies, other unions could organize them under the first-come-first-served rules of the Labour Relations Act. So CSAO lost its instant access to all provincially-funded workers, and had to beat the bushes with organizing drives, or lose out to other unions. Even the civil service wasn't locked in forever. CSAO was an omnibus structure, almost a One Big Union. It represented hundreds of distinct groups of workers who had one common bond – the same employer. Often, that wasn't enough. Scores of groups, from plumbers to nurses, felt they had more in common with people in their trades or professions, and could be better represented by a body dedicated to their special needs. CSAO was worried that competing unions and associations could scavenge the public service, and pick up choice pieces of the CSAO membership.

That's how CSAO got into the fight of its life for union security. Competition, the lifeblood of commerce, was also the prod behind CSAO's new-found zeal for the methods and machinery of unionism.

In 1966, to keep hold of Department of Agriculture staff transferred to Guelph University and outside the civil service domain, CSAO registered itself as a union for purposes of organizing in the private sector. The decision to license CSAO as a union under the Ontario Labour Relations Act, Bowen told the board, would have a "sharp impact on future operations of the Association."

This was truer than he perhaps knew. Apart from any formal name change, organizing is what keeps a union in fighting trim. Organizing forces a union to rely on activists rather than count on passive support, to win over majorities, not just add them up. And organizing brings in new blood with no respect for the old ways. It's one of the most subversive things a union can do, as some of Bowen's critics quickly learned.

In 1967, CSAO beat out its arch public-sector rival, the Canadian Union of Public Employees (CUPE), and organized workers at the Niagara Parks Commission, also newly independent from the civil service. The resulting collective agreement, CSAO's first, has a standard passage defining CSAO, "hereinafter referred to as 'the union.'"

Workers at Guelph, active members in CSAO since 1922, rejoined in 1967, because they preferred CSAO to a traditional union. A year later, they were on strike. It was CSAO's first, and the first at any Ontario university. The strike also made the record books as the first where workers rode horseback on the picket lines. Guelph workers struck again in 1969, with a 92 per cent vote, for better wages and union security. The strike featured demonstrations co-sponsored by student activists, including future CSAO/OPSEU researcher Jim Onyschuk. The students boycotted classes, and refused to scab by cleaning up their residence rooms. One campus rally of worker-student unity had everybody singing "Solidarity Forever" and "Hold The Fort," two of labour's most rousing anthems. Strikers also went door-to-door in town with a petition demanding a public inquiry into the university's waste of public resources. Despite these efforts, the strike went badly, and the branch later left CSAO.

CSAO was also pushed into outreach mode to keep tabs on former Provincial Institute of Trades staff, absorbed in the new community colleges that opened their doors in 1966. Apart from the legislative change which granted them independence from the civil service, support staff from the old institutes saw no big change in their lives. "You wouldn't have known from the Friday to the Monday," says Neil Pollock, formerly at George Brown. CSAO didn't lose a beat picking them up as members.

Once in, however, they had to be looked after. "CSAO had no idea of how to handle it," says Pollock, now a staff rep with OPSEU. Servicing the far-flung college system required staff reps spread across the province, and spelled the beginning of the end of CSAO's days as a centralized Toronto-based operation, with outposts in Thunder Bay and North Bay. Servicing also required separate and independent bargaining teams based strictly on occupational groupings, again cutting across the grain of CSAO, which Bowen had patterned on less confrontational ministry lines, playing down a clear-cut bargaining focus. "It didn't occur to us at the time that we were Bowen's nemesis," says Pollock, shortly to become one of Bowen's foremost opponents. "He didn't want any cohesion in bargaining teams."

When the province took over county jails in 1968, CSAO tried to win over 856 guards from CUPE's traditional bailiwick. To strengthen its claim, CSAO signed up 61 per cent of guards across the province. But it couldn't make much of a dint in CUPE's stronghold at Toronto's Don Jail, and only signed up 41 of 229. In January, 1968, Don Jail guards wildcatted. They were used to CUPE, which gave its locals lots of space and autonomy. They didn't want to be forced into a mushy civil service association that was too big and too centralized to answer to their special needs. They returned to work only when promised that Judge Walter Little's commission on provincial bargaining policy would look into their standing.

In February, CSAO promised the guards they'd be able to keep their identity. In July, they got a province-wide branch, a structure that allowed them to run their own show and positioned them for collective bargaining. That was a big exception for CSAO to make. Until then, it paralleled the government's organization, set up branches by ministry and by geographic area, not by occupation, the decisive factor in serious bargaining. Again, CSAO was structuring itself along union lines.

Little or nothing

Judge Little's investigation of civil service labour relations turned on two elements of union security. The first and most obvious was the question of automatic membership and dues, the Rand Formula for union security, a standard issue for all new unions. The second and special issue was the security CSAO needed as the sole bargaining agent for civil servants.

All unions have to deal with security of financing for two simple reasons. Unions cost money to run. Many people who benefit from the union would rather pocket their dues money than give it to the union. The Rand Formula, concocted by Justice Ivan Rand to settle a militant strike by Ford workers in Windsor in 1945, solves the problem neatly. It gives the union security by making all workers who benefit from its services pay into it, just like paying taxes for government services. Employers who want to keep their unions on the defensive, strapped for cash and unable to make long-term plans, want their unions to remain insecure, and oppose the Rand Formula. Workers who want their union to be able to afford good staff and programs support it.

In this respect, the CSAO was no different from other unions. As soon as it got into serious bargaining, it got into union security. It started delivering on a full-fledged program of bargaining in 1965, with all the overhead costs that involves, such as research, member education and grievance handling.

"Collective bargaining is possible only between parties of equal strength," *CSAO News* claimed in 1966, pushing for a big dues increase. Without money to back up bargaining efforts, CSAO would only have "collective begging" with the employer. Without union security, it was forced into individual begging with members, draining its energy in the grinding exercise of hitting up members one at a time for a voluntary dues contribution. With a ten per cent yearly turnover rate in the civil service, chasing down new members could easily take up more time than constructive work such as bargaining.

There was a more serious aspect of union security at issue. CSAO's brand of union security meant the exclusive right to represent the entire civil service, preventing the drain of key occupational groups to other unions. Without that right, the civil service would be balkanized into scores of unions that spent more time fighting each other than the employer.

In 1967, union security became an urgent matter. CUPE and the Canadian Labour Congress called for the civil service to be covered by the same labour legislation that covered all other workers. That meant the right to bargain and strike. It also meant that workplaces could be organized one at a time, by whatever union scraped up a majority in a workplace. This was the opening shot in CUPE's campaign to oust what it called "Roberts' company union," and replace it with a real union, CUPE.

The next year, the nurses' association made a bid to represent nurses in the psychiatric hospitals. A hot new group out of North Bay, the United Government Workers of Ontario (UGWO), signed up 2,000 institutional care workers. Many North Bay attendants, recently laid off from the railroads, were used to a more aggressive union style than what they saw in CSAO. And CUPE was lurking in the background.

CSAO desperately needed to fend off these trespassers. At the same time, changes within Ontario government operations put new question marks around the special relationship between CSAO and the government. Increasingly, government planners were coming under the sway of private-sector lawyers like Robert Hicks, founding partner in a new firm that sold labour relations counsel to managers. Hicks liked the cut and thrust of hard-edged private sector bargaining. He didn't like the more amicable relationships he saw in government.

Once the Joint Council ceased to be a "talkshop" and took up routine union claims, management wanted the same tight standards that governed other union operations. Anything could be discussed when the Joint Council was all talk. But when it became all bargaining, some boundaries had to be set. All of a sudden, it mattered which side supervisors and professionals were on, the employer's or the union's. And management rights were not up for discussion now that the discussions were formal.

Thus, management was more than open when CSAO raised the Rand Formula at the bargaining table in 1967. Managers indicated, according to CSAO minutes, that they wanted "to couple negotiations on the Rand Formula with certain items known as 'management rights.'" The downside of this swap didn't appeal to CSAO, whose members left a May meeting convinced that it was "only a matter of time before it is politically possible to do away with the Joint Council and move to the industrial concept."

In all likelihood, there was no need for CSAO to trade off anything for the right to represent the entire civil service. Management liked having an in-house association that could settle all bargaining matters in one fell swoop. There was no percentage in opting for scores of unions, some of which would try to outbid others with their militancy. Hicks even dropped a hint that CSAO should start signing up workers at the Workmen's Compensation Board. CSAO missed the hint, and lost the WCB to CUPE.

For the rising generation of government officials, a new relationship with CSAO offered the best of two worlds. They could act tough just like in the private sector, and not feel beholden to a paternalistic relationship with workers. And they didn't have to look over their shoulders, because a CSAO monopoly guarded them from outside attack. For the government, union security was a means of avoiding a union, not creating one.

Conciliation

Serious discussions between the government and CSAO started in May, 1967. Managers said they wanted a study done of the issue. Judge Walter Little, approved by both sides, was appointed special advisor in July. His terms of reference went way beyond the Rand Formula. He was also to report on who belonged in a bargaining unit, the range of topics that could be bargained, and ways of negotiating in a "bargaining system in which compulsory arbitration is a final means of resolving disputes."

Walter Little was the senior labour conciliator in the province. His father, a Scots stonemason active in his union, always taught him that every conflict could be settled. His own experience proved that too. Working as an insurance lawyer in North Bay during the 1930s, he cut deals to avoid court costs. After the war, Ottawa made him a judge in Parry Sound, where he faced problems that required common-sense solutions and "seat of the pants justice." The small county court left him lots of time to build a lucrative practice as a moonlighting labour conciliator.

Judges were picked to conciliate labour disputes during the 1950s and '60s because they were disciplined to be neutral, not because they were legalistic, Little says now. He was not trained in labour law, and he relied on a few rules of thumb in his dealings with managers and unions.

"Don't make people lose face. That is the big thing," he says. "In labour matters, you have to get behind the scenes to settle problems." It is his opinion that professors of law, not judges, have bungled up labour rulings with abstractions and hair-splitting.

Little used all his conciliator's skills when he worked with the provincial government and CSAO. He told both sides he needed their help if he was going to settle the problem. He refused to recommend any changes that both sides didn't agree to. He knew most of the government's lawyers personally, and knew how to tell them it was time to give. "When you know fellows like that, you can talk to them like a Dutch uncle," he says. After some horse-trading on who would be in and out of the union, there were no disagreements. The right to strike "wasn't a big deal," he says. That was a lucky break, since the terms of reference for his appointment ruled out the right to strike.

In November, 1967, CSAO asked Judge Little to grant it automatic dues and membership for all new employees, the right to represent part-time and unclassified workers, and to bargain all conditions of work. To strengthen its case, CSAO started a massive recruiting drive. By the time Little reported in May, 1969, CSAO had signed up 27,640 members, 56 per cent of the entire civil service.

Aside from the membership recruiting drive, Bowen made no appeals to the public or the membership to put pressure on Little or the government during the hearings. In fact, he did his best to keep the hearings secret. CSAO had to be sensitive to the political pressures the government was under, Bowen told the board in June, 1966, before the campaign got under way. The politicians couldn't afford to be embarrassed by unions charging they were frozen out of a closed-shop agreement. CSAO members themselves didn't have to know about Little's appointment, Bowen told the board in July, 1967. Other unions might get wind of it and start butting in. Word had already leaked out "and the Association had to act very discreetly in order to have this suppressed," he said. For the same reason, the matter was kept out of the board's report to the 1968 annual general meeting.

Little's report, Collective Bargaining in the Ontario Public Service, came down in May, 1969. It addressed all the major issues of labour relations. He recommended giving CSAO representation rights for the entire civil service and management sole control over decisions on merit and job classifications. And he would exclude professionals and managers from union membership. Though denial of the right to strike was a given, spelled out in the terms of reference for his report, Little took it upon himself to deliver his opinion. Citing a recent report by Ivan Rand, he called civil service strikes a "harbinger of social disintegration."

In arguing against the right to strike, Little did not make the case that government workers were essential, and couldn't be spared from their jobs. That didn't enter his argument. His argument rested on a principle, the supremacy of elected governments. "Governments are elected to formulate policies and make decisions for the benefit of the whole community," he wrote. "No individuals in the community," especially workers hired to carry out government policy, "should be able by concerted action, to impede or frustrate such implementation, in order to enforce their will on the citizens as a whole." Though government workers didn't have a right to strike, Little said they did have a right to an arbitration system that delivered benefits equal to what they could get if they worked in the private sector.

Premier Robarts was less concerned about sovereignty. In explaining why Ontario did not follow Quebec and federal laws granting civil servants the right to strike, he said: "If you give a man a new toy, you must expect him to play with it." Indeed, if sovereignty of elected officials were uppermost in anyone's mind, the concern would have been over how compulsory arbitration takes away the legislature's right to set workplace policy and determine government expenses, and grants that power to an unelected arbitrator.

In June, the *CSAO News* expressed disappointment that Little excluded professionals from membership and pensions from bargaining, and wished that he had said nothing on the right to strike. The less said about strikes, the better, Bowen reasoned, believing that silence at least left the door open.

The only academic analysis of Little's report, by arbitrator and professor of labour law Harry Arthurs, attacked it for its lack of vision and the "limited changes [it had made] within the context of the present system in order to formalize and regularize it." Neither the government nor CSAO opted for real change, he wrote. "Obviously it is in the government's interest to have only a single, semi-militant employee representative to bargain with and obviously the CSAO wishes to be that representative. Thus each party bolsters the other's position by maintaining that the present system is flexible and workable."

Little was one of the last judges to affect government labour policy. A royal commission in 1971 condemned the use of judges on conciliation work. To get around the law banning judicial moonlighting, the government paid Little $100 a day for out-of-pocket expenses, exactly the same fee that professional conciliators got. "This is the sort of subterfuge in which neither governments nor judges should be engaged," commissioner J.C. McRuer said.

In October, 1969, the government acted on Little's recommendations to exclude managerial, professional and confidential staff from CSAO. It also granted CSAO the automatic dues checkoff for its current members and all new employees. In November, the other shoe dropped. Premier John Robarts appointed a Committee on Government Productivity (COGP) to draw up a blueprint for government re-organization. The ground that old-style labour relations stood on was about to shift, just as the rules were set.

Quiet revolution

The 1960s are known for raunchy rock, frisbees, hippies, the youth revolt, the drug cult and a mania over a prime minister who wore sandals and said the state had no place in the bedrooms of the nation.

The decade isn't known for its cult of experts who took government everywhere but the bedroom, while making it more bureaucratic and remote. Nor are the '60s often seen as a decade of labour revolt, or a time when civil servants came into their own. Yet all these features of the decade figured in the evolution of the Ontario government and the CSAO.

The Tories, entering their third decade of uninterrupted rule, were rejuvenated by the baby boom. They presided over the biggest expansion of government services in the country's history. They delivered hard services like roads and sewers to connect to new suburbs. They also set up a rash of soft services that fed into new demands of a work world based on complex and interdependent service industries and automated process technology. Health institutions were revamped. Schools, colleges and universities were built – in 1963, enough for one politician to have cut a ribbon a day for 15 years. All told, government expenditures jumped from one billion dollars in 1962 to 2.5 billion a decade later.

Government employees were busy in hundreds of new projects that reflected new obligations and new power bases in society. Lands, forests and highways, representing traditional public works, barely grew at all. Real growth was in education, where budgets went up five times, health up four times, and social services eight times. This shift from public works to good works is commonly known as the rise of the "welfare state" or "service state."

Tories did not hold back on this expansion. On the contrary, according to K. J. Rea's *The Prosperous Years*, "they were remarkably quick to pick up new ideas, including fads and fancies of the time, whenever it suited their purposes. They embraced, without evident concern for consistency, 'planning,' conservation, public ownership, education, health insurance, regional government, industrial promotion, urban transport, counter-cyclical budgeting, the war on poverty, the fight against inflation, and neo-conservatism, as the occasion and practice elsewhere recommended such policies. They were more often trendy than conservative."

What kept this rash of reforms still distinctly Ontario Tory? Partly, it's that no one noticed them. Keeping government out of the limelight was one of the Tories' secrets of success. No trumpets meant no scrutiny and no pressure to deliver more.

Quebec in the 1960s had its famous Quiet Revolution. Ontario, because it was Tory, changed more quietly. But in substance it went through no less a revolution.

Of course, in Quebec the French majority had a language problem and a have-not problem that went with it. Politics there was about hearts and souls, not just meat and potatoes. In Ontario, the English majority didn't have a language problem, and the have-nots didn't dream of separating. Nor did Ontario have as much catching up to do. Nationalizing Hydro, which sent Quebec politics on a wild ride in 1965, had been ho-hum in Ontario for 60 years. What both provinces had in common was the rise of a new "state middle class" of experts. In Quebec, they announced themselves boldly. The new government workers felt themselves a breed apart, contemptuous of the nuns, priests and party hacks they replaced, and bitter at the Anglo business elite they came up against. They wore their up-to-date expertise as a badge of modern nationalism. Ontario Tories, by contrast, kept their experts under wraps, though this did not dilute their influence, or reduce the scale of changes they introduced.

In 1964, the province set up the Ontario Housing Corporation, and built 70,000 subsidized units in the next eight years, to become the second largest public housing agency on the continent. For Centennial Year in 1967, Ontario opened the Science Centre, a hands-on showplace that mixed science with fun. In 1970, the province became a broadcaster under the Ontario Educational Communications Authority, and pioneered in taking educational programming far beyond televised lectures.

Tory budgets didn't just add and subtract public revenues and expenditures. By 1966, the government embraced fiscal budgets, designed as instruments to shape the entire economy. This wasn't seen as radical. In 1967, the Ontario Committee on Taxation described government action to promote full employment, equality and price stability as "so generally recognized as falling within the purview of government that an enumeration is almost superfluous."

In every area, government programs were on the cutting edge of new ideas. Money was no obstacle. Ironically, many of these innovations ended in disaster, flawed by their technocratic design. Many also heightened conflict between civil service workers and managers. Those three elements of Tory reform – dynamic experimentation, technocratic design and worker alienation – are the fulcrum for understanding the evolution of CSAO in the late 1960s and early 1970s.

Education was the showpiece of the new Tory order. The race was to catch up with Russia's Sputnik and the science and education that made the first space satellite of 1957 possible. Following the 1968 publication of *Living and Learning*, the manifesto of school principal Lloyd Dennis and Supreme Court justice Emmett Hall, schools loosened up. Memory work was downgraded. Students got to pick options. Uniform grade 13 exams were ended. School inspectors became program consultants. The Ontario Institute for Studies in Education, a temple of progressive educational theory, opened in 1962. The race was on to catch up with the fleet of new, self-starting para-professions and trades that rode in with the new service economy. This kind of creativity meant breaking free from the schools' historic regimentation.

But these reforms also had a hidden curriculum that fostered the rise of a new educational elite, centralization of power in Toronto, and tighter limits on the choices given poor and working-class pupils. Streaming shunted "slow learners" into dead-end courses. Ever-higher degrees became the basis for teaching credentials. On the other hand, to promote equality of opportunity, education minister Bill Davis amalgamated rural school boards, slashing their number from 2,419 to 1,037 in 1968. Little red schoolhouses were put up for sale to weekenders; children spent an hour a day on a bus to take advantage of better equipment and specialized teachers in bigger centres.

Like most of the Tory reforms, educational changes sparked a backlash among those who preferred the human scale of small, personal and neighbourly. "Wiseacres at Queen's Park," the Simcoe *Reformer* editorialized in 1968, were scheming to wipe out the hometown talent.

"Eventually the County Boards will become Regional Boards with the source of their brainpower and high-salaried experts in Queen's Park. Local autonomy will become a relic of the past both in educational matters and in the whole range of civic administration." Like most of the Tory reforms, education changes sparked union-type organizing. Teachers started organizing for collective bargaining.

Experimentation as part of reform even extended to the province's relations with Native people. In 1960, the social services ministry granted band councils on Indian reserves the same right to administer welfare that municipalities enjoyed. In 1966 this policy was applied to child-care services. A variety of community development projects brought improved water and housing onto the reserves and helped provide jobs in local industries. The province set up an Indian Development Branch in 1966 to carry this work forward. For a provincial government, these were unprecedented moves that recognized Native sovereignty.

Although the province had set aside its own funds to support these projects, premier Robarts balked at picking up the entire tab when Ottawa refused to pay its share. The whole initiative was cancelled in 1969, sparking a revolt from the Indian Development Branch. The entire staff of 16 resigned in protest and picketed Queen's Park in May, throwing the legislature into an uproar. An Opposition motion to censure the government was defeated by the solid Tory majority, and Robarts held firm on his decision. According to an official history of the ministry, "It was the first occasion departmental staff staged a public protest against departmental action or rather, inaction." There is no record of the CSAO having offered support.

Caatacomb

In 1965, Minister of Education Bill Davis launched 22 community colleges to provide "the fullest possible development of each individual to the limit of his ability." As a place to upgrade adults and train youth in high-end skills, the colleges "captured my imagination," he said. "I have no intention of permitting any group of young people to be forgotten and deprived, or of any group of adults needing retraining for a new world of work in a new age to be neglected. The new era is golden with promise, if only we prepare in time for it."

The community colleges were the centrepiece of a massive investment in education by the Tories during the late 1960s. In the five years before 1971, capital budgets soared from 2.5 to 63 million dollars, and operating expenses rocketed from five to 100 million dollars.

The colleges filled a huge hole in Ontario's education system. Both universities and high schools had turned their backs on students who wanted skills training. The bias of high schools toward the university elite was intensifying. In 1945, the university stream soaked up 63 per cent of high school funding. By 1960, it was 89 per cent. All that money went to the nine per cent of students who proceeded to university. Few were encouraged to go on with training. In all of Canada, only 8,300 students took post-secondary technical courses in 1960. John Porter denounced this tradition of elitist bias and "educational poverty" in his critique of inequality in Canada, *The Vertical Mosaic*. It was forcing the sons and daughters of Canadian-born workers into unskilled jobs, and bringing immigrants to fill the skilled jobs, he charged: "No society can move into an industrial epoch with so much of its creative potential incarcerated in ignorance."

The colleges were ready to take up the graduates of high school technical and commercial streams established by then-education minister John Robarts in 1961. Their post-secondary educational treatment, however, was decided in a squeeze play by two established elite groups.

Industry wanted a new species of trained workers. The demand for skilled trades grew by 38 per cent during the 1950s, a good 14 per cent above the demand for labour in general. These new jobs required conceptual ability as well as manual dexterity, in the view of a 1963 select committee on manpower training: "The challenge of developing this type of worker will no doubt prove more demanding than the relatively simple task of upgrading workers in the more traditional skills." Schools had to teach "learning to learn" so graduates could adjust to lifelong change.

But conceptual learning was not what university presidents had in mind for colleges. Robarts gave university presidents the power to decide on Ontario's future college system in 1962. Not surprisingly, they wanted funding to go to universities, on which "our future productivity, our national security and our health" depend, as the presidents saw it.

The university presidents vetoed the idea of U.S.-style junior colleges, which provided a side-door entrance to university for late bloomers and the poor. That would "dilute" the excellence of universities, they said. Students with "little academic ability" needed a terminal institution "for which many of them are better-suited." It would offer the bare minimum of academic work, as much "as they can possibly be cajoled into taking" to protect them from chronic unemployment. Letting universities decide the future of colleges resulted in Ontario being one of the few places in North America where colleges are not part of the system of university preparation.

Despite their promise, the Colleges of Applied Arts and Technology in Ontario were denied such standard features of post-secondary education as independent charters guaranteeing freedom of inquiry and independence from government, or faculty choice over chairs, deans and presidents. They were given the nickname of "community colleges" to make sure there was no confusion with U.S.-style junior colleges. But they had none of the features the name suggests: appointed business executives, not elected education trustees, dominated their boards of directors; and they were run centrally by the province.

Like most reforms of the Tory era, the colleges rode a wave of expansive hopes and liberatory rhetoric. Most of these reforms were captured by forces that reduced possibilities for local and direct consumer and community control.

More for the mind

Humane reforms were the order of the day in jails and institutions.

After a tour of the Renfrew jailhouse in 1967, Corrections minister Allan Grossman told reporters that such jails, built purely for punishment, "don't belong to this century." Only two years earlier, when he was first appointed minister, Grossman had refused to talk with protesting prisoners, claiming they would subject him to their "manipulative tendencies."

Grossman's job was to turn jails into correctional centres, and recoup the ministry's public standing after a riot at the Guelph reformatory in 1952 and three further riots in 1958. The last riot led to the resignation of the deputy minister, Colonel Hedley Basher. A subsequent review of the Guelph jail by Anglican chaplain and sociologist William Mann blamed Ontario jails for their emphasis on production of farm and other goods which could be measured in reports, rather than rehabilitation and training which could not.

Under Grossman, community programs were started and a new training college for staff was opened. Guards were re-named "correctional officers" and psychologists were hired as senior advisors in the notoriously paramilitary department. On the theory that self-respect encouraged rehabilitation, inmates were supplied with a few luxuries like mattresses and deodorant. In 1968, the province took over county and municipal jails in an effort to upgrade the standards for both guards and inmates.

Psychiatric care was transformed under the influence of the Canadian Mental Health Association's 1961 study *More For The Mind*. A new generation of psychiatrists had worked their way up professional ladders since the 1950s. One of them was Dr. B.H. McNeel, chief of Ontario's mental health branch. They had at their disposal a new generation of drugs for controlling the behaviour of people formerly sent to mental hospitals for life.

Cyril Greenland, appointed Director of Social Work for all provincial psychiatric hospitals in 1962, had a mandate from McNeel and health minister Matthew Dymond to develop treatment strategies for home and community care. This took some political courage on Dymond's part, since many of the attendants at Whitby, where Greenland experimented with new reform ideas in 1958, were Dymond's patronage appointments.

Whitby, Greenland says, was "a snakepit." A top supervisor pocketed money for supplies. Some patients were so scrawny they looked like concentration camp inmates, while others were overweight, a sure sign that the strong were stealing from the weak. Most male inmates walked around naked. Hospital-issue clothes, one size fits all, were too loose. Since no belts were allowed – inmates might use them to hang themselves – it was easier to go natural. Nudity, a trademark of insanity in the public's mind, was in fact induced by the asylum. Greenland solved the problem overnight by bringing women into the male wards.

The old male-only wards had been run by attendants who "controlled the wards the only way they knew," Greenland says. Sometimes, violent patients were taken to pavilion 2B for a beating. Both patients and staff were demoralized by the wretched conditions. The only difference between patients and staff is that patients get better, Greenland told one group of visitors. His joke was picked up by the press and made him an outcast at the hospital.

Spirits were so low, no one believed Greenland when he said he had a blank cheque to bring in needed equipment. When he asked attendants for an estimate of how many toothbrushes should be bought for each ward, they suggested five; that would make for shorter lineups than when inmates shared just two. Attendants couldn't believe their ears when Greenland said he had the connections to get a toothbrush for each patient.

Greenland created shock waves when he brought female nurses onto male wards – a bid to create a more normal civilian atmosphere, and set professionalism in motion. Female staff were nurses, while male attendants had little formal training. He also introduced new "wonder drugs" that allowed behaviour to be controlled chemically, which drastically cut back on staff. Previously, four attendants were needed to hold down patients for camphor, which cooled them out by inducing a fit, for electric shock therapy, and for swaddling violent patients in wet blankets. The combination of drugs and integrated wards doomed the attendants as an occupational group with any future. The hospitals no longer needed big, strapping men to control violent patients, says Fred Upshaw, a Whitby nurse who later became president of OPSEU.

Greenland also worked to discharge healthier patients. The attendants "hated my guts for letting those patients out," he says. They counted on the better patients to take charge of making beds, cleaning up and working the hospital farm, and so had a vested interest in keeping high-functioning inmates in.

The impact of reform wasn't always what Greenland hoped for. Some reforms stifled human warmth and individual care. Although unskilled attendants did at times apply "reality therapy" and rough treatment, it was also quite common, says Upshaw, to sit down with patients, share a cigarette, gain their trust and talk about their problems. Under the new regime, staff only worked with patients after they were docile under the influence of drugs, he says. And in the new medical model, farms on hospital grounds were declared unsanitary and abolished. Contrary to the normalization and self-reliance Greenland promoted, the new medically-controlled hospitals left patients idle after they'd been doped up. Greenland, who still works in the mental health field, says he often wonders whether all the changes have been for the better.

The urge to regionalize

The most politically-charged and electorally-costly Tory reform of the era was regional government. The drive to regional government was directed by Municipal Affairs minister Darcy McKeough, later the most important player in government re-organization during the 1970s.

Beginning with the amalgamation of Metro Toronto in 1964, 70 regional governments were planned to replace 90 municipalities. That way, the theory went, a broader tax base could pay for universal standardized services to poor and rich neighbourhoods alike. Sure of itself, the government never considered the possibility of opposition. However, though no referendums were allowed, resistance was so bitter and widespread that the Tories threw up their hands and gave regional government up for dead in 1973.

Regional government often brought professionalized services and provided modern public buildings. A review of its progress noted that, in the Waterloo area, for instance, standardized social services led to major increases in welfare allowances at the request of professionally-qualified staff. But the reforms cut two ways. Expertise in social policy came at the expense of local control. Councillors in one-horse towns were political amateurs who usually donated their time to their community and made decisions after a chat with their neighbours. Small-town officials were easy to put down, but they gave government a human face, and somehow operated a social service system that didn't require foodbanks and didn't produce homelessness.

Big government

The wide-ranging agenda of 1960s Conservative reformism is sometimes seen as evidence of "Red Toryism" or "creeping socialism." More likely, it's a case of "sprawling capitalism," evidence of new methods of social control and new power centres within the Ontario elite. It's worth saying a few words about this, because it sets a framework for understanding the reaction of the Ontario public and public sector workers to the changes that were introduced.

Big government was not just a response to social needs. The political theorist Claus Offe argues that cooped-up chickens that need their fix of antibiotics and infrared lights are not suffering from rising expectations. They are victims of dependency.

Nor were reforms in prisons, psychiatric hospitals and schools merely a response to humanitarian pressures. The kind of discipline and obedience needed in an era of service industries and process technologies had to be based on lightweight "technologies of power," not heavy-handed bullyings. French historian Michel Foucault made this link in analyzing the rise of individualized medical treatment in European asylums and jails. The dawn of more sophisticated factory production required a new "disciplinary grid," he writes, that relied on minimum expenditures of power for maximum returns in self-discipline. The new code of discipline in society at large led to the repudiation of old-style asylums and jails, he writes.

Foucault's perspective also throws light on the philosophy taken up by business circles in the 1960s: "human resource management." It didn't fit with straw bosses and regimentation, but combined well with progressive education, progressive discipline, and personnel policy. It also smacked of a view that human beings were another "resource" to be processed.

In 1969, the Tories did to the central civil service what they had done to local government and education. The new-age reforms did not empower workers any more than earlier changes empowered citizens. They gave rise to a new elite, which came down as hard on civil servants' workplace autonomy as regional government did on local government.

A thousand points of bureaucracy: the COGP

Whatever Ontario Tories lacked in political theory, they made up for with consultant reports. Like Adam Smith on "the invisible hand of the market" at the dawn of capitalism, Ontario had its Committee on Government Productivity (COGP) for corporate analysis of the state.

Appointed by Robarts toward the end of his career, the COGP became, according to Davis aide Ed Stewart, "the general point of reference for anything and everything that changed in the Ontario government" after Davis became premier in 1971. In ten reports published between 1969 and 1972, the think tank of top business executives and civil servants laid out a blueprint for an entirely new style of civil service. Their wholesale re-organization was designed to make government more efficient and responsive by introducing "improvements that can be adapted from the business community."

The consulting commando group gasped at the speed of change that had overtaken the province since 1960. One and a half million new people, many of them immigrants. A "barrage of technological advances" that tripled economic output to 42 billion dollars. At 66,000, twice the number of civil servants. Government expenses up six times to five billion dollars. A roster of 250 government agencies that "surpassed anything conceptualized by old-line socialists, let alone those devoted to laissez-faire government." Expansion so out of hand, "it [was] impossible to predict if or when a new line [would] be drawn" around what belonged in the private sector.

Demands for government action, the COGP said, "merely reinforce the argument in favour of a new management style which can deal effectively with a set of revolutionary circumstances and issues quite different from those with which any government has had to deal in the relatively evolutionary decades in the past."

The politicians had dreams of grandeur. In 1971, Davis dubbed the first batch of committee recommendations "the most comprehensive restructuring of government in this country" and, at the committee's bidding, he handed out 17 ministerial titles to the chosen among 22 old departmental secretaries. Seven reports and a year later, Darcy McKeough, put in charge of several ministries as a result of committee recommendations, called the changes "probably the most revolutionary re-organization of any government anywhere in Canada at any period in history."

With hindsight, the committee's results more closely resemble a counter-revolution. But there's no denying the sweeping and fundamental changes. The committee started its work while the country was in the throes of Trudeaumania, of participatory democracy and the Just Society. It completed its work in the wake of Trudeau's use of the War Measures Act, in the era of the Club of Rome, limits to growth, wage controls, and neo-conservative-inspired government cutbacks.

Confronting disorder everywhere, the COGP looked to revamping government organization as a bastion "capable of change to meet the demands of society, while at the same time being able to preserve a degree of stability." It sought harmony in hierarchy, reason in ledgerbooks, and calm in bureaucracy.

Until the COGP, remote and businesslike efficiency were not trademarks of the Tory personal style or the Tory formula of political success. Ontario Toryism dealt with people's problems hands-on. Rules were made to be broken. The NDP's gadfly Morton Shulman once asked Provincial Treasurer Charles McNaughton why he flouted a court order and refused to garnishee wages of a government employee. The garnishee was against a widow raising four children and struggling to pay off medical bills, McNaughton replied. He was proud to defend poor widows, he said.

Though premier John Robarts was often sneered at for his chairman-of-the-board corporate style, he worried that faceless bureaucrats were increasingly stealing the show from elected politicians. "Either we control the government or we don't," he'd rant. He hated the endless meetings that were supposed to handle a "virtual maze of interrelated decisions."

Insiders say he made no secret to cabinet that the motion to strike the committee was forced on him. It's said that top budget chiefs Carl Brannan and H.I. Macdonald were fed up with the way government policy was set by political pressures at budget time. They introduced PPB (planning/programming/budgeting) in 1967 to counter this drift by insisting on costing entire packages of reform in advance. They wanted the doctrine to spread.

Though the committee was first set up with a limited mandate as a Productivity Improvement Project, it went far beyond that. "In official publications reflecting, I suspect, the fact that the bureaucrats had gotten hold of the matter," Ed Stewart wrote after his retirement from government, "the objectives were described as the need to address the challenges 'arising from the accumulation of social, technological, economic and demographic change,' [which] 'clearly required a thorough investigation and restructuring of Ontario's governmental system.'" In short, once they got their foot in the door, they went for the whole shooting match.

The COGP was made up of senior deputies and senior business executives from Gulf, Noranda and Hockey Canada, directed by Harvard Business School graduate and York University business dean, James Fleck and chaired by Labatt vice-president J.B. Cronyn. There was not a woman, unionist, government worker, person of colour or politician among them. Naturally enough, the committee looked to private sector, business-style hierarchies to "prepare the managerial ground" for policy development and internal control of government.

Applying managerial science, ministers would no longer groan under the weight of meetings and administrative trivia. They could concentrate on policy by offloading this detail work to parliamentary assistants. Filled with clear-headed ministers, cabinet would accept the discipline of "priorities." A new Management Board – the very term "board" recalls the turn-of-the-century effort to replace political decisions with neutral expertise – and a new policy and priorities committee of cabinet would see to it that one program wasn't added willy-nilly to another. This would mean the end of shopping sprees encouraged by federal cost-sharing programs in housing, education and health. New programs had to stay within the bounds of government revenues that were bottoming out after a decade of taxing business to the limit, the COGP insisted.

Challenged to a broader overview than any one minister could have, three new super-ministers of social development, resources and justice would oversee the whole spectrum of issues and manage the way they interlocked. They would make sure, for instance, that roads were linked to industry and tourism and not just go their own way. They would also keep control firmly at the top, and clamp down on ministers and staff who got carried away with their pet projects.

The COGP also wanted the government to make effective use of the province's "most valuable asset, its human resources," by adopting less rigid supervision over skilled technical staff. This gave the nod to the new experts in personnel management who knew how "to get the maximum performance from their human resources and conduct their programmes with maximum efficiency and effectiveness, which, at the same time, would permit the career and personal needs of the individual to be fulfilled."

The bottom line was government productivity, for want of a better, private-sector, word like "profitability." This is where the number crunchers came in. Obsessed by the prospects for boosting productivity, the COGP set up experimental projects "designed to produce measurable increases in productivity."

"Output budgeting" and "program analysis and review" were then all the rage in management circles, though in Ontario the fad went by the name of PPBS, Brannan and Macdonald's planning-programming-budgeting system, a series of checklists to help define aims and resources. "It is a keystone recommendation," one report said, "that the Government adopt a similar approach to the management of its employees."

By imposing business methods on the civil service, program managers would be held responsible for budgets, and routine and clerical work could be subjected to work measurement. Pay levels would match outputs. This, in the view of one report, was how work got done in the private sector, not by paying for duties, qualifications and experience as the government did.

The PPBS idea was probably borrowed from the federal government's Science Council of Canada. There, it was part of an effort to get away from the Lester "We'll burn that bridge when we come to it" Pearson style of incremental decisions. PPBS, by contrast, let mathematician-kings sit back and ponder options, and stopped governments from being led around by pressure groups.

Another borrowed term was "Request For Proposal," originally coined by the Pentagon, but brought to Ontario by Ernest Manning (father of Preston Manning), who stepped down as Alberta's Social Credit premier in 1967 to launch a crusade for a national party of true social conservatism. RFPs were seen as a boost to privatization. Since they defined work to be done in terms of snippets of cost rather than public accountability, they were perfectly designed for contracting out. The COGP was aware of the new word, "privatization," and promoted organization of many government offices along corporate lines to ease the transition to private sector sell-offs.

The ten reports of the COGP amount to a manifesto by the new class of mandarins who took over the corporate heights in the 1960s. As described in Carl Derber's *Power in the Highest Degree*, they shared credentials from university management schools, a passion for quantitative methods, and contempt for intuition. The COGP's most obvious parallel is with the people who surrounded U.S. president Jack Kennedy and who were put under the microscope by David Halberstam's bestselling *The Best and the Brightest*. They all liked "neat, cold, antiseptic statistics, devoid of blood and heart," mixed in with a can-do approach that almost always led to disastrous errors, most notably the war on Vietnam, Halberstam writes.

֍

Farewell to reform

The Committee on Government Productivity may have had the best and brightest Ontario could muster, but it ranks as one of the great fiascos in the government's history. It started off on the wrong foot. The title page of the glossy brochure announcing the new era of precision in the civil service spelled "government" wrong. A Freudian slip, some said.

The opposition parties had only a glimmering of what the COGP was about. In 1969, the NDP's Pat Lawlor welcomed the COGP and urged Ontario to catch up with the leader of PPB budgeting in Ottawa, Simon Reisman, later Canada's negotiator for free trade with the U.S. Yet, in 1971, when the first series of bills arising from COGP came up for adoption, there were some critical voices. The Liberals' populist Eddie Sargent saw the writing on the wall for "the executive group controlling the legislative process." The NDP's Stephen Lewis feared "the government has surrendered itself to a frame of mind of the management consultant." New Democrat Donald MacDonald spotted the opening for privatization in the government's separation of its policy and delivery functions, which "can undercut its own employees and can destroy the solidarity of the civil service and any union group." Nevertheless, the NDP didn't vote against the raft of COGP-inspired changes in the government's bill. According to Lewis, "the bill doesn't carry with it a sufficient relevance in public terms to get one excited enough to oppose it."

Though it passed easily, nothing seemed to work out once the COGP's measures were put into practice. The first super-ministers, the people who were supposed to exercise foresight in co-ordinating issues across various ministries, were rivals to Davis's leadership. The post became a sort of pasture, except in the case of Darcy McKeough, who had to be dumped for conflict of interest. Few ministers ever became masters of far-seeing policy, since Davis kept shuffling them, if only, according to arch-critics like Morton Shulman, to keep them new at the job and immune from responsibility.

Streamlining was also botched. Responsibility for personnel policy was split between the Civil Service Commission and Management Board. Many ministries were forced to house opposing interests. Consumer and commercial relations were put together, a sure way to prevent an emphasis on consumer protection. Natural Resources looked after parks and logging, which spoiled it as a champion of parks. It also handled promotion of mines and protection of miners' health and safety.

Nor was COGP able to transform the management style in the civil service. COGP experts didn't think civil service managers were up to snuff. They weren't generalists and they weren't very analytical. Only 30 of 97 had experience outside one ministry. They made decisions on the basis of experience and intuition, not hard measurements. Although PPBS had been around since 1967, "the quantitative approach is not accepted by many managers," a COGP report complained. The deputies lacked training in statistics, distrusted them as dry and arid, and, worse still, "regard the whole process as chicanery and sedulously avoid it." For their part, 279 managers surveyed in the late 1970s found the COGP's system "too controlling." It led to "excessive meddling" and left them swamped in paperwork.

After a decade of rapid change in the 1960s, the COGP bid farewell to reform. All great experiments ground to a halt under the new order. The Ontario Housing Corporation, for instance, wound down its role in the housing business in 1973. The only new megaproject thereafter was Ontario Hydro's full-scale embrace of nuclear power, touted by a special task force of the COGP in 1974. Nuclear power, unlike conservation and renewable energy which have been shown to be at least as efficient, is dependent on experts, higher mathematics and centralization.

Despite its many resounding failures, the COGP succeeded in its fundamental aim. It made the civil service the kingpin of government, and made it a bulwark against change, a house of sober second thought. The legislature, still referred to in politics textbooks as the centre of democratic government, operated on a budget of one-fifth of one per cent of provincial expenditures.

Although the new men of power were covered by ministerial responsibility, the real power lay with a bureaucracy that ran on remote control. By 1972, according to a report of the Ontario Economic Council by conservative academic James Gillies, the notion of ministerial responsibility was just an "old dogma," because bureaucracy had become "the

Civil Service Review

ISSUED BY THE CIVIL SERVICE ASSOCIATION OF ONTARIO

In 1929, CSAO's annual "Field Day and Basket Picnic" was held at the Ontario Agricultural College in Guelph

Fred Beardall, CSAO president 1928-29, 1932 and 1944 (page 31)

Ontario's first Joint Advisory Council firmly controlled by premier George Drew (seated), May 18, 1944 (page 38)

President Harold Bowen (centre), already in his fourth term in 1956, shows off CSAO's logo (page 52) with Dave Holmes and future president Bill Harper

W. C. ("Bill") Harper, president 1958-60

Smiths Falls branch executive, 1956. Fifth from left, front row, is Ev Sammons, first vice-president/treasurer of OPSEU from 1980 to 1984

Moving day, 1959: June McCallum and Greta Kerr help CSAO move from 17 Queen St. E. to 1 Carlton St., Toronto

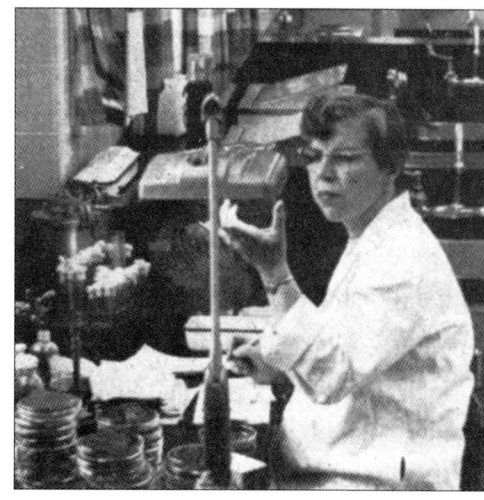

New public health lab in North Bay, November 1959

Director G. W. Ockwell confirms what Don Jail members already knew: Their pay was too low (March 1961)

Harold Mace, president 1961-64

50th anniversary annual meeting, 1961

1964 board of directors. Harold Bowen, now full-time executive secretary, is seated third from left, next to president Wilf Foster. Future president George Gemmell is seated at right

Annual luncheon, King Edward Hotel, Toronto, November 1963

The Trillium captioned this photo "A bevy of beauties at the Registration Desk" (1963 annual meeting)

"Harold Bowen: As hard-nosed as his counterparts in Quebec." –Toronto *Telegram*, March 11, 1966

W. J. ("Wilf") Foster, president 1964-66 (page 84)

George T. Gemmell, president 1966-74

One of the earliest demonstrations for higher pay: Hospital workers rally at Queen's Park, Nov. 7, 1966 (page 86)

CSAO's first strike, University of Guelph support staff, April 10-16, 1968: Ken Blackwell and Robert Marshall do picket duty on horseback (page 88)

Members' children (Doug Powell and Chris Blythe) join the second strike at Guelph University, November 1969 (page 89)

CSAO secretary-treasurer Merion Clement in 1970 (page 135)

May 1971: First VP Sid Oxenham, president George Gemmell and general manager Harold Bowen plot strategy against Darcy McKeough's five per cent wage ceiling (page 129)

"C. F. George" national officers, 1971; Ontario representative Sid Oxenham is 5th from left, standing (page 205)

Long-time activist Charlie Lockwood leads Queen's Park picketers against CECBA, May 16, 1972 (page 144)

Ron Morse, Bowen's successor as general manager (1973-74) (page 148)

Hospital delegates to the 1973 annual general meeting welcome their transfer to CSAO from "CSAO National" (page 195)

Community college teachers demonstrate against CECBA's "stacked" arbitration board, March 6, 1974 (page 151)

Public service ambulance officers picket health ministry offices for a better wage offer in February 1974

G. G. ("Jake") Norman, "the Arnold Schwarzenegger of CSAO" (page 149), the union's last general manager (1974-76)

General Manager Jake Norman explains bargaining strategy to delegates to the Public Service "gen ops" category demand-setting meeting, Sept. 21, 1974 (page 165)

Jake Norman and Chris Trower (r.) perform for a province-wide audience at CSAO's "Electric Union" meeting, Nov. 18, 1974 (page 166)

Jake Norman (left, leaning across table) leads CSAO's face-off with the government over CECBA, June 11, 1974. Management Board chair Eric Winkler (right, in shirtsleeves) soon lost his jovial mood as confrontation mounted (page 153)

CSAO's first appearance in Toronto's Labour Day Parade (1974) featured imprisoned civil servants

Jim Fuller at the 1974 annual meeting: "I am seldom civil and I am a servant to no man" (page 157)

First vice-president Mary Coates drops the puck at the 1977 OPSEU Cup Peewee Hockey Championship (page 193)

Allan Millard, drafter of OPSEU's constitution and head of the grievance department, 1975-77 (page 171)

Charlie Darrow, president 1974-78

OPSEU's first province-wide strike, by college support staff, January 1979. Shown are picketers at Northern College, Kirkland Lake

President Sean O'Flynn (r.) grits his teeth as OPSEU agrees to join NUPGE, "a sewer we had to crawl through to get into the CLC" (page 206). At left, NUPGE president Bill Jackson with CLC president Dennis McDermott

Halton-Mississauga ambulance workers torch an effigy of their manager during their six-week strike in 1979 (page 227)

President Sean O'Flynn is surrounded by well-wishers as he emerges from Toronto's Metro West Detention Centre, Jan. 25, 1980 after serving 23 days of a 35-day sentence for supporting jail guards' three-day illegal strike (page 217)

OHIP's 1980 move to Kingston, widely seen as a bribe to win votes for Tory cabinet minister Keith Norton, was immortalized by *OPSEU News* cartoonist Roy Carless

OPSEU's first equal opportunities committee, forerunner of the Provincial Women's Committee, meets Oct. 26, 1980

Equal opportunities coordinators Neil Louttit, Debbie Field, Daina Green and Frances Lankin

OFL secretary-treasurer Terry Meagher, Local 559 member Ross Morra, Labour Council president Wally Majesky, steward Jeff Hartman and OPSEU president Sean O'Flynn during their eight-day sit-in at Centennial College, June 1981 (page 218)

OPSEU members and staff bar entry to Mini-Skools' Mississauga daycare centre during Local 588's eight-month strike – the union's longest (page 250)

Bob DeMatteo, OPSEU's senior health and safety officer (pages 253-255)

With senior researcher Bob Hebdon, Sean O'Flynn argues against premier Bill Davis' wage controls at the legislature, Oct. 19, 1982

OPSEU members join Goderich citizens in torchlight parade Jan. 21, 1983 to protest closure of the Bluewater Centre for the developmentally handicapped (page 258)

Canadore College faculty member Wayne Ayotte on the picket line during the union's largest strike (7,600 members), Oct.-Nov 1984 (page 268)

The O'Flynn era ends as James Clancy takes over as OPSEU president, November 4, 1984

interpreter, the funnel through which the information flows to decision makers in government." Though it bathed itself in the rhetoric of neutrality, he said, "the bureaucracy must be seen for what it is: a major source of political, economic and social power in our society."

The invisible government preached the neutrality of the civil service. It made its points with technical and quantitative methods. But this was just a ruse, wrote George Szablowski, the only author of a COGP dissenting report. His 1971 working paper denounced the obsession with efficiency, precision and rationality for overriding "all other values, including those of participation, openness and wider access to public policymaking."

The quest for efficiency went in the wrong direction, Vernon Lang wrote in a study for the Ontario Economic Council in 1974. Efficiency leaned toward the Big Brother state, not the fuss and muss of service and involvement. "Just as men have tamed the atom without devising appropriate social controls on a world-wide scale, so, on a national and provincial scale, they have socialized some important public services without learning at the same time how to democratize them," Lang wrote.

John Donahue, in *The Privatization Decision: Public Ends, Private Means*, says the application of private sector standards of efficiency misses out on what government is all about. Public services are based on inputs of skill, resources, honour and accountability, not outputs of widgets, he argues. Comparing the two is like judging an axe like a shovel.

Bill Davis came into his own just as the COGP was in full swing. His election as Progressive Conservative leader in 1971 marked the first use of computers for a fast and neutral tally of the vote of convention delegates. The computer misfired and the counting was held up for hours. The Big Blue Machine Davis created after his election as leader was the perfect counterpart to the COGP. There were problems keeping in touch with the man on the street when the old political radar and intuition of grassroots leaders was replaced by layers of bureaucracy. "The influence of the new COGP structure was one of reducing the political inputs around the premier and increasing the bureaucratic and systemic drive behind policy development and implementation," claims Hugh Segal, a key member of the BBM. He quoted an old-time partisan who claimed that "the Harvard Business School [a direct reference to Fleck] has done more to destroy democracy than the Communist Party."

But the BBM did not restore influence to the community grassroots or even the Conservative rank and file. It merely provided a two-track system, one for policy pro's and one for political pro's who were masters at advertising, mass manipulation and trend-reading, and who furthered the centralization of power and knowledge in the premier's office.

The art of governing through a political party was being lost.

Death of a servant

It's no accident that CSAO's lurch from association to union coincided with the phasing-in of COGP recommendations.

It's not that the COGP fomented a clash between workers and union bashers out to whip them into shape. They were more subtle. Following the latest fashion in industrial psychology, they talked up "meaningful and relevant job opportunities." Government had to keep up with a new generation of educated workers with minds of their own and a desire for fulfilling careers, not just steady jobs. The COGP supported pension plans that were indexed against inflation, better sick-leave plans, more flexibility in selecting hours. Bargaining was to be done in "an atmosphere of co-operation and common interest. Any shift to the adversary system – whereby employer and employee take up opposing positions which make compromise difficult without mediation or arbitration – should be foreseen and avoided." The government also took pains to minimize individual losses resulting from COGP-inspired transfers by "gold-circling" any workers who got transferred.

Nor did the CSAO see the new changes as a management plot. The

CSAO News gave the COGP a rave review in November, 1970, and urged its members to help out. In 1972, the *News* reported government promises of job security in the wake of any COGP-inspired re-organization.

CSAO leaders seemed unaware of the COGP's impact on shop, office and institutional floors. The effort to make government more productive, more output-conscious, destroyed the civil servants' sense that they were somebodies. It also destroyed the sense of a career service, that hard work and loyalty would be rewarded with advancement. Once the new order of credential-based promotions came in, those who started at the bottom of the ladder got stepped on by people with degrees. If workers didn't lose money, they lost face and faith. It ended what the sociologist Max Weber called "traditional domination" through status and custom, and replaced it with formal, rational legal domination.

The old order had its problems with low pay and petty tyrants. But camaraderie on the job made those problems a bit like slipping into an old pair of slippers or sliding into a favourite easy chair. Re-organization took away workers' autonomy on the job that gave them pride, the sense that their work was part of their life, not just a way of making a living. With that psychic income gone, workers' patience with low wages was tried beyond the breaking point.

Almost all the old hands in the civil service still have a strong sense of before and after the deluge of mandarins. They make it clear that the COGP set the psychological stage for unionism by turning the term "civil servant" into a badge of servitude, not service.

When the Department of Transport was merged with the Department of Highways, the old transport crew, used to wearing a uniform and having the power to take away a person's licence, felt downgraded. The merger "neutered us," says Mike Rowett, then a leader of Windsor driver examiners. And the testing lots were turned into production lines, he says. From 1970 to 1972, the time for a driver's test shrank from 25 to 15 minutes.

After the re-organization that turned Lands and Forests into the Ministry of Natural Resources, district managers ran their operations by the book and stopped consulting workers. "It was no longer what should we do, it's what will we do," says North Bay district veteran Neil Lang. The managers pulled rank. "There was too much of that at the top, and consequently it wasn't near as nice a place to work anymore." Workers were no longer asked to pitch in wherever help was needed. They were kept in one job and "segregation started setting in," he says. Their job title changed from "forest ranger" to "resource technician." "You didn't have the same sense of being needed," he says.

"You almost had to get authority to start a truck up," says George Kerhanovich, with Highways in the Sault. At the OPP garage in Toronto, mechanic Pat Rooney saw the changes through a wall of glass. When the car and motorcycle garages were amalgamated, the new garage had a raised glass office for the manager, allowing him to oversee everyone.

Where autonomy wasn't taken away by individual managers, it was taken away by the process of promoting only those with credentials. Old files from Quetico Park in northwestern Ontario tell the legends of the park's most beloved naturalist, Shannon Walshe. His trials began in 1973, when district lines were changed and "a whole new order came in." Walshe hated turning in his old Lands and Forests uniform for the new "jumpsuit." He hated filling out forms. Most of all, he hated the new university-trained parks planners who didn't understand a park, where nature was in charge. But "if there's anything Shan loves, it's taking a park planner on a canoe trip and driving them into the ground," the file on him at Quetico claims, allowing "what a dull bureaucratic world it would be" without characters like Walshe.

Jack Armstrong worked as a game warden in the far northwest. Until 1970, he issued limits on fishing and hunting based on his wildlife counts. After 1970, he was told his job was to provide a count for the ministry biologist, who would make the policy decision. This change was linked to a new job classification that "broadbanded" ministry staff as technicians. To Armstrong, that reclassification packed the simple message: "The professional people will run the government and the technical people will do the work." This remained a sore point with him until 1985, when a classification grievance he spearheaded on behalf of slighted conservation officers led to a major pay increase. The COGP's various re-organizations took away the sense that workers and managers were involved in a common enterprise. The sense of all being in the ship together had muted the power differences between them. The new regime bared that difference.

The new district managers were "pencil pushers," says Lang, who never wandered far from their offices. University qualifications ended the old pattern whereby someone could work their way up on the basis of practical experience in the woods. They planted, as they had learned, by the book, and didn't listen to the likes of Lang who told them that white pine need shade to stay free of blister rot. "After the re-org," he says, "you weren't working together. You were working in the field."

For firefighters like Roy Storey in Beardmore, the 1970s saw a change from the days when entire crews drove in to the fire, slept in the same tent, ate from the same pot. After 1972, managers flew over the fire area to survey the damage. "In an old fire you went in and did what you thought you had to do. In a new fire you went in and did what someone else thought you should do from a much removed location...having never seen it," he says. Before, "the senior fire technician would be out there on the fire with you. In 1972, when things started to change, you would probably not see that person. All you would hear was him on the radio."

It was the same in eastern Ontario, where Bill Craig worked on the roads, boarding with the whole crew in out-of-town projects. When he started, "everybody was like a great big family, especially in construction, the supervisors right on down. You were on the road together. You lived together. You partied together. And that's the way it was. Project supervisors dropped in once a week." That changed in 1975, when engineers took over from project supervisors. Roadmen resented the raw graduates "walking in and taking over or stepping on their turf." To add insult to injury, they had to teach their new bosses the twists and turns of practical roadwork. A manager was no longer one of the guys. He was an outsider. That's as potent a force for creating us-versus-them unionism as wages.

DON'T CALL ME SERVANT

The Purple People Eater

Not only did the new system formalize work relations, it formalized the system for dealing with workplace problems. Mike Rowett's buddies referred to the new purple-covered manual of administration as "the purple people eater," a reference to a popular rock song of the day.

At OHIP offices, brought under the Ministry of Health in 1971, the old "loosey-goosey" style of an independent commission was replaced by "management by dictate," says former clerk Jim Tait. Everything about how to handle a claim was specified by elaborate manuals, "and all of a sudden, you had the purple people eater imposed on you." Once the system was made uniform, workers wanted the benefits of uniformity too, he says. Before, workers in each operation had their own deal. One group got two coffee breaks a day. Another got one. Another had none. "Little things like that impress themselves upon the worker," Tait says, and local CSAO activists began pressing for consistency.

In the North Bay area, grievances became "more of a hardcut fact" and supervisors had to play by the rulebook even if they personally preferred discussions, says Neil Lang. Their response to grievances was that "they didn't want to deal with the union." The old days when he could cut a special deal were gone.

But if managers wanted to run the workplace according to the bottom line, the bottom line was that workers wanted more pay. And if managers wanted to live by the book, they could die by the book. If managers wanted to deal from on high, then "union" became the way to get to the top. Relations based on give and take, mutual obligation and trust, were replaced by rights and duties under a contract.

Bill Craig was a hockey player who turned union pro. After high school, his coach thought he had the stuff to play NHL and pulled a few strings with local Tory broker Jimmy Auld. In 1963, Auld got Craig a highway job that didn't leave him too tired for hockey practice. After a crack at the minors in the U.S., Craig came back to Ontario and the new order. When he got turned down on a $12 expense claim, he went to see a CSAO steward, who taught him how to cross-check with the grievance procedure.

Vic Williams, an office worker in Kenora, had a typical boss of the 1970s, a university grad who started at the top, not an oldtimer who worked his way up. "He didn't run an office. He ran a prison camp," says Williams. At first, Williams tried to handle the problem one-on-one. When the boss docked workers for being late, Williams gave him late slips for supervisors who came in late. "Just helping you out," he explained. When the humour on double standards went over the manager's head, Williams figured he'd have to go higher up to get some action. "I was at the bottom of the stairs. He was at the top where he could hit me pretty easy." Williams ran for the CSAO board, where he joined up with union backers from down south.

In the institutions, it was the modern authoritarian management style, not the old paternalism, that provoked protest. "On my first day at Kitchener Jail, I was given a tour, given the keys, and left on my own to run the jail," says Vic Cooper. "The jails were simply holes, they were old and crumbling around our feet." The old jails were dilapidated and authoritarian, but there were lots of nooks and crannies where guards could set up a personal relationship. "Before the jails were taken over by the province," says Cooper, "we were able to work around the rigid system. As guards, we taught inmates how to cook, clean, cut hair, do laundry, do landscaping, gardening and carpentry work. Once the government saw this as a way of saving money, they hired special rehab people and we lost these duties." The loss of personal space happened at the very moment when jails took in more hardened and hostile inmates, which made the guards' lack of control more frightening, he says.

In Thunder Bay, a new administrator from the U.S. centralized administration. "He broke the kingdoms, the little individual kingdoms. There was only one kingdom under him, and that was him," says Mel Vezina, a long-time maintenance worker at the psychiatric hospital there. Still bitter over the college-trained nurses who relegated attendants to being "uniformed secretaries," he calls the changeover "the white power movement," a reference to medical uniforms.

Not all grudges were directed against managers. Workers fought among themselves too. Jan Holowka, one of the first college grads to start at Northwestern Regional Centre for the mentally retarded, got broken in on the job her first day. Attendants asked her to untie one of the inmates and feed her lunch. The chronically violent inmate beat the hell out of Holowka. Take that, college grad.

In Smiths Falls, a new personnel head introduced a big policy book to run the mental retardation centre. Workers nicknamed him "Captain Morgan," and local union activist Ev Sammons called her yappy chihuahua "Captain" in his honour. A new medical director wore coverings over his shoes when he walked the wards and pulled out a hanky to turn doorknobs. He sterilized human relations with the same zeal. When she first came to Smiths Falls in 1965, says counsellor Joyce Earl, a "whole lot of things" made it less harsh than it seemed. Smiths Falls was seen as a world leader in treatment of the retarded. It had the latest equipment, and took up rare problems no one else could handle. Female aides helped patients with their makeup and hairdos, and helped them prepare for the annual Christmas concert, one of the town's main events. "Nobody really said what you should do. You just did what you thought was the right thing to do," she says.

Under the new regime, violent patients were subdued with drugs, not cold packs. That meant calling in doctors for authority. Rules were set by people who worked far from the scene. Every six months, program evaluation prescribed routines for each worker and inmate. Workers ridiculed the "tickey-off sheets" they had to fill whenever inmates went to the bathroom. But the hurt couldn't be laughed off. "We'd raised our own kids, worked here for years without supervision," and "all of a sudden we weren't good enough any more," Earl says. "It made everyone aware that management was often wrong, very often wrong in the kind of rules that came down."

Garnet Rowe started working on the grounds at North Bay Psychiatric Hospital in 1963. "It wasn't a job, it was a position," he says. Workers commonly worked on Sundays, used their free time to take patients shopping or bring them home to see their farms. In the evenings, they took patients skating or bowling. "The thing that broke the nutshell," Rowe says, was the new policy ordering staff volunteers to pay for their own hot chocolate after skating. That was it. The outings stopped, and "then they had to get a recreation department that cost a lot more than hot chocolate," he says.

At Oxford Regional Centre in southwestern Ontario, a worker wrote *CSAO News* in January 1972 to complain about penny-wise changes there. Subsidized bus service, free coffee at break time, cheap meals at the cafeteria, clothing allowance, all went in economy moves. These were the little perks, the social wages, that helped workers cope with low pay and feel they were valued by someone "up there" who cared.

The economics of the changeover were drastic for casuals, many of whom worked seasonally for the government every year. Casuals were the fastest growing group of government employees in the 1960s, up 25 per cent, according to the calculations of economist Meyer Bucovetsky. In many areas of the province, this was part of the life cycle. Subsistence farmers worked the roads and laid-off loggers planted trees every summer. "With the re-organization, people didn't care about the experience or anything. It was just a body out there," Neil Lang says. Planters were put on piecework, a change that upset the whole organization. Before, the best planters were assigned to the worst soil, where their speed paid off for the group. With piecework, the green thumbs demanded time on the good soil, and supervisors had to ride herd on slow planters.

Wayne Campbell started as an elevator mechanic in Sudbury district in 1970. He marvelled at cleaning staff who kept rundown buildings spic and span. "We truly owned it. It was our goddamned equipment," he says. Then cleaning and maintenance jobs were contracted out, and "there was no longer the sense of pride and ownership."

A former factory worker and steel worker, Campbell didn't think this work reality jibed with the A in CSAO. "I didn't know what the hell an association was. An association is something that professional people join. I thought this is crazy. We're all sweathogs, damn good sweathogs. We need a union."

Once the new regime took away ownership of jobs, the rights that went with ownership had to be transferred to a union. And what was once custom had to be fought for as a right.

Women office workers may not have experienced downgrading as sharply, probably because the strict division of labour inspired by the COGP did not become technically possible until the "electronic office" tied women to their work stations a decade later. After a long break from the paid workforce, Isobel Bird took a secretarial job with the nursing assistant training program in 1961 when she was left widowed with four children to raise. "I felt my work was important and I enjoyed doing it. The work was never a bore," she recalled. "With people coming and going, you had that sort of rapport with people which wasn't dull. It wasn't like it was strictly all office work." Another secretary who asked to remain anonymous, recalls a similar work regime in the 1960s at the Ministry of Agriculture. "One call will be about a man who's had his acres and acres of corn absolutely wiped out and there's going to be a terrific claim for damages, and the next phone call will be from a balcony gardener whose tomato plant was failing and what could she do about it. There was quite a bit of public relations, because you really had to be civil to one and all."

Whatever was missing in rapport with male managers was made up for in close relations with other workers. Another secretary from the '60s who also asked to remain anonymous had a boss who was "not very bright" and "a real party hack." She says: "I tried to maintain a boss-secretary relationship and I would get so angry I would have dreams in which I would call him names. That was, I guess, the way I was venting my frustration. On the other hand, it was an absolutely incredible office because there were three other secretaries there and another assistant and the four of us got along incredibly well. We had a wonderful time. We laughed all day long through our work. We were very close."

The courts were exceptional in providing managers an opportunity to turn clerical work into repetitive and uninterrupted drudgery because of the huge amounts of uniform tickets, fines and written instructions that were sent out. Once the court system was centralized in 1968, a law reform study noted in 1973, "the initiation of appropriate studies to segregate and analyze the whole range of problems that confront and beset the administrative function of the court system" became the order of the day. "The dispensing of justice under law is not to be equated with product manufacturing," the commissioners allowed. "That is not to say, however, that all devices and procedures by which efficiency is achieved in the business world are irrelevant to some aspects of the court system." Female clerks had to go down the street when nature called. In retaliation, CSAO steward Rusty Fawcett stole the lounge key, made copies for each of the clerks, and told them to sit down for their rights. "They were pissing four times an hour," he says, until management relented.

Faulty pillars

Around 1971, the roof fell in on the old CSAO. Premier Robarts resigned, and CSAO leaders lost their pipeline to political influence. The new hands in the premier's office and in government personnel departments had no feel for the old ways of doing business. The CSAO had to find new ways of getting its views to the top.

Formerly, the CSAO and the Civil Service Commission were something of a mutual admiration society. They propped each other up, even though they were on different sides of the employee-employer fence. They found common cause in the fight to override ministers and despotic deputies in their hiring and employment practices. To jealous deputies, the Civil Service Commission was as much an intruder as the CSAO. The commission officially encouraged workers to join CSAO, and welcomed delegates to CSAO gatherings. It backed CSAO's call for dues checkoff as early as 1965.

The relationship was a little incestuous. In the 1960s, Harold Mace gave up the CSAO presidency to become a senior commission staffer. In turn, the CSAO snatched up Dorothy Homuth (who handled grievances for the commission in the 1950s), to handle workers' grievances in the 1960s. Homuth, a former secretary to Lady Eaton, hobnobbed with the high society set. A secretary once left her a note saying Laura Thomson had called. "That's Lord Thomson," Homuth said stiffly.

The buzz among CSAO militants was that this cosy relationship made the joint council a "tea and crumpets affair." That's a slander, says Bob Hebdon, a CSAO researcher who attended many council sessions. Only coffee and blueberry muffins were ever served. They were "the finest I've ever eaten," he says, "but it was not tea and crumpets at all."

Hebdon joined the CSAO staff in 1968. Harold Bowen asked him two questions in his job interview. Do you have your MA in economics? When can you start? Three weeks later, Hebdon faced his first wage arbitration board, where CSAO battled the government for wages to match those paid in the private sector. Hebdon's counterpart at the commission prided herself on the independence of her research. Her statistics showed that government workers lagged as much as 30 per cent behind their private-sector equivalents. "All we did was play a supporting role," says Hebdon, when the Treasury Board's lawyer tried to challenge his own witness.

New era managers wanted firmer hands at the labour relations helm. The need for expert direction was signalled by Justice Ivan Rand's 1968 royal commission on labour disputes in Ontario. Unprecedented advances in science and military technology had destroyed all notions of people's place, morality and responsibility, he said, leaving in their wake "an unlimited field of demolished inhibitions." To counter demands for ever more luxuries and rights, to install some procedures for "adjustment to societies of order," he wrote, "persons of high gifts, sound judgement and thorough training" were needed in labour relations. Judge Walter Little's report on civil service bargaining came on the heels of Rand's commission. He too urged the government to join the professional leagues in labour relations matters.

The switch in titles from "human relations" to "human resources" put a name on these changes. In bargaining, that meant formal negotiations that proceeded from a management agenda. At a time when European industrialists planned a comeback based on co-management and worker involvement, North American industrialists and governments wanted top-down scientific management.

Government managers, not CSAO leaders, were the first to replace co-operation with conflict. In 1969, the Ontario government spirited J. R. ("Rollie") Scott from the chemical and forestry giant, Domtar, to head the government's bargaining team. He convinced the politicians to stay away from the bargaining table, and let the labour relations branch get down to serious negotiating.

Legal advice came courtesy of Robert Hicks, charter member of Hicks Morley Hamilton, the country's first law firm to specialize in corporate labour relations. The firm broke from the British tradition of gentlemen barristers, who only represented clients in court. Instead, it "really got in there with the client," doing hard bargaining as well as legal work, one of the firm's present partners says.

Though well-connected to leading Tories, the firm's gladiatorial style fitted in with the Toronto Board of Trade, which Hicks chaired. The firm gave clients practical advice; its philosophy was to take the law to the limit, and force workers and unions to fight for every right. In 1968, when community college bargaining legislation was still in limbo, partner Fred Hamilton refused to call the contract a "collective agreement." It was a memorandum of understanding, he insisted. Hamilton gave nothing he wasn't forced to, according to Bob Hebdon, who assisted in the bargaining.

Partners in Hicks Morley Hamilton represented the government at the Little hearings, handled public relations for the COGP, and wrote the bargaining legislation for civil servants and community college teachers. Though private-sector experience taught them that unions were a fact of life, that didn't mean workers had to be mollycoddled. Tough bargaining with a weak union might leave employers further ahead than paternalism, an intricate system that demands constant maintenance and frequent gifts.

Oldtime Tories were paternalistic. They had a sense of duty and caring for those who served them, a sense of two-way responsibilities over and above the exchange of cash for labour, and a sense for when rules could be broken to suit particular circumstances. Paternalism modified old Tory authoritarianism. The new executive class was autocratic, not paternalistic. It formatted labour relations on an adversarial and formalistic basis that led to union-style conflict and arbitration. Arbitration did two things. It replaced big P political interference with the small p politics of handing power over to neutral experts. It also removed the onus on politicians to take the rap for hard bargaining. Management was free to take a strong stand, in opposition to CSAO, without having to accept responsibility for the final settlement.

Politicians were nervous about the risks of this new course. It meant, after all, granting final say on wage settlements and conditions of work to arbitrators, who weren't accountable to the public and who had no stake in the well-being of the governing party.

In 1970, as the new regime was being launched, provincial treasurer Charles McNaughton floated the idea of a six per cent guideline on arbitrated settlements. His advisors told him that instructions like that undid the basic principle of arbitration – that a neutral should judge on the merits of a case – and McNaughton dropped his idea. Senior policy advisors had a harder time using quiet persuasion on McNaughton's successor, Darcy McKeough, described by one aide as "forceful, dynamic and autocratic."

McKeough faced off against CSAO as it geared up for a major campaign in 1971 wage negotiations. The government was the province's biggest employer of minimum wage labour, CSAO charged, and most cleaners and support staff could do just as well on welfare. CSAO wanted a 40 per cent wage hike.

In April, McKeough brought down a budget that *Canadian News Facts* described as the "highest spending program in Ontario history." He promised to create 100,000 private sector jobs by slashing taxes and cutting out what he called the "distortionary" effects of government spending. A supply-sider a decade ahead of his time, he okayed an unprecedented $415 million government deficit to cover the loss in tax cuts designed to spur on private spending.

The recipe for government changes outlined in the budget was lifted straight from COGP reports. Strict accounting and streamlined decision-making would "pay off in terms of a more efficient public service, more value for public money spent and more resources for use by the private sector and by taxpayers themselves," McKeough promised. For good measure, he threw in a five per cent limit on public service wage increases.

Over at CSAO, Bowen was furious, with the kind of anger that flashes only in family disputes, says Hebdon. He called an emergency CSAO executive meeting, which called an emergency CSAO convention. Within two weeks of the budget, delegates voted 251 to 5 to reject any wage ceilings, and to launch work-to-rule and rotating strikes while building for a public-service-wide strike vote in mid-May. A special issue of *CSAO News* used words like "bullyboy," "dictatorial," and "big daddy paternalism" to describe the government. A strike would be legal, Bowen explained, since government had killed the arbitration system that substituted for strikes. "Having sown the wind, the Government will reap the whirlwind," Bowen warned.

On May 14, three days before the strike vote deadline, CSAO leaders met a sheepish McKeough. The arbitrator had made it clear that he would not be influenced by any government guideline, and McKeough's staff had already scolded him for making a farce of arbitration.

With cameras flashing around him, McKeough said he'd been taken out of context. He had no intention of interfering in arbitration. He had only issued a guideline for his own negotiators. Moreover, he wanted CSAO input on Bill 217, the government's new bill to formalize labour relations and compulsory arbitration. The year-old bill was just a "rough draft," he said.

The CSAO went to press that day, celebrating the members' "finest hour" and "bold new spirit." It even used the u-word, claiming "a union forged in the crucible of adversity is that much tougher." For the first time, the CSAO had flexed its union muscles and felt it had a politician's scalp to show for it. Unbeknownst to the CSAO, however, it had burst heroically through an open door. McKeough's five per cent wage cap was the most expendable item in the game plan to re-organize government along business lines. CSAO's protest provided the occasion for the government's rising stars to replace Bill 217 with a new law that more clearly reflected their COGP-based agenda.

But that was precisely what the Conservative strategy was: to rejig the role and structures of government along the lines set out by the Committee on Government Productivity. CSAO's outbreak only caught on to five per cent of that larger agenda.

A management bill of rights

True to his word, McKeough let Bill 217 die. It was so one-sided in granting all rights to government – one clause gave cabinet blanket powers to forbid negotiations on "any matter or any position or classification" – that it was an embarrassment. The *Globe* called it "unfair, ill-conceived and offensive."

Killing Bill 217 was not just a concession to CSAO. It didn't fit with government plans either. The bill politicized labour relations, and put the politicians on the hot seat at a time when executives were groping toward an impersonal rule-based system that operated on automatic pilot.

Rollie Scott and Robert Hicks drew up a new Crown Employees Collective Bargaining Act (CECBA) that was truer to COGP principles. The bill was introduced in May, 1972 by Charles McNaughton, chair of Management Board, the new cabinet position created at the behest of COGP to take charge of technical control over the civil service. McNaughton called the bill a "landmark" and "watershed" that spelled out union and management rights in law and kept political interlopers at bay.

The bill spelled out more management than worker rights. It banned bargaining on 21 exclusive management powers, "such an impressive list of items," according to the authors of *Provincial Governments as Employers*, "that one wonders what is left over to be negotiated." Everyday workplace policies like training, classification, job evaluation, staffing levels and pensions – which, in turn, touch on a score of health and safety, quality of working life and technical change issues – were vested in management.

In the view of James Renwick, speaking in the legislature for the NDP, the bill missed the point of democratic legislation, which is supposed to strengthen the rights of people, not rulers. Everything was gutted except pay and a few fringe benefits, he charged. "I would have to say that the employees' rights are virtually everywhere in the bill except where they are excluded," McNaughton replied. "Except where they are needed," New Democrat Ian Deans shot back. Asked to explain the government's refusal to bargain over training, McNaughton told MPPs to read the COGP's report on human resources. New Democrat Mike Cassidy took him up during the break in debate, and came back to describe the bias of the report as "almost a class system." McNaughton made no reply.

The Crown Employees Collective Bargaining Act was introduced on the heels of McKeough's March 1972 budget, a slashing exercise that signalled the end of the glory days of government expansion. CECBA was designed for a government moving toward a shutdown, not new adventures, in public enterprise. Once again, the handiwork of the COGP is evident.

"Creeping government control rubs every fiber of his person the wrong way," the *Globe* wrote in a budget-eve portrait of McKeough, then wrapping up a speaking tour to spur the private sector to take over more government programs. He has "an unfortunate tendency" to speak "in terms like cost-effectiveness, planned budget programming and delivery of services," the *Globe* noted, without identifying this programmed language as the mantra of the COGP.

The *Globe* traced McKeough's passion for this language to a return visit the year before to his old private school, Ridley College in St. Catharines. It caught McKeough's fancy that the work once done by college staff was now contracted out. He immediately grasped the possibilities. "There are armies of people in the civil service who are cooking meals and cleaning halls," McKeough said, and "maybe it would be better to go out and buy that service because the private sector can probably do it and make money and save the taxpayer some money." In an echo of the COGP, he declared that "the best workbench for curing some of our social problems is the private rather than the public sector."

CECBA was not well-received. The *Globe* thought it failed to come to grips with the causes of public sector labour unrest then sweeping the country. A common front of Quebec government workers had just sparked the biggest general strike in North American history. In Ontario, hydro workers brought the province to the edge of brownouts with a series of wildcat strikes, while garbage piled up in Toronto parks during a strike by municipal workers. This strike fever "does not give the government the right to treat other workers as faceless, rightless peons," the *Globe* wrote. "Indeed, these excesses should spur the government on to devise a more satisfactory formula to govern and resolve labour disputes." Both the *Globe* and the *Star* argued that the scope of bargaining should be broadened to make up for workers' loss of the right to strike.

Liberal leader Robert Nixon attacked the blanket prohibition on strikes. If teachers, hydro and garbage workers could strike – subject to back-to-work laws in event of public emergency – then provincial employees should have the same right, he said. Nixon blamed the bill's petty and small-minded spirit on McNaughton, a "hardheaded seed dealer from Goderich – he knows what that implies." Not so, said McNaughton. He'd sold seeds in Exeter. McNaughton didn't say what that implied.

NDP leader Stephen Lewis heaped scorn on the bill as "some sort of permanent indentured labour," which denied the right to strike and to bargain workplace rules. "It is beyond dictatorial!" he yelled. Opposition fury went for naught. McNaughton volunteered only one amendment in the legislature. A section made it legal for managers to pressure workers for political donations if they were "employed or proposed to be employed in a managerial or confidential capacity." Since any individual might be deemed "proposed to be," this loophole allowed anyone to be strong-armed, Deans complained. McNaughton, in a bid "to show you how co-operative we are on this side of the House," said proposed managers wouldn't be pressured.

The committee that read the bill in detail came back with two minor amendments. One granted workers the right to grieve management decisions related to dismissal, appraisal and classification. This amendment shouldn't have slipped through, says Rollie Scott, the bill's drafter. (Ironically, the amendment became part of OPSEU folklore, and has been widely interpreted as forcing the union to take all grievances to arbitration. This reading of the law has allowed political leaders to avoid taking responsibility for OPSEU's unique policy.) Another amendment carried in committee gave CSAO the right to bargain mileage rates when workers used their own cars on government business.

The CECBA bill was rammed through three readings in three weeks and passed May 30, 1972. CSAO did very little to lobby against it. This put New Democrats in bad temper. They stuck out their necks to defend the rights of CSAO, instead of taking up the complaints of CUPE or other unions, many affiliated to the NDP, who lost out most as a result of the monopoly given to the CSAO under CECBA. Yet the CSAO had not one person in the galleries to cheer on the NDP's gallantry.

Deans called the bill "the worst piece of legislation that I have ever seen," and said the CSAO was "part of this legislation." No other worker organization in the province "would have accepted this kind of legislation," he said, "that the CSAO has accepted." For Lewis it was hypocrisy to call this a bill for collective bargaining. "It is a bill to straitjacket Crown employees. A bill to arrange for a serf relationship with government for Crown employees. A bill to establish the unilateral rights of the crown in the bargaining process. A bill, at the very least, to establish compulsory arbitration for its employees." McNaughton couldn't afford to ignore the NDP's criticisms, Lewis charged, unless he'd already cut a deal with CSAO. He "is so self-satisfied," Lewis said, "clearly having the pre-arranged acquiescence of the civil service or at least of the association."

Deans moved to re-title the bill "the Crown Employees Compulsory Arbitration Act." The motion was defeated 54 to 32, and CECBA became law.

※

Keeping up with Jones

It wasn't anything as pitiful as a sweetheart deal that kept CSAO activists away from the legislature where their future was debated. The no-show had a sorrier explanation. "We were too busy stabbing ourselves in the back," says Bob Hebdon.

CSAO was a case study of what historian H.C. Pentland calls "the most novel and revealing feature of the labour militancy of the 1960s – the frequent revolt of union membership against their leaders." Rebel voices cascaded on an organization that had to work through difficult internal changes, open up to new occupational groupings, and adjust to harsh new bargaining realities. To add to the mess, CSAO had its full share of what Hebdon calls "organizational crud." From 1968 to 1973, it ran out of control.

In the 1960s, CSAO "was more like a family than a complex organization," says former senior staffer Jim Keatings. But Bowen knew best. In 1970, Keatings was ousted after a family feud. Bowen had hired Keatings and Gren Jones, both leaders of the Toronto Don Jail branch, in 1960. They did not match the standard image of jail guards. Keatings hated capital punishment, and wanted a first-hand look at the prospects for prison reform. Jones, an experienced British bobby, had turned down a job with "Toronto's finest" because he couldn't stomach the sight of police "jackbooted, with gun to their belt. They looked exactly like the

SS." He got hired at CSAO, no questions asked, when the interviewer found out they'd served in the same regiment during World War II.

From day one, Keatings and Jones preached union. In 1961, Jones asked the CSAO board to re-organize around ten bargaining groups. CSAO couldn't be all things to all civil servants, he said. Managers grumbled about belonging to a "sweepers' union." Working stiffs sneered at the company union. Either kick out the managers, or the workers will break away or sink into apathy, he said.

As director of education, Jones produced some of the first union videos in the country. The first show, made with a home movie camera, starred Bowen's secretary Merion Clement. The second told the story of Britain's famed Tolpuddle Martyrs, farm labourers banished to Canada for organizing a union. The film was shot in London, Ontario's Fanshawe Cemetery, where some of the exiles are buried.

Jones and Keatings were at the height of their CSAO careers in 1967. Jones was seen as Bowen's heir apparent. Then CSAO directors started wrestling with policy changes to keep pace with new organizing and bargaining realities. They hired a professor, a lawyer, an insurance agent and an accountant as consultants. If CSAO didn't broaden its base, they warned, the members pushed out of the direct civil service would go over to CUPE. But "the real basis for concern" was the government's push to bargain on occupational lines. "The Association must re-align its internal structure in order to dovetail with the suggestions generally proposed by Government," the consultants said, and added that CSAO also needed districts and branches and regional staff reps to cope with local problems.

This advice went against the grain of directors elected along ministry, not job or geographic, lines. In 1968, the board voted to stay with the old ways.

Holding fast on CSAO's internal structure didn't stop CSAO from shedding its old skin as a social, service and self-help organization. Bargaining and organizing were the order of the day. So much so that in 1969, CSAO broke a 42-year-old tradition and shut down its employee-run cafeteria in Queen's Park. It also cancelled recreational activities and the annual Christmas choir concert "in line with its recent policy to remove itself from all commitments which were not those of a bargaining agent." Whatever its structure, the organization was singing a different tune.

The problems wouldn't go away. But the answers weren't easy to find. Getting the right structure for a public sector union is harder than it looks to private-sector eyes. In the private sector, if there's one plant with one employer, then it makes a lot of sense to organize industrially on the principle that "in unity there is strength." The local is where the organizing drive takes place. It is where decisions are taken, and where the problems have to be solved. And the local is the focus of bargaining. This only starts to get complicated when one employer – General Motors is an example – owns several plants and makes common decisions for all of them. Then the workers have to figure out what's local and what's general.

In government, structures are not so straightforward. No one local office, no one ministry, sets policy on wages or working conditions. But structuring a civil service organization around job groups is no easy matter. A secretary in Toronto rarely bumps into a secretary from Thunder Bay, in her ministry or not. What they have in common is a job title, not a workplace or community.

Working through the dilemmas of union structure for CSAO took good will, just what CSAO didn't have much of. After 1968, Bowen became obsessed with a structure that would keep CSAO under his thumb, most staff and activists say. Kevin Burkett, fresh from business school, says he picked up Bowen's bargaining load so that Bowen could keep a hand free to deal with staff and board critics.

Bowen quashed any groups that might rival him in power or influence, says long-time CSAO accountant Helen Silinsky. He broke up the Queen's Park branch, a virtual empire unto itself with as many staff and programs as CSAO-central. Except for $500 in petty cash, funding for branches was doled out through Bowen's office. He resisted staffing large, union-style branches of institutional workers in North Bay and Smiths

Falls. And should anyone get into badmouthing the CSAO leadership, "Bylaw 66" provided for expulsion of any member who "[acted] in a manner prejudicial to the association."

Bowen wanted the branches kept lifeless and dependent, says Garnet Rowe, a mainstay of the North Bay branch. Rowe wrote Bowen to ask "where head office was at" in terms of the local demand for its own staff rep. Bowen wrote back that head office was at 15 St. Mary Street in Toronto. The North Bay local demanded an appearance from CSAO president George Gemmell, then did their best to humiliate him.

Becoming politicized

Gren Jones tried a more intellectual route. He hoped to force the pace of change by organizing community college faculty, a drive he still considers "the most significant thing that [he'd] done." He counted on the college faculty to bring in new blood and bold thoughts. He lucked out. The very act of bargaining for college staff threw a monkey wrench into Bowen's plans, as had already been shown when college support workers joined CSAO.

Bowen's CSAO had 325 branches that included all government workers in an area, regardless of occupation, ministry or work site. Branch members had little in common, and less that they could do about any problem they did share. The almost-inevitable result was a social club with lacklustre attendance, leadership and accountability.

The colleges couldn't help but break up this clubhouse arrangement, George Brown trades instructor Eric Lord told Jones. College staff would have to be organized and serviced around a common employer and common workplace. "You're going to turn this association into a trade union," Jones remembers Lord saying. "As soon as you get everybody together who've all got the same complaint, then you've got some strength to do something about it. If you do this thing in the colleges, all the remaining members are going to want the same thing."

College faculty didn't gravitate to CSAO in the way support staff had years earlier. They had neither an old sense of belonging with CSAO nor a new sense of belonging in a union. "There may have been a less militant group in Ontario," says Cam Hopkins, who taught chemistry in Sudbury's brand-new Cambrian College, "but I don't know who they'd be."

The college trademark was hands-on learning. Many teachers, like Lord, came from skilled trades with a tradition of unionism. More came from professional and executive backgrounds where unions were looked down on.

First-time teachers turned on to the "tremendous sense of mission and purpose, that we were building something from scratch," says Bill Kuehnbaum, a math instructor at Cambrian, later vice-president of OPSEU. "There was an excitement that overrode workload considerations, often even salary conditions. It was just a helluva lot of fun being in the colleges then."

Everything was top-of-the-line. Many companies were so keen to help out, they donated equipment and manuals. University professors who visited college labs wept, Lord says. "That was in the days when if you thought you should have this piece of equipment you'd order it, orders went to Queen's Park, and the stuff arrived."

A stuffy civil service association was okay for time-servers, but not much good in the colleges, many thought. The Ontario Federation of Community College Faculty Associations, backed by Ron Martin at Oakville's Sheridan College and Floyd Laughren at Cambrian College, had a good run at beating CSAO. "It was the professionalism thing," says Martin. But CSAO had a leg-up organizationally when it came to a province-wide drive. CSAO recruiters signed up 35 per cent of college teachers in 1971. That meant teachers had a choice to mark their ballot for CSAO or nothing, not CSAO or another group. CSAO won by a large margin.

The CSAO drive peaked just as the college romance was fading. When the dust on the great experiment had settled, business administrators were firmly in control. College presidents were recruited from industry, not academia. They appointed a bevy of deans and chairs who conducted themselves like private-sector supervisors, not university chairs elected by their peers.

"It is of interest to note how many of the colleges borrowed from industrial models in developing their organizational structures and their policies," William Stoddart wrote in a study for the Council for Leadership in Educational Administration in 1974. Communications were "deplorably weak," Arthur Porter wrote the same year, in an inquiry into Kitchener-Waterloo's Conestoga College. "All they did was re-invent the pyramid," says Kuehnbaum.

Almost half the college staff were under 35. The management style didn't sit well with hang-loose arts and social service teachers who had just graduated from the counter-culture. When Cambrian president John Koski gave a drab lecture to his faculty, a long-haired, social services instructor in blue jeans leaned over his chair and asked, "Fuck, John, what the fuck does all this mean?" According to Hopkins, "This undermined the dignity of the president's remarks."

When Cambrian faculty started to compare pay cheques, they found that the administration was taking advantage of them, arbitrarily paying some far more than others. Confronted with this, the president asked to meet faculty association president Hopkins privately and informally. "I'm like the Pope, I only speak *ex cathedra*," Hopkins told him. The president explained that the college's duty to give equal pay for equal work was expressed as a "shall," not a "must." These are the kinds of hairs that professional union negotiators get paid to split.

College presidents put the "you" in union for a shocked teachers' bargaining team when they hired management lawyer Fred Hamilton to negotiate the first round of province-wide bargaining in 1972. Hamilton refused to negotiate terms for part-timers or for student-teacher ratios. These topics, he insisted, were none of the union's business, as defined by the Colleges Act (which his firm drafted). "When I saw the cavalier way our negotiating team was treated by the government lawyers...I'd never been treated that way," says bargaining team member Ron Martin. "It began to politicize me, and the college began to lose its lustre."

A week after the contract was settled, George Brown College laid off 11 teachers and was ready to lay off ten more. Under CSAO banners, 150 teachers marched to Queen's Park demanding the government "fire poor administrators, not good teachers."

Injured innocence turned quickly to rage. The new college members – feisty, self-confident, some would say self-important – wanted a CSAO that expressed their anger and aspirations. They were not about to be locked away in one of Bowen's divisional catacombs. That, coupled with the intellectual and radical bent of many college activists, made it impossible for Bowen to steer a steady course from a milquetoast employee association to a "bread and butter" or "business" union. A year after their entry into CSAO, college leaders were major players in transforming it.

Jones did not get to see these fruits of his college organizing. His showdown with Bowen came too early.

Bowen was starting to "lose it" by 1970, Jones says. Bowen felt "the whole world is yapping at his heels and they're all trade unionists," Jones says. He and Keatings were seen as a fifth column. Feelings of persecution were coupled with a sense of omnipotence, and Bowen increasingly referred to CSAO as "my organization." Jones claims that Bowen told him: "I want CSAO to be a monument to me."

A few days before the 1970 annual meeting, Jones met with Bowen to talk him out of his proposed bylaw changes that would have squelched free speech and limited membership control. Jones had consulted a lawyer, who advised him that CSAO was still a corporation, as it was in 1927. That meant individual members, not delegates, had to vote on bylaw changes. In his back pocket, Jones had a statement from his lawyer confirming that individual members could sue to block the controversial changes. Bowen's jaw stiffened, and he turned deathly white. "From that moment on, I was a marked man," Jones says. Bowen assigned Jones to a room at the King Edward Hotel. Jones checked in early the next day, and stumbled onto a man bugging his room.

Bowen's changes to CSAO's bylaws, presented as democracy in motion, carried the day at the annual meeting. "The change from begging to bargaining necessarily required change in CSAO internal structures," Bowen reported. "Without such a change, the members ran the risk of facing, internally, a bureaucracy as frustrating as that imposed by the employer."

Once the convention was over, Bowen demoted Jones, a senior CSAO manager, to training officer. That was a mistake. The CSAO staff had unionized in 1969, and Jones gained protection from arbitrary firing. A short time later, Bowen fired Jones and his two suspected allies on staff, Jim Keatings and Norma Maclean. He fired another staffer, Ben Coffey, for sending out a press release protesting the firings.

A year later, an arbitrator reinstated all but Coffey. When they returned, Bowen fired them again. The three settled for a cash buyout. Jones also demanded a glowing letter of reference. "I made him eat shit," he says. Jones was rehabilitated when OPSEU asked him to chair its 1978 and 1984 presidential elections. He kept his legal letter and the bugging of his room secret until interviewed for this book. "If I'd wanted to destroy the organization, if it'd come to the point where I was disloyal, I could have done it easily," he says.

※

Four Horsemen of the Apocalypse

Bowen couldn't fire CSAO's elected leaders, who mutinied in 1972.

A new set of leaders came to the fore after 1970 who were quickly branded as "the Four Horsemen of the Apocalypse." Future "horseman" Neil Pollock received a "deep throat" telephone call inviting him to a top-secret meeting shortly after he was elected to the bargaining team for community college support staff in 1969. He went to a sleazy downtown Toronto hotel where he met unnamed members and staff – "it was secret contact and I mean secret," he says – who "felt they had no control" over CSAO. Dissidents were encouraged to run for the board of directors and to fight to democratize the board. Pollock was elected to represent community college support staff in 1970.

"Horseman" Jim Tait, a Toronto OHIP clerk, joined the board in 1972. While waiting for the first meeting to start, he leafed through a copy of *Last Post* that featured an exposé of Jones's firing by Bowen. "Horseman" Ron Haggett, a psychiatric aide from Brockville, sat down beside him, struck up a conversation, and now they were three. The fourth was Vic Williams, a Natural Resources clerk from the northwest. The four often rode with Debbie Julian, a hospital technologist from Peterborough, and Charlie Darrow, an attendant from Woodstock.

The "gang of six" had a better idea of what they were against than what they were for. "Our aim in life was to challenge Bowen as often as we could," says Pollock. "He sat at the end of the table, very well dressed, and sat there like a bat. He was an evil man." He says the group came together when board members demanded to see the text of a contract Bowen signed with CSAO staff before approving it. "That was the start of the challenges. That's how basic it was," Pollock says. "Absolute power corrupts absolutely. He was living proof of that." Though Pollock had been a union activist in Britain, "I don't believe the people sitting around that table thought CSAO was going to become a union. They weren't trade unionists. It was a question of democracy, even for myself."

Williams remembers it the same way. "Democracy was the issue of the day," he says. He wanted to "get the elected leadership first," then deal with the changeover to a union. Haggett thought democracy and unionism were linked. "I wanted to take the union by the horns," he says. Tait thought the real issue was the Tory and Masonic links of board members tied to Bowen and his cosy relationship with government.

Even president Gemmell felt the pressure from below. "The advent of collective bargaining made me more aware of the need for participation by the members in decision-making," he told the 1970 annual meeting. He noted that health workers had picketed CSAO offices to protest the settlement agreed to by the board of directors and Civil Service Commission.

By 1972, Gemmell knew the opposition had the horses to carry the day. He came to a board meeting looking haggard and soaking wet. "Excuse my appearance," Williams recalls him saying. "I've been up all night and just had a shower, but I decided that Bowen shouldn't run the organization any more."

In March, the board voted itself the power to hire and control the top three staff, and to make them subordinate to elected leaders. Bowen and Clement called their bluff, and resigned immediately.

Rumours flew through the building. Researcher Bob Hebdon led a staff delegation demanding job security for all staff and a year's extension for Bowen so he could arrange a smooth transition in the last months before his retirement.

The board held firm, and Bowen was ousted. Hebdon was then named assistant general manager with authority of general manager, "the longest job title in North America," he says. It didn't last long. On May 4, without so much as a tipoff, Hebdon learned that CECBA was before the legislature. He rushed into Gemmell's office. Gemmell said there was no reason to get upset, and left Hebdon to field media calls. On an emergency basis, Hebdon called a special general meeting of members for May 13 to consider CSAO's response. Then he started working up a brief on CECBA.

Bowen's supporters seized control of the May 13 meeting. CSAO needed a steady hand at the helm in this time of crisis, delegates insisted. Bowen had to be brought back. Debate on the new bargaining law got short shrift. Delegates decided CSAO should oppose the limits on bargaining, and should campaign in a way that suggested strike action might be taken.

As the meeting dragged to a close, someone moved that all CSAO staff retire at 65. It passed. Bowen was a lame duck, with seven months to go in office.

No media reported on the meeting, and CSAO put on a bold face for public consumption. Advertisements were published in 58 dailies across the province:

> WE KNOW YOU'RE TIRED OF STRIKES
> SO WE WON'T STRIKE
> IF WE GET FULL BARGAINING RIGHTS

CSAO's position won editorial support from the *Star* and *Globe*.

On May 16, a small circle of CSAO staff, nicknamed the "donut brigade," carried placards outside Queen's Park while the legislative committee readied CECBA for final reading. "Government workers gazed out the windows wondering what we were up to," says Mike Rowett. "Let's shoot the damn thing down in flames," one placard read. "If bargaining rights you deny, then you'll hear the union hue and cry," claimed another. Gemmell threatened a protest strike.

He didn't convince any workers. They "stayed away in droves," a special edition of *CSAO News* reported. "Which is more important: your noon-hour card games and the shoppers' specials at Eaton's, or your working future?" Gemmell didn't even convince himself. The next day, he conceded a strike was unlikely. Bowen said CSAO would have to live with the act. "The issues are such that we might have difficulty generating sufficient enthusiasm among the members," he said.

The battle to control CSAO seemed to be over. The battle against CECBA had just been a sideshow. When CECBA went through its final reading, no CSAO members showed up to protest.

Though the annual general meeting that fall seemed to leave Bowen fully in control, his days were numbered. A group of board members who blamed their political defeat on Bowen's interference got the board to hire a private detective to prove Bowen and his staff aides had strong-armed members. This was a staff-bashing witch-hunt, the staff charged. The board refused to call off its private eye. Staff voted unanimously to prepare for a strike.

Bowen came to work on his 65th birthday. His office was locked. Security guards escorted him out of the building. Staff gave Gemmell 30 minutes to remove the guards and call off the investigation. Gemmell held firm. Staff walked out.

Through a bitterly cold February of 1973, they picketed CSAO headquarters. After two weeks, they were ordered to come back. If they didn't, they'd be fired. Bowen came to the next strike meeting. He urged the strikers to stay out. "Show that the staff run the union, not the board," he said, according to Hebdon.

Hebdon washed his hands of the strike, and booked off on holidays. Fourteen other staffers crossed the picket line.

In March, a special CSAO meeting voted overwhelmingly to fire the 36 remaining strikers. In April, the labour board called the strike an illegal wildcat and upheld CSAO's decision to fire them. Bowen left the CSAO a broken man, retired to his farm in Minesing, and died eight years later of cancer.

Lorne Kenney was new to CSAO staff when the strike began. A manager called him out, he says, and "I was never really sure what was going on." He lost his job. "The only thing I regret is... the five months I was there was such fun. I thoroughly loved the work I was doing. Representing people, involved in a cause, awakening a sleeping giant. I don't think I've liked working quite so much ever since."

Chapter Four

Raging Bull

His first day on the job, negotiator Andy Todd asked to see the CSAO's collective agreements file. A researcher said that Bowen always kept them to himself, that it might not be proper for Todd to look through them. Todd rifled the files, but found only lists of salaries. There was no sense of direction or building toward strategic goals.

Switchboard called. A Mr. Haggett says he has an appointment. Todd said he'd never heard of Haggett. Haggett picked up the phone, said he certainly did have an appointment, pal. Todd agreed. That's when he learned that members, even board members such as Haggett, weren't allowed in the building without staff permission.

The next caller didn't bother to introduce himself. "I'm at home," he said. "That's nice," Todd said. The member said he worked at the Brantford School for the Deaf, that the pay always came late, that workers were staying home until they got paid even though the CSAO general manager had told them to go back to work. Their pay was couriered from Toronto in the afternoon.

The next day, tollgate operators in Burlington took their time making change and created a five-mile traffic jam to protest layoffs they'd suffer when the bridge went toll-free.

They seemed the only people taking their time to make change in the fall of 1973. This was make-or-break time for CSAO. The staff strike and firings left a clean slate, there was no one to say that this wasn't the way things were done, and a new union popped up overnight, "like a peony bud where the flower opens instantly," says Mike Rowett, hired as a staff rep that fall. "It was tremendously exhausting but tremendously exhilarating. A marvellous two years. We can never get them back."

When the mainspring broke, the only casing that stopped everything from blowing in the air was the Crown Employees Collective Bargaining Act, passed the year before to stop the union clock from ticking. Charles McNaughton, chair of Management Board, had an inkling that might happen. NDP leader Stephen Lewis says he overheard McNaughton mutter that CECBA would prove the government's Achilles heel. Just so.

The government miscalculated, and got more than it bargained for with CECBA. It got a structured adversarial system. By ruling out negotiations on many workplace concerns, CECBA forced bargaining onto straight wage issues, the clearest rallying point for any union. By hiving off middle managers, it removed the filter that up-and-comers might have put on demands from lower-echelon workers. By denying the right to strike, it gave CSAO leaders a free hand to go for their full wish list, without fear of spoiling serious talks and ending up on the bricks. And the money that most unions hoard in a strike fund was free for a war chest to fund public campaigns. The campaigns could be centralized and focussed, since bargaining rights were granted to CSAO, not its locals, as was the case in the private sector. The government got the union it deserved.

Of course, CECBA might have worked out better for the government. The same law might have undermined union activists, kept them weak and fragmented. For a while, it looked as though that might happen. CSAO was in shambles from its staff strike and the loss of its 20-year leader. Its internal politics were wrecked by splits over membership control, not straight-up union principles.

To catch its breath, the board hired Ron Morse as general manager. Morse was raised in a union-minded Welsh mining family, had been active in the British civil service association before emigrating to Ontario, and had been a CSAO local president before he was promoted to management and put in charge of pollution control. Seconded from management to head CSAO in the spring of 1973, he was praised by *CSAO News* for his ability to wear both worker and management hats, though he was "predominantly Union-oriented." According to one lawyer who worked for CSAO, Morse's life at CSAO was a bad dream and he was afraid of his own shadow. He was "an English officer, not a Canadian sergeant major," says George Richards, hired by Morse as a grievance officer.

The government did not take the changes in CSAO seriously. President George Gemmell and Morse met with Management Board to protest lack of consultation when COGP changes led to layoffs. Gemmell told government managers that CSAO was "not going to tolerate our members being uprooted and pushed around as in the past." Right after the meeting, Management Board chair Eric Winkler wrote Gemmell to say how much he'd enjoyed the meeting and looked forward to more.

Triumph of the will

Morse and the CSAO board looked around for a manager to handle membership representation, and hired G.G. ("Jake") Norman. "That was like hiring the sorcerer's apprentice," says John Ward, hired by Norman to handle public relations. "Shortly, the whole room was awash." In a year, Morse was gone, and Norman was in charge.

Norman personified CSAO's Great Leap Forward in 1973 and 1974. No one doubts that. But opinions vary widely on what he did and stood for. He pulled CSAO up by the bootstraps, says Ev Sammons, a longtime CSAO and OPSEU board member. "He made people stand up for things they'd never done before," she says. "But the only thing he had was the gift of the gab," says long-time CSAO and OPSEU researcher Bob Hebdon. "He was just a bombastic Bowen."

Norman was the Arnold Schwarzenegger of civil service unionism. He had a fierce face centred around a Fu Manchu moustache, and was built like a Sumo wrestler, with arms like tree trunks. He'd been a champion gymnast and boxer and had a black belt in karate. "His office was filled with pictures of him throwing people through the air," says researcher Jim Onyschuk, who couldn't help noticing there were no pictures of anyone throwing Norman in the air. He wore loud suits, "like a used car salesman in a Monty Python movie," says Sudbury college teacher Bill Kuehnbaum. He knew how to use his body to show off his tough style of unionism. At meetings, he'd rip off his jacket, roll up his sleeves, light up a cigar, and take over the room. "Straight out of Central Casting," OFL secretary-treasurer Terry Meagher whispered when he saw him move into action.

"He takes the power. That's just the way he is," says former CSAO and OPSEU accountant Helen Silinsky. "Everything Jake Norman did was big and glamorous." He had a power office on the top floor, and "everything had to be big and plush for him," she says. It was a foot bigger than the president's office and was known as the Taj Mahal. It adjoined an executive washroom and a board room with full-length mirrors and a meeting table so long it had to be lifted by crane and brought in through the windows. It was known as "King Kong's skateboard."

A former talent director for the CBC, he was probably the most media-wise union leader in the country. "I had a tremendous 'optic' for what you could do with images and pictures. I used it extensively in CSAO," he says.

This was the age of Marshall McLuhan, of Greenpeace confronting U.S. destroyers with little dinghies, and Norman understood it. He classed the old CSAO as a "tea and crumpet" association that did "collective begging," counting on people to recoil from their past in disgust. He wowed his first CSAO convention with a slide show that showed how civil servants had been ripped off. He took a loaf of bread to meetings to show what crumbs workers were getting, and why they had to double their dues to get a bigger slice. "Militant" was his favourite word.

Some of this bravura may have covered up the hurt of his youth. His mother took sick when he was six and he had to be sent to a foster home in Ottawa. "It was the most traumatic experience of my life," he says. His foster family spoke French, so he had to learn a new language. The experience, he says, "made me extremely independent, not reliant on others to do things for me, made a mover and shaker out of me, instilled a need to survive and succeed."

Some of his exaggerated images came back to haunt him. His plush Taj Mahal office was really standard middle-management size, with a fibre rug and bark wallpaper that peeled off. Yet his opponents used it as a symbol of his arrogance and privilege.

Before coming to CSAO, Norman worked as a labour relations manager for the CBC in Montreal, where he fought Andy Todd and John Ward on the union side. But he'd already carved out a career for himself as a troubleshooter, a hired gun who specialized in turning organizations around. He did that for five employers before coming to CSAO, and did it for another nine before he retired. "When other good men have tried and not been successful, it just made it challenging. No amount of money could substitute for that feeling," he says.

As soon as he was hired at CSAO, he phoned up Ward and Todd in Montreal. "The CSAO is in a bad way," he told Ward, and asked him to prepare a brief for an all-out attack on CECBA.

Norman had to move fast to get out in front of militant members. In December, 1973, 225 college teachers arranged their own meeting in Oakville to denounce the "arrogant, power-seeking bureaucracy" that usurped power with CECBA. It is "demoralizing, demeaning and dehumanizing" to be placed under the act, lead speaker Ray McAfee said, because class size and teaching conditions can't be bargained. "We are professionals, and this act is the antithesis of the concept of the rights of professionals held by our society," he said. "We are not here to talk about money, but about the preservation of the quality of education, and the restoration of rights which have been lost under this act."

The meeting denounced 20 per cent increases in class sizes in some colleges, and demanded a limit. Peter Churchill, a member of the bargaining committee, said the team should refuse to bargain under the act, which classed many working conditions as exclusive to management decisions.

The meeting set up an ongoing committee on quality education, centred in the colleges. A college teacher from Welland, Sean O'Flynn, said the CSAO had just hired some new talent, and should be called on to organize the fight. "It's not much of an organization, but it's all we've got," O'Flynn said. Someone at the head table said Jake Norman had offered CSAO's support for a broad fight against CECBA, and contacts were quickly made.

Early in 1974, a hundred college teachers threw up a picket line in front of the Royal York Hotel where the arbitration of their collective agreement was taking place. The college bargaining team refused to cross the picket line. Former Sudbury college teacher Floyd Laughren, by then an NDP MPP, issued a press release celebrating the action. They "are doing what all Crown employees should be doing," Laughren said. "The CSAO has been slow to react to the more offensive aspects of Bill 105, and the faculties of the colleges are in the forefront in a battle to restore integrity to the bargaining process for all civil servants." Later that year, college teachers organized a "study session" that had all the earmarks of a strike. The teachers studied until the arbitrator appointed by a management-stacked board resigned, and was replaced by an arbitrator whom both union and management could respect.

College teachers weren't the only ones to jump CSAO's delayed gun. Wayne Campbell, an elevator mechanic working out of North Bay, heard that premier Davis was coming to town. He organized a protest. "It was the good old days when you grabbed a goddamned packing box and a stick and out you went," he says. Davis stayed calm and walked over to Campbell to shake hands and ask about his concerns. As camera crews zeroed in on the two, Campbell said "I'll not shake the hand of the man who stole my rights." The next day, Campbell was chewed out by CSAO headquarters in Toronto. He'd just stolen the thunder from a CSAO press conference scheduled for next day. "I hadn't thought to kick the thing off. But there you are. You can't hide from the press," Campbell insisted. Campbell and his crew eventually became CSAO's notorious "flying squad," which hounded every Conservative who entered the north with bullhorns and moose horns. "We became pretty expert at nailing politicians that weren't doing good," says squad member Garnet Rowe.

In February, 1974, the CSAO board called for an emergency convention to launch a $600,000 campaign to "eliminate" CECBA, and gain union recognition under the more generous Labour Relations Act. In April, Norman held the convention spellbound, his talk illustrated with 4,000 slides flashed from front and rear projectors, designed to "light a fire of pride in these people." Four hundred delegates voted to double union dues to two dollars a week, and set aside 25 cents for the fight against CECBA, "the most repressive labour legislation in Canada." CSAO geared up to pull out all the stops. The union would take on CECBA in the media, the courts and in bargaining. "The only way the union can truly represent its membership is to stop trying to make the CECBA work," a position paper said.

"Free the Servants"

Jake Norman delivered a slick, professional, high-profile campaign. There were "Free the Servants" billboards, bumper stickers and buttons, featuring handcuffed trilliums. There were Davis Dollars, issued by the Bank of the Big Blue Machine, which paid civil servants 63 cents on the dollar. Activists carried a safety kit, with deodorant and Clorets to ward off the government's stench, and Alka-Seltzer and Tums for indigestion caused by management. Norman wanted staff to sport blue jackets with gold insignia, but was pulled up short by his assistant Frank Eastham, who reminded him CSAO was a union, not IBM. Public relations, Norman thought, were "the soft underbelly of government. They didn't expect this. They weren't used to having a lot of static coming from a union. It had never been challenged before."

But behind closed doors, CSAO gave out conflicting messages. In May, Gemmell wrote premier Davis to "respectfully request" a meeting where CSAO could present its brief. Davis suggested that CSAO meet with Eric Winkler, chair of Management Board, which Gemmell took as a slight. He threatened to go to the press if Davis brushed him off on a mere cabinet minister, and Davis relented. In the end, all they did at the meeting was pose with the cabinet for a photographer with the in-house civil service newspaper. Two could play the game of public relations.

In June, Norman presented a brief demanding 24 changes to CECBA's "one-quarter of a bargaining system." Without the right to strike, civil service wage gains had lost ground and now lagged a good ten per cent behind the private sector. CSAO wanted to make up for lost time by having the right to choose between arbitration and striking, the brief said. It's "time for your government to pull its head out of the sand," Norman told Eric Winkler and his staff. Then, according to minutes of the meeting, Norman extended the olive branch. We'd live without the right to strike if you gave us the right to bargain management rights, he said. CECBA can be changed: It doesn't have to be thrown out, he said. Winkler said it was too soon to change the new act drastically, but promised that smaller changes were in the works.

Norman left the meeting and headed over to a downtown hotel, where he hosted a media extravaganza, with lunch laid on for reporters and "rip and read" soundbites at the ready for radio stations. He announced the CSAO's $600,000 campaign to win the right to strike and political freedom for civil servants. Both demands were non-negotiable, he said. "We're moving from a tea-party organization to a respectable and respected union," he said.

A blitz of media ads followed, slamming the government's low wage offers at a time of 11 per cent inflation. On July 2, a special meeting discussed possible strike action. The next day, Norman and his team met senior government negotiators. No cabinet ministers showed up. "We've been slighted," Norman shouted. "This is an absolute insult. Winkler sent in third-line quarterbacks." CSAO wasn't prepared to go through "three or four filtration procedures" where demands were watered down before the last stage of talks, another union rep said.

The government negotiators were dumbfounded. "You're being unkind to impute to us that this is not vitally important," one of them said. "You can prove the system doesn't work, or you can have intelligent discussion," added Rollie Scott. "We are inviting Winkler to the next meeting," Norman said. "Your views will be made known," Scott replied.

Shortly after, the CSAO board met at the Ramada Renaissance Hotel, in northeast Toronto. Norman and his assistant Frank Eastham made the case that CSAO had to move fast and hard. Gemmell and Morse balked at that, Eastham says. Then the Four Horsemen, the group that once bucked Bowen, announced they weren't coming to any more board meetings until Gemmell and Morse resigned. They got up and left, and waited outside in the lobby. The Horsemen considered Gemmell incompetent – he fell asleep at one meeting with a cabinet minister – and Morse a mouse. "We wanted someone to get the place up and running," says Jim Tait. Gemmell tried hard, and Morse was a gentleman, but neither "had the ability to ramrod an organization," Norman says. By the end of the day, Morse resigned and was replaced by Norman, while Gemmell stepped down and was replaced by first vice-president Charlie Darrow.

A paratrooper during the war – he enlisted at the age of 17 – the adventuresome Darrow kicked around the mines in northern Ontario and the Arctic during the 1950s. He'd been active in both Mine-Mill and the Steelworkers union. In 1960, he used his connections with a Tory power broker to settle down with a steady attendant's job at the Oxford Regional Centre in Woodstock.

Friends called Darrow the "run silent, run deep type." He was a union PR nightmare. At press conferences, he usually answered "Yep" or "Nope." In relaxed settings, he was hail-fellow-well-met. But once he said "Yep" or "Nope," he stuck to it. Andy Todd was with him when a strapping correctional officer grabbed him by the scruff of the neck and threatened to throw him from the tenth floor of the union headquarters. "The answer's still Nope," Darrow said.

When members saw Darrow, Todd remembers, they said: "One of us has made it to the top." Those were exactly the thoughts of Fred Upshaw, then a psychiatric attendant in Whitby, later a president of OPSEU. "When I saw him, it was an inspiration. Here was an attendant who became president. I thought there was hope for everybody." The takeover by Darrow and Norman "was not just a palace coup, it was a major realignment," says former CSAO/OPSEU researcher John O'Grady.

Government brass got wind of the change immediately. On August 1, Rollie Scott wrote all personnel directors to tell them CSAO's president and general manager had been forced out and that new leaders were intensifying their attack on the government. As discussed in the recent seminar on staff relations, he wrote, we won't get into a "war of bulletins and press releases" with CSAO. "But from time to time we will supply you with information which you may want to pass along to the employees. The employees are quite capable of distinguishing between fact and fiction and will govern themselves accordingly."

Government managers found CSAO's new-found militancy hard to take. The common attitude, says Don Carter, who then served as an arbitrator of civil servant grievances and was privy to management discussions, was that of frustrated parents. "It was sort of like trying to deal with a teenager in your house when your mild-mannered child turns into an aggressive terror," he says.

On November 5, Norman launched the direct action phase of the Free The Servants campaign. As long as it was just a matter of informing the media and politicians, the campaign could be run from CSAO headquarters. "Now the real power of your union must be unleashed."

A whirlwind tour of 35 locations, designed to build anti-CECBA committees, attracted close to ten per cent of CSAO members to rallies. Rusty Fawcett cherishes his memories of the feeling at meetings in eastern Ontario. "At last, we were going to act like a union, instead of a bunch of bloody cream-puffs."

To get the blood pumping, CSAO put out its own record, "Sixty Thousand Voices."

> Sing out for my brother!
> We've been silent far too long;
> We must help one another,
> We are one and we are strong.
> Sing out for my sister!
> The time has come to right each wrong;
> In the cause we will enlist her,
> We are one and we are strong.
> Sing out now together!
> Build the future with our song;
> Throw off every tether,
> We are one and we are strong.
> Sing with sixty thousand voices!
> We are joined now hand to hand.
> Sing of freedom, rights and choices,
> Spread the word...it's time to stand!

Taking advantage of every loophole in the Public Service Act and CECBA, Darrow's message on the record jacket urged members to join a political party, work in the campaigns, ask questions at public meetings. The act's prohibitions on union politics left these individual activities as grey areas.

"This was the start of Madison Avenue trade unionism," says Peter Slee, a Hamilton journalist hired on staff midway through the campaign. But it was more than that. Norman was looking for shock value, he was applying shock therapy to the timid, self-effacing civil service personality, jolting members to face the biggest employer in the province. The glitz was part of building that self-confidence.

Those whose jobs and lives had been demeaned as a result of changes brought on by the COGP soaked up the Free The Servants rhetoric. At the 1974 convention, meat inspector and former sergeant major Jim (Foghorn) Fuller got a ten-minute ovation when he yelled: "I am seldom civil and I am a servant to no man." Andy Todd says: "It struck a chord with everybody there. Yeah, that's us. We're tired of being meek-mannered civil servants hanging around the corner waiting for a handout from the boss. We're sick and tired of that. And we're not taking it any more."

The campaign hit the government hard. It couldn't pretend not to notice. Contrary to Rollie Scott's advice, politicians got drawn into open battle. In October, Winkler issued a brochure claiming that government wages had kept pace with inflation. He praised the old CSAO for its tradition of frank and forthright discussions. "It can only be in the interests of the people of the Province that this co-operative relationship should continue and that the tactics of confrontation should not become the prevailing style," he wrote. The CSAO denounced Winkler's brochure as a $10,000 effort to interfere in union affairs, and described his wage survey as lying with statistics.

In November, goaded by the NDP's Michael Cassidy, Winkler accused CSAO of hiring a Montreal advertising firm and spending $600,000 to tear the government apart. He attacked "the new leaders of the CSAO," who "have decided on a course of confrontation regardless of what we do." He remained confident, however, that the civil servants of Ontario "are very, very high-class people."

Winkler said it was unfair of CSAO to attack the government-appointed arbitration board that oversaw CECBA's operations. The government only appoints people who are unbiased, Winkler said: "The government is still of the view that non-partisan boards are more appropriate than partisan boards in public sector collective bargaining." His statement betrayed a fundamental misunderstanding of what labour relations were about. Arbitrators in labour relations are always chosen by nominees of both sides. One side doesn't get to appoint people it considers impartial. By the end of his speech, however, Winkler did say the government was open to changing its approach to CECBA's arbitration board.

Three weeks later, Winkler invited Charlie Darrow to a hastily-called meeting about CECBA changes. The two jousted. Darrow said he hadn't been consulted on the recent staffing freeze. Winkler accused Darrow of provoking the government into cancelling meetings, "since the CSAO embarked on its campaign of personal attack on the Government through the media." Darrow shot back that "we will no longer sit meekly at the feet of the almighty and accept the condescending paternalism of the employer; we want to discuss such matters as an equal partner." Norman joined in and accused the government of calling a quick meeting to legitimize its own political decision to change CECBA.

The CSAO met Winkler's staff in early December, one day before Tory amendments were scheduled in the legislature. It was too late for dramatic changes, government officials said, but CSAO's input was welcomed even at this late date. "There are some imperfections. Our combined talents would make it read better," an official said.

Close but no cigar

In December, 1974, the government announced ten changes to CECBA. College staff got out from under CECBA, and got their own Colleges Collective Bargaining Act with the right to strike and the right to bargain everything except pensions. Civil servants won the right to negotiate job classifications, promotions and layoffs, subjects previously immune from union influence. Workers also got the right to take their union with them if they were transferred out of the civil service into the private or broad public sector. The CSAO won the right to nominate its own representatives to the Public Service Labour Relations Tribunal and to a new Grievance Settlement Board.

Aside from changes to CECBA, adopted in early 1975, the government made a number of other gestures to conciliate CSAO, or at least head off toe-to-toe confrontations. Better insurance benefits were provided. The Tories also reclassified Hamilton property assessor Brian Charlton to a position that allowed him to contest the provincial election as an NDP candidate, thereby depriving CSAO of the legal case it was preparing for the Supreme Court. (Charlton later became Minister of Energy and chair of Management Board in the NDP government.)

CSAO turned thumbs down on the changes. "We came out empty-handed," Norman griped. Darrow dismissed the changes as "window dressing and political diarrhetoric." Vital issues, such as the right to strike, or to bargain over pensions and technological change, were unchanged. "The mountain has moved and produced a mouse," he said. "We must show government we won't be bought off with the crumbs it is offering us."

Norman cheered one advance, the decision to tender the contract for group insurance benefits for civil servants. Confederation Life made a better offer and took the contract away from London Life, just as it did with the community colleges two years earlier. "We have broken the back of that old consortium which for nearly ten years has received millions of dollars from the government employees' insurance plans," Norman said.

The insurance change certainly touched a nerve. Within days, a citizens' coalition was formed to fight the advance of public sector unions. Key backers included former Ontario premier John Robarts, former Alberta premier Ernest Manning, and Colin Brown, the London Life agent who lost his commission. Jake Norman denounced the grouping as "a confused web of insurance companies, corporations and politicians working for very selfish interests." Norman charged that Brown organized a charter flight to take Robarts and Davis golfing. The phone number given out for further inquiries was Rollie Scott's, Norman charged.

This consortium was the forerunner of Colin Brown's National Citizens' Coalition, one of the most successful union-bashing groups in the country. In 1984, the Coalition launched a Charter case against OPSEU that challenged union rights to use dues income for community and political campaigns. Some called the case a grudge match.

It wasn't just false modesty or political posturing that led CSAO to refuse credit for the 1974 reforms. The Free The Servants campaign was only one point of pressure on the Conservatives. Changes to CECBA were one part of a general overhaul of labour relations undertaken by Davis that year. The overhaul was designed to stabilize, not revamp, labour relations, to ride out what OPSEU negotiator André Bekerman calls "the long con," rather than take the short-term savings but long-term risks of the "short con."

Labour unrest

Davis's hard line against unions in the early 1970s caused him as much trouble as it caused the unions he hoped to contain. CECBA wasn't the only case of an anti-union law turned to seed, creating instead of quelling labour unrest.

Changes to the Labour Relations Act in 1971 also backfired. They literally courted disaster. Labour code changes forced unions to sign up 65 per cent of a plant's workers before gaining automatic certification. This ensured bitter and drawn-out organizing drives. Individuals who claimed that their religious scruples freed them from paying union dues got the green light from code changes. That tied up the labour board with endless disputes of a crackpot character. The code also imposed a duty of fair representation on unions, an attempt to tar unions with the brush of Mafia-style repression of member grievances. The raft of petty grievances that followed cost unions and employers a fortune.

With runaway inflation and a tight labour market, unions racked up strike after strike, and put Canada over the top as the most strike-prone country in the world. "The premier's office was intimately involved in labour relations because it was a number one problem," says labour law professor Don Carter, then just starting out as an arbitrator. "There was a tremendous amount of labour unrest, and it made the government look bad because it couldn't handle the situation," Carter says. "The old guard was suddenly on the outs. They were regarded as having no new answers."

The old system, in which a small club of judges knew all the players and how to make them play, couldn't cope with the changes. Davis brought in Tim Armstrong, law partner of David Lewis, to head the labour board and take charge of the labour ministry as deputy. In 1975, constructive changes were introduced to the code, as the Tories rushed to show themselves progressive. "To stay in the middle, they couldn't afford to be seen as anti-labour," Carter says.

Strong-arming didn't work with high school teachers either. The Tories resisted granting the right to strike, and faced mass rallies at Queen's Park. One overflowed Maple Leaf Gardens. Eddie Goodman, a member of the Big Blue Machine, worried about entering an election with an anti-labour reputation, and convinced Davis to grant teachers the right to strike and to put fact finders and conciliators in place to reduce the need for strikes.

With teachers playing one board off against another, the province didn't want school teachers leapfrogging over college teachers. Davis wanted college faculty off his payroll, off his back, so he wouldn't get the rap for setting any pattern in teacher wages. The province was willing to meet the rates set by boards, but it didn't want to set rates itself, says Rollie Scott, head of civil service staff relations.

New college legislation was drawn up on the run, closely modelled on the law for high school teachers, and sped through the legislature to avoid any chance of overlapping bargaining rounds. The government was in such a hurry to get the bills passed together that college workers, including support staff, got the same legislative guarantee of scab-free strikes as teachers. (Strikebreaking is considered an educational no-no, since it creates havoc among students, who shouldn't be forced into taking sides with one group of teachers against another.) However the power of the teachers' lobby was such that CSAO almost got caught in their model of having principals in the bargaining unit.

In all likelihood, civil servants also benefitted from walking down the legislative aisle together with teachers when the government decided to index pensions to inflation. The reform didn't give workers bargaining rights over their pensions, but it far exceeded the monetary gains won by unions that did have bargaining rights.

The government also had its own reasons for replacing CECBA's original Public Service Grievance Board (PSGB) – the same one that continued to deal with complaints from non-unionized managerial employees – with a Grievance Settlement Board modelled on standard labour relations lines. The new board had a union as well as a management nominee, and an arbitrator sensitive to the procedures of unionized environments. "The most notable feature of PSGB decisions is their brevity, their lack of any detailed reasoning, their failure to canvass relevant published arbitrable jurisprudence, and their lack of any dissenting opinions," a CSAO brief claimed. Management had its own complaints. CSAO grievance officer Grant Bruce could work his charm on the board and get mercy for workers on a compassionate basis, says Dave Beatty, chair of the new board. "The system drove people crazy," he says.

Management and its lawyers wanted predictability. They also wanted a board with enough clout to impose modern ideas and order on some of the fiefdoms – Corrections was the example most often given – that had never been brought under centralized bureaucratic control. Having a board impose order relieved central management of that responsibility, and took away the bad taste of giving the union credit for any improvements, says Don Brown, a leading authority on arbitration who was close to the government scene. An even-handed board was one way of keeping the union at arm's length in the workplace, replacing participation and conflict with bureaucratic rules. When all was said and done, legal reasoning corresponded to the impersonal logic of a committee-on-government-productivity-style management.

By his personal style, the chair of the new grievance board, Dave Beatty, seemed more suited to the television show "Night Court" than to a government grievance board. A brilliant legal reasoner and co-author of the standard text on arbitration, the University of Toronto professor enjoyed the support of both union and management. By a quirk of fate, he had just finished nine arbitrations at Stelco, and had ruled in management's favour nine times in a row. Robert Hicks, the government's talent scout for a new chair, thought that showed a sound legal mind. He met Beatty over breakfast and said this would be a wonderful opportunity to make the rules for a large organization. Hicks approached Steve Goudge, a rising labour and environmental law star retained by the union, and suggested Beatty. Goudge knew Beatty as a "bleeding heart" when it came to discipline, and agreed.

Beatty put the new board to work in 1975 to clear up what was in those days considered an intolerable backlog of 16 cases. He insisted on his own office in a separate building from management to remove any taint of dependence. To assert his neutrality, he wanted to report to the legislature, not Management Board. Tim Armstrong, then chair of the Labour Relations Board, came to a meeting where Beatty lobbied for this change. "I remember thinking what the fuck is he doing here," Beatty says. He ended up reporting to the Minister of Labour, a supposed guarantee of neutrality.

His aim was to turn the Grievance Settlement Board into a school to teach managers and workers about the meaning of union relationships. He thought 95 per cent of workplace problems were "how-to-get-along problems," and wanted a permanent board that would get the feel of government workplaces and push the lessons of how to deal with conflict down into the workplace. He did not want a board dominated by abstract legal reasoning.

Beatty lasted in the job one year, until Armstrong replaced him with George Adams. Adams established a larger board that met less regularly. Without the consensus that develops when boards work toward an intimate understanding of human problems in the workplace, the Adams board quickly came to rely on legal parsing and precedent. In the end, the 1974 reforms to workplace grievances worked to consolidate the workplace style set in motion by the Committee on Government Productivity, not the Free The Servants mentality promoted by CSAO.

One clear-cut victory among the 1974 amendments was won with parish pump methods, quite unlike those of the Free The Servants campaign. In Brockville, psychiatric attendant Art Lane got an inkling that the government might get out of direct responsibility for psychiatric hospitals. If that happened, Lane wanted to make sure the union would stay with the workers and continue to protect them when they were transferred.

Brockville was a government town, a strong and loyal Tory town, and it always got one local member appointed to cabinet. Lane went to see his local member, Jimmy Auld, a man with a genuine concern for his constituents. Auld shared Lane's fears that a shakeup was on the way. Lane lobbied the local Progressive Conservative riding association and persuaded Auld to sponsor a "Crown Transfers Act" that guaranteed union succession in the event of a major transfer or privatization. Within a few years, when cutbacks were in full swing, this change ranked as OPSEU's salvation.

The 1975 changes to CECBA were the last of any consequence until 1993.

❋

The year of bargaining dangerously

The Free the Servants campaign brought the new CSAO into the world of political campaigning. The union also wanted to make a show of what it could do on the bargaining front in the same year.

To turn CSAO into an instant union, Jake Norman hired top guns from other unions. Chris Trower was one of the first. A high school dropout who worked in the lumber camps and mining towns of British Columbia, he led the rough-and-ready Trail local before joining the staff of the Steelworkers. Later stationed in Toronto, he was a bit too free-wheeling to fit the Steel mould and was assigned to work with community groups. Trower wanted to go to law school, but the Steelworkers wouldn't give him the time off. When Norman heard this, he hired Trower, and promised to send him to school if he'd put in one all-out year with CSAO. He was put in charge of the "general operational" category, a far-flung group of mostly blue-collar workers.

With inflation running at 11 per cent in 1974, wages were the only issue. The contract had a strict deadline, December 31. "It was an ideal bargaining situation for setting up some sort of power play," Trower says. He asked researcher John O'Grady to concoct a case for the biggest wage demand possible. O'Grady did his best, and came up with a rationale to back the demand for a 51 per cent increase. Not high enough, Trower said. O'Grady did some more research, and came back when his numbers reached 64 per cent. Trower found that more reasonable. "My theory was that if you want to get something you start with something big, and if you want to get attention you start with something outrageous," Trower says. If the demand was outrageous enough, the media would spread the word better than the union could to members scattered across the province, he says.

He stage-managed the meeting of "gen ops" delegates brought to Toronto to set bargaining goals. Trower and Norman stayed up with Charlie Darrow all night while he rehearsed his speech. Trower brought in 15 staffers, assigned them to seats scattered throughout the hall, and gave them copies of Darrow's speech, clearly marked so they would know when to stand on their chairs and cheer spontaneously.

Darrow began. "Strike talk! That's what I've been hearing in the halls last night when I spoke to delegates. Strike talk!" Delegates cheered, and passed the demands unanimously. Trower guessed that his outlandish bargaining position would "create an upscale climate," and lead members to expect something really big if they united behind the union. He also thought it would put management on the defensive. "It was too high to logically knock down. It's much easier to explain why something should be 8 per cent instead of 10 per cent. It's almost impossible to explain why something should be 10 per cent rather than 64 per cent," he says.

At the first bargaining session, John O'Grady gave a slide show outlining CSAO demands. Before managers could react, Trower said "We'll await your offer," and left the room. The government fell into Trower's first trap. It offered an 8.25 per cent increase, three points below the rate of inflation. Trower took the insulting offer to the members, and asked for a strike vote.

Management Board's Eric Winkler was outraged. He called voting on a first offer "extreme bad faith," which gave workers no choice but to strike. "The government will not be intimidated by such provocative and reprehensible tactics," he said.

Trower organized an "electric union show" for the strike vote. Closed circuit television gave members a province-wide union meeting. From Toronto, the sound and fury of 3,000 workers hooting and stomping to labour songs by the Travellers were beamed to Kenora, Cornwall, Cochrane and points between.

The union's TV debut was also carefully scripted. Workers only got to speak through the hookup if staff gave an advance signal that they were militant. Otherwise, they just spoke to their own small crowd. The secret ballot also coloured the results. A white ballot was dropped in the box for strike, a black for acceptance. "No matter how you folded them, they were still black and white," says snowplough operator Roy Storey, who watched from Thunder Bay. Storey liked it. "It was the first time anyone ever said No to the government and put together some type of campaign," he says.

Workers voted 92 per cent against accepting the government offer. The mood was building for "no contract, no work." Even as the strike vote on the first offer was being organized, government officials insisted there were better offers to come. They fell into Trower's second trap. They proved his case that tough talk and hard organizing got results.

The looming civil service strike was a great media story. Most reports and editorials sympathized with workers who'd been held down too long. The cameras played up the drama. Trower had a huge cast on a leg he broke after slipping on some ice. The cameras panned to his cast, and Trower threatened to cripple the province if the government didn't give in.

The National Citizens' Coalition ran full-page newspaper ads urging the government to hold firm against the grasping union bullies.

It was late December before talks got serious. The two teams met round the clock at the Four Seasons. Across the street at the Park Plaza, government bargaining director Rollie Scott sipped coffee, waiting for calls from his negotiator. He had a mandate from the government to go up to 20 per cent. He didn't think many workers would honour a CSAO strike call, but enough would to cause disruption. "So it was nail-biting time," he says.

Trower was determined to break 20 per cent.

Then the government set a trap for Trower. It offered a 25 per cent hike to jail guards, as long as he accepted 20 per cent for everyone else. Trower had feared this. Of all the "gen ops" workers, guards were most likely to strike, and most likely to create an emergency if they did. Trower needed that threat to boost the strength of the others. "The first thing I didn't want was a potential division within our ranks" that would create a stampede to solve special problems, he says. He wanted to stampede the other way, force the government into an across-the-board settlement that would knock the wage grid out of whack. In later years, when militancy might not be possible, workers could go after increases based on classification disputes, not raw power.

Long after midnight, Rollie Scott looked down from his suite and saw NDP leader Stephen Lewis walking out of the Four Seasons. "That introduced another element," says Scott, still unsure what Lewis was doing there. Lewis's role is the "untold story" of that bargaining round, says Todd. He convinced the government that a strike was possible, and that CSAO wasn't bluffing. "He got the government to put a deal together and pulled Jake's chestnuts out of the fire. Jake was hanging on for dear life, like the proverbial guy who's yelling 'let me at him,' hoping the men holding him back will hold tight." Norman's assistant, Frank Eastham, agrees. Jake got nervous as the bargaining went down to the wire, he says: "We knew the strike was a bluff. We couldn't have pulled it off."

At 8:30 a.m., the government offered a 21.5 per cent increase for all, and threw in an extra 5 per cent for the jail guards. The union team, tipped off beforehand, had a pre-meeting champagne breakfast and filed in behind Trower, who wore a white plantation owner's suit with a rose in the lapel, and puffed on a cherub cigar. The management team was red-eyed and haggard. Trower allowed that the $37 million offer was enough to declare a victory.

At 10:45, the bargaining team got to the International Centre on Airport Road where 5,000 Toronto-area members, linked up with workers from across the province on television hookup, awaited the results. Members voted 70 per cent to accept. The normally unflappable Trower remembers feeling like Rocky at the end of his boxing match. Exhausted, with reporters swarming around him, he dragged himself from the stage and called out for his wife. "I just wanted to be taken home and tucked into bed," he says. After going the distance, Trower tripped. Shortly after the settlement, he told Toronto *Star* reporter Rosemary Speirs that the government had fallen for pure bluff and could have got off a lot cheaper. The story made front page news.

"It was like Mulroney's 'roll the dice' speech after Meech Lake," says one union negotiator. "It showed that Steelworker attitude that civil servants are nothing." The bargaining team called for Trower's head. Trower recuperated in Hawaii for two weeks, came back, and was hand-delivered a letter telling him he was fired. He hired a lawyer, who reminded Norman of the deal to send Trower to law school after a year at bargaining. Trower was kept on until fall, then sent to law school at CSAO expense.

The episode left a bad taste in the government's mouth. Rollie Scott feels the government should have held out for a bigger margin for jail guards. That might have prevented their wildcat strike five years later, he says. That time, the union warned that a strike was in the offing, but the government wasn't about to have the same trick pulled on it twice.

For most CSAO activists, the results felt good. People were really pumped up, says Jack Armstrong, a resource technician in the northwest. "We were winning something for a change. We weren't sitting back and saying okay, that's all they can give us. We had made up our minds that we were going to be paid a fair wage. It was exciting."

Opinion is divided on whether there could have been a strike. It would have been touch and go, many say, especially after the government broke the 20 per cent barrier. But militants were certainly waxing poetic about their new-found power. D. L. Redick, a snowplough operator in Alviston, left this record of his love of Canadian winters as the deadline approached:

> December 31 is the set time
> For us to form our picket line,
> If then Bill Davis doesn't give in,
> The civil service will sock it to him.
> What will happen we do not know,
> We'll just hope for a hell of a snow,
> To fall upon our striking days,
> And then watch Davis raise our pay.

Ross Withers, a worker at Kingston Psychiatric Hospital, had these feelings the night before strike deadline:

> 'Twas the night before New Year's,

    And all through the wards,
    The staff were preparing
    To walk out in hordes.
    Old Santa Davis
    Has not come across,
    And the staff were all saying
    "We'll show you who's boss."

Former researcher Bob Hebdon says the 1974 "gen ops" bargaining made CSAO a union, put it on the map as a union that would stick it to the boss and make it stick. "Changing to OPSEU was just a name change. The real change was the beginning of confrontational bargaining," Hebdon says.

A new constitution

In November, 1974, CSAO had its last convention. Free the Servants defined the union's new campaign style. Hard-driving confrontation defined its new bargaining style. A new name, the Ontario Public Service Employees Union, formalized the shift away from the confines of an association beholden to a civil service identity.

A new constitution enshrined the values of a new generation as well as new union rules of order. Industrial unions tended to be top-down organizations, a reflection of their origins as a strike force of "organizing committees" that picked up members after structures and officers were in place. Standard union terms, such as "rank and file" and "brass," suggest the military style and marching solidarity needed to battle the captains of industry. And most unionists of that generation were raised in a culture that expected strong, even authoritarian, leadership. By contrast, new unionists coming into their own in the late 1960s and early 1970s were raised in a culture that valued participatory democracy and a tolerance of diversity.

For the first time, delegates elected a president from the floor of a convention. Until then, presidents had been chosen in the back rooms by the board of directors. Charlie Darrow won a hands-down victory over Mary Coates, a switchboard operator from Ottawa who was considered to be old guard in her thinking. For the first time, the vice-presidency was defined as a full-time job, with the time to put the membership's stamp on financial management of the union. Sean O'Flynn, a college teacher from Welland, won that post.

Allan Millard wrote the new constitution. He was the son of Charlie Millard, the architect of industrial unionism in Canada during the 1940s, and national director of the Steelworkers. In his own right, Allan Millard rose to the top staff position in the Canadian Union of Public Employees. CSAO hired him in the summer of 1974, shortly after he was fired for squealing on a deal made by CUPE leaders at the 1974 Canadian Labour Congress convention. Millard charged that CUPE brass sold out a planned showdown with U.S.-dominated unions in exchange for a top CLC post for one of its own, Shirley Carr. Millard was sacked for denouncing the deal at a CUPE caucus, he says. Todd and Ward had worked with Millard when they formed the new broadcast division of CUPE in Montreal, respected his constitutional savvy, and arranged to have him hired by CSAO.

It's sometimes said that Millard's feud with CUPE led him to draft OPSEU's constitution as the opposite of CUPE's. In fact, he just drafted a constitution that reflected inherent differences between the two unions. CUPE's central office is sometimes referred to as a "beached whale," a reference to its fierce tradition of local autonomy, natural enough in a union that came out of a merger and that's based on municipal workers from diverse communities. "It's really a confederation masquerading as a union," Millard says. By contrast, the pull in CSAO went toward centralization, appropriate in a union that has most of its dealings with one centralized employer. Millard drafted a constitution that reflected these differences.

Allan Millard also passed some of his birthright on to OPSEU. He was raised at the knees of one of Canada's leading social unionists. Charlie Millard always saw union office as a pulpit for issues of social conscience, an opportunity to lift workers up so they could play a leadership role in their communities and in politics. Allan Millard had the same hopes for OPSEU.

The old CSAO had "a narrow sense of its mandate," he says. "Parochial's too mild a word. Everything was in-house, incestuous almost." Since the right to strike wasn't on the horizon, the new union needed scope to exercise its view of the world, or face slipping back to the old narrow ways. He had this "very much in mind," he says, when he structured the executive board so that it dealt with public policy issues one step removed from direct bargaining, which was handled by members from each occupational group. Millard was also keen to define a role for "divisions" – the very word sounded like unity abandoned, to oldtimers – within OPSEU. Women's and retiree divisions, he thought, could "juice up an issue," and bring activists into contact with social movements in the broader society.

Millard's distrust of wheeler-dealers and his respect for pluralism also showed up in the constitution. Apart from his experience at CUPE, he'd seen the backroom power-plays of slate makers in the Ontario NDP. Once an "official slate" was announced, it was virtually impossible for dissidents to "break" it, no matter what support they enjoyed from the folks back home. To offset this administrative control, Millard made sure that the seven geographic regions in OPSEU elected board members in their own area, before elections for top officers were held. Regardless of population, each region had equal representation on the executive. Millard wanted to make that executive smaller, but his membership advisors insisted on a 28-person board, just as in the old CSAO. "They all wanted to make sure they all got back," he says.

Despite the hurry to break from the CSAO's past, discretion was deemed the better part of valour when it came to legal standing. CSAO was formed as an incorporated organization in 1927. Unionists didn't like the business ring of "incorporation." But relations with the government were so tense that no one wanted to risk a major legal change that might give the government cause to demand a new organizing drive for a brand new union. Thus, OPSEU remained one of the few incorporated unions in the country, and continued to hold annual general meetings, as required under the Corporations Act – although it now called them conventions.

The constitution passed with little debate. It was a blue-sky convention, with all attention fixed on the new union horizon. National labour leaders welcomed OPSEU to the ranks. Norman held the convention in his hand for an hour and a half as he highlighted the changes that unionism would bring. "We are now going through the stage that many unions in the private sector went through 20 to 30 years ago – the stage of recognition," Norman said. "It's a rough stage. But it's a necessary stage if we hope to convince management they are at last dealing with a real union and not with a tame association."

Jake and the Kid

Norman wasn't ready for OPSEU's next necessary stage, when elected leaders decided to run their union.

When O'Flynn was elected vice-president, the buzz on the convention floor was that war was coming. Both O'Flynn and Norman were determined personalities. Putting them close together was "like putting them in a cage," says board member Vic Williams.

Norman and O'Flynn were OPSEU's odd couple. Norman called O'Flynn "the leather man," a jibe at the leather jacket he always wore, and "the bearded one," a putdown of his devilish goatee. When O'Flynn reported for his first day at OPSEU, Norman gave him a desk in the hallway, handed him a policy manual, and told him his job was to keep it up to date. When the board put O'Flynn in charge of staff, Norman's traditional bailiwick, Norman brought O'Flynn to a meeting and said "this asshole's going to be in charge of staff." When O'Flynn came to a meeting of department heads while Darrow was away, Norman ordered him to sit in silence. O'Flynn gritted his teeth and said "I'm here representing the president."

The Four Horsemen reared back into action in support of elected control. Every vote on the board was a cliffhanger, and feelings ran high. Both sides fought like alleycats. Meetings broke into screaming and shoving matches. At one meeting, a board member had a nervous attack and was dragged out choking.

One weekend, Darrow and O'Flynn snuck into union headquarters at 1901 Yonge St., Toronto, and moved their offices from beside Norman on the tenth floor down to the seventh. Negotiator Andy Todd, who got bumped from the seventh up to the tenth, knew Norman's jig was up. "Wherever I was, was where the power wasn't," says Todd.

Charlie Darrow supported O'Flynn, but backed off from a premature confrontation. "Charlie was the chess player," says Norman's assistant Frank Eastham. "He had a game plan, to get a full transformation to a union run by the elected leaders. But he knew Jake was needed for a time. Jake was a business unionist and we needed a business unionist. Jake was a packager, and we needed a packager," says Eastham, now a vice-president at the University of British Columbia.

Norman had devoted supporters too, organized as the Committee of Concerned Members, or CCM. They tended to be civil servants and moderates – some said Tories – who respected Norman's managerial abilities, and felt the need for his firm hand at the throttle. Like many members, they credited Norman with all the union's successes.

The CCM called a special meeting to deal with OPSEU's internal crisis. Their battle cry was "Send O'Flynn back to school." The CCM accused the anti-Norman forces of stealing from the union, and demanded a union trial. O'Flynn took a camera, they said, Darrow took a pair of cufflinks, Jim Tait stole some T-shirts, and Ron Haggett forged a union cheque. The charges were petty, easily explainable, and would normally have been laughed out of court. "I was the only legitimate thief," Haggett says. A board member from Brockville Psychiatric Hospital, he arrived in Toronto after closing hours on the night before a board meeting. He was broke, had a date that night, found the unsigned expense cheque that had been prepared for him, and forged Darrow's signature on it.

The CCM forces drew first blood. As members of the North Bay flying squad patrolled the room with chains and bats, the trial committee brought down charges against all Norman's opponents, save Darrow. "They stayed clear of regicide. They just wanted to kill the Dauphin," says Eastham. "We came out of that meeting with our tail between our legs," says O'Flynn.

The next morning, Darrow called a meeting of supporters at his hotel. One witness says that lightning struck, and the lights went out. Darrow said he'd decided this was the last straw, that it wasn't going to happen again, that Norman was going. "Charlie was one of the most astute country politicians I've ever known," Jim Tait says, and he started doing the math on the support he needed to do Norman in. Norman had pushed too hard, and had been spotted with his hand in the political till, lining up members for the vote, something staff in a civil service union aren't supposed to do. As a prelude to laying formal charges against Norman, affidavits were sworn out by witnesses who claimed to have seen him lobbying delegates. Then Vic Williams did his own count of the board lineup. Why bother, he said, let's just abolish his position.

At the board meeting next day, Williams moved that the position of general manager be abolished. There was a long silence. Maxine Jones, a community college teacher from Windsor, seconded the motion. It passed by a vote of 25 to 3. Norman was paid off and went to work as an industrial relations manager for Rothman's.

Norman says he left quietly because a full-scale battle over the alleged corruption of his enemies "would have left the union a shambles." Others say he knew his jig was up. Many members were starting to resent him, thought he lived too high on the hog, that his office was too plush. One member even accused Norman of plotting to have his own union-paid barber when he ordered a "clipping service." Norman would have lost if he went to the membership, they say.

For O'Flynn, getting rid of Norman was OPSEU's rite of passage. "For the first time, we had a president, Charlie Darrow, with full authority to run the union, and we joined the ranks of healthy unions that are run by their members," he says.

It was also the end of the glory days for many staffers.

Under Norman, most staff pushed themselves beyond the limit, fuelled by the excitement and romance of building from scratch, going where no one had gone before. "It was like discovering sex," says Peter Slee. "You walked three feet off the ground most of the time." In a young organization, "nobody's worried about mistakes, everybody's shooting from the hip, there's no laid-down procedures, you're going out there to do the best you can and there's no need to cover your ass. It's like the underdog football team."

Norman also knew how to run a high-performance team. "He made sure everyone was involved. We felt part of it, and there was a unity you wouldn't believe," says Mike Rowett. Norman always backed staff who took risks and made mistakes. "When you're out on a limb, you don't want to hear a chainsaw," says Slee. As a manager, Norman was schooled in the latest progressive methods. When he worked for the federal ministry of labour on the west coast, he lapped up ministry courses on experiments in Scandinavia, called "direct industrial democracy" there but imported to North America as Quality of Working Life. It taught delegation to autonomous work teams that were given the tools and held responsible for their activities, so they would feel pride and ownership in their work.

That approach to staff came to an end with Norman's departure. Staff came to be seen as a threat to membership control. When Norman's staff-management functions were absorbed by the president, says chief negotiator Andy Todd, an "us-them" relationship grew between staff and elected leaders. Staff were defined as technicians who had to be kept in check, says Pauline Seville, a senior staffer who's served several presidents as assistant. "As a Jew, I find it especially offensive when a Jew is racist," she says. "I have that same sense of expectation and disappointment when a civil service union treats its staff like a civil service." In other unions, says Peter Slee, staffers are looked to for political leadership as well as technical know-how. By the same token, Slee admits they follow the administration line. Whatever the advantages and disadvantages, OPSEU's unique way of defining staff roles comes from the Norman experience.

Norman, now retired, has no regrets. "My time at CSAO-OPSEU was the achievement of a lifetime and probably some of the happiest times in my life," he says. "I was right up to my elbows. My timesheets show I worked 90 hours a week. If you lead in that fashion, it's surprising how many people will follow," he says.

Going the extra mile

To judge by the noise level of the Free The Servants campaign and the gen ops strike threat, a boisterous and militant union burst onto the scene overnight. The campaigns spoke to a new mood, but they were also something of an illusion. They were "marvellous pieces of theatre" with "outside experts to put on a show," says grievance officer George Richards. But, he says, the lack of "deep bench strength" in the new union showed up in more complex situations. Experience with the 1974 round of public service bargaining over working conditions and with nationwide wage controls confirms his judgment.

Collective bargaining was seen as the engine of the union, says chief negotiator Andy Todd, "but I was trying to put a Ferrari engine into an Austin minivan." While Trower got to strut his stuff on a wage breakthrough, Todd got the nuts-and-bolts job of negotiating the first genuinely union working-conditions agreement for the civil service. He worked with leaders of each team to hammer out basic labour relations rules that could make the union part of everyday work life.

Todd's first job was to take workplace rules out of the Public Service Act and put them into a collective agreement. As long as rules were laid out in an act, he figured, workers would suffer an inferiority complex, see themselves as merely an interest group lobbying an all-powerful government. Todd wanted workers to get the feel of treating the government as just another employer. He wanted the government employer to know what it was to deal with the union as an equal, as is the case in the private sector. He started by translating the Public Service Act into the language of a collective agreement, just to make his point that form was as important as content. Government negotiators balked.

Little details gave the full measure of the changes that unionism brought. Unionism meant holding bargaining sessions in a hotel rather than in free government boardrooms, a simple gesture of two equal parties meeting on neutral ground, as well as a neat way of making sure the government side lost immediate access to all its files. At the bargaining table, it meant an end to idle chitchat with employer representatives. Be polite and businesslike, but no fraternizing with the enemy, Todd told his team. The rude boy of OPSEU, he stayed glued to his seat when cabinet members came into the room, another effort to show that unions don't stand for inequality. Usually, Todd was the only team member to sit on union ceremony.

At first, Todd and Norman, who had bargained fringe benefits for the entire civil service, staged a walkout a day, each one scripted in advance. The scripting was a courtesy to union researcher Bob Hebdon, embarrassed when he was left in the lurch with ten minutes' worth of files to pick up after everyone else had walked out.

Todd's 30-person team turned the Brownstone Inn into home sweet home for 18 months. Each bargaining session was preceded by a three-day caucus. Todd taught Bargaining 101. Jim Fuller put meat on the union bones. A meat inspector, he brought the wares of his trade, and team members took turns cooking specialties from their native lands, washed down with homebrew.

The rubber hit the road in a fight over mileage allowances for approximately 5,000 workers who drove their cars as part of their job. If management said cars were a condition of employment, Todd would make the case that management had to pay a hefty mileage rate for their upkeep. If management said cars were an option, then workers otherwise denied the right to strike could bring their operations to a virtual standstill by walking out on the job. If welfare field workers in rural areas refused to use their cars, for instance, their daily visits would be cut by at least half.

Management bargainers stalled. They refused to allow cars that had "Free The Servants" bumper stickers into government parking lots. To that extent, they treated workers' cars as management property. But managers didn't want to pay mileage rates that reflected that responsibility. Todd got NDP leader Stephen Lewis to ask in the legislature if cars were a condition of government employment. Winkler, chair of Management Board, said no. The next day, Todd read Hansard to management negotiators and served notice that the union was pulling cars off the road until the government paid decent rates. The union's bargaining team, worried that workers weren't ready, was as nervous about the threat as management.

To show that workplace protest wasn't a joyride, managers made sure that workers' last calls were far out in the boonies and hours from home. Strikes are nasty, Todd told bargaining team leaders buckling under protests from stranded members. When the union won increased rates, managers were sore losers. They applied the increase retroactively, so that workers who defied the union ban – about two-thirds of the workforce – got a nice bonus, while union loyalists got nothing for their pains.

In the fall of 1975, Trudeau's Liberals introduced wage and price controls to be imposed by the Anti-Inflation Board (AIB). Called "wage and wage controls" by OPSEU, they knocked the wind out of union bargaining, just when public sector unions were starting to make major gains. The limited bargaining rights gained in the early 1970s didn't become a way station on the road to free collective bargaining, labour analysts Leo Panitch and Donald Schwarz wrote of this period. "At the same time that the way station was reached, the roadbed was beginning to crumble."

The controls came in just as OPSEU was in mediation on behalf of three bargaining groups. Major gains for women workers and casuals were in the works. Premier Davis had promised that the government's nominee to the arbitration board wouldn't fight too hard against a major raise for women secretaries. Wage controls allowed no exceptions for workers who were poorly paid, and Davis's promise proved empty.

OPSEU's November convention, held shortly after controls were imposed, denounced controls as a "wage measures act," a reference to Pierre Trudeau's Draconian moves against civil rights in his use of the War Measures Act in 1970. "For OPSEU, it's the greatest challenge in our history," Darrow wrote in *OPSEU News* after the convention. "And we're ready for it."

OPSEU was the first union in the country to endorse the CLC's alternative program of price and profit controls, and kicked in 25 cents per member to finance the CLC campaign. It also campaigned for a membership vote in support of the CLC's call for a "day of protest," a one-day general strike against the controls.

Pete Slee marshalled the campaign for a strike vote. The government pulled out all the stops to defeat the vote, and threatened mass firings if workers broke the law prohibiting strikes. The vote to strike was defeated, 5,580 to 3,480. Militants scored big victories in institutions and in locations far from Toronto. But the margins weren't big enough to counter the massive no-vote in Toronto. "I was almost torn limb from limb at the OHIP office in Toronto," Slee says. "It broke my heart. I was up to my bald spot in it." Workers at head office don't like to stick their heads out, says Slee, because the presence and power of bosses is everywhere and the countervailing force of solidarity is weakest in the rat-race atmosphere of head office.

Slee sees the AIB strike vote as a downturn for defiant unionism. Pauline Seville, fresh from a disappointing CLC campaign to organize white collar workers, was "astonished" that 40 per cent of the workers, without the right to strike at any time and with no strike experience, were prepared to cast their fate with union solidarity at a time when OPSEU wasn't even in the CLC. "It just proves that unionism doesn't happen with one event. It has to grow," she says.

Ontario under wage controls wasn't a place to stand or a place to grow for a new public sector union. Controls encouraged the drift to team-based bargaining that made the case for increases on catch-ups with workers getting better pay elsewhere. That's the argument that goes down best with arbitrators, says respected arbitrator Ken Swan, so the natural course of arbitration is to make parity – not other measures of equity – a principle.

The Ontario government "glued itself to the federal controls" for the three years they were in place, says Andy Todd. Unlike many private-sector employers who continued bargaining as usual and let the feds slap down their agreements, provincial government bargainers refused to offer more than the federal guidelines allowed. OPSEU responded by taking all its teams to arbitration, hoping to find an arbitrator who would pry open the few loopholes for exceptions that AIB allowed. The effort only worked once, in 1978, when an arbitrator allowed an above-average increase for workers in isolated areas.

Bang bang Maxwell's silver hammer

The federal government's 1975 AIB program was a speed bump on the union's way to aggressive wage bargaining. The provincial government's McKeough-Henderson report, which put massive cutbacks on the agenda one month later, was a brick wall.

The report ushered in a decade of cutbacks, blessed a neo-conservative approach to government services, and entrenched cost-accounting methods that put civil servants on the debit side of government ledgers. "The last vestige of government paternalism died with that report," says former bargaining researcher Bob Hebdon. Members learned that their security rested with their union, not their employer. Activists learned that their union would have to be built as a community force defending high-quality government services, not a "business union" that centred its demands around wages alone. The ground shifted before OPSEU ever got a feeling for traditional unionism. It became a "social union" at the core of its being.

The McKeough-Henderson report was one of the first shots in the battle of the bulge against growing government expenditures in the mid-1970s. In Britain, Margaret Thatcher became the "iron lady" of the new Conservatism, but even the governing Labour Party imposed major cuts in 1976 at the behest of the International Monetary Fund. In New York, the new financial orthodoxy was masterminded by the Rockefeller-funded Trilateral Commission, which pulled together tycoons from Europe, Japan and North America in 1973. The Commission, which included Darcy McKeough and the Ontario government's favourite consulting firm, Coopers & Lybrand, on its board, issued manifestos on the "excesses of democracy" and the need to roll back social legislation. In Canada, federal financial agencies slowed down the money supply from the Bank of Canada in 1975 and officially repudiated Keynesianism in 1976. The Business Council on National Issues spoke for 150 Canadian chief executives fed up with welfare state excesses. The AIB, best known for capping wage increases, was part of this counter-offensive. Little public attention was drawn to the AIB's menu of government cutbacks, notwithstanding Trudeau's notorious speeches on the need to lower public expectations.

Premier Davis caught wind of the new mood in May, 1975. While on a pre-election swing through Niagara Falls, he announced the formation of a committee to review government expenditures. In the election campaign that August, Liberals and New Democrats attacked his free-spending ways. Robert Nixon for the Liberals, leading the polls until well into the election, hammered Davis's "gutless approach to inflation," and called for $300 million worth of cuts. Stephen Lewis brought the NDP onside with restraint, claiming "even I say they have gone too far." Davis squeaked through with a minority government, the first setback for the Tories since 1948. Party hardliners blamed the poor showing on his lack of ardour for free enterprise.

The Davis appointments to the committee reviewing government spending put Ontario's social, cultural and health programs at the mercy of some of Ontario's worst reactionaries. Second in importance only to the Committee on Government Productivity, this new committee defined the government's agenda for a decade.

Chairman Maxwell Henderson personified the central place granted to accounting, not accountability. When he was federal auditor general, his annual reports made him a folk hero in the war against government waste. Terms as secretary-treasurer of Bronfman-controlled Seagram's and chair of the Canadian Chamber of Commerce gave him access to the entire business establishment. Since issuing the Committee's report, he's worked for such far-right think tanks as the Toronto-based Mackenzie Institute, for landlord lobbies against rent controls, and for the National Citizens' Coalition.

Lieutenant-General William Anderson had served as Canada's director of military intelligence during the 1950s cold war. After retiring from the military, he became a ranking officer in charge of Ontario's civil service in 1969. Davis recalled him from retirement in 1982 to command Ontario's public sector wage controls program.

James Fleck, former director of the Committee on Government Productivity and secretary to the cabinet, had been in a huff about runaway public sector wages for some time. At the time of his appointment, he told a Toronto conference on government labour relations that government workers have no discipline to bring their demands in line with reality. Fleck popped up again in 1978, as the owner of Fleck Manufacturing near London, Ontario, scene of the province's most celebrated all-women strike and the most expensive police strikebreaking operation in the province's history. After the company was unionized, Fleck pulled up stakes and started again in Mexico.

Robert Hurlburt, president of General Foods and a senior member of the Business Council on National Issues, brought the perspective of a leading multinational. Eric Winkler, the Exeter seed retailer who chaired Management Board, represented the management arm of cabinet. Betty Kennedy, star of CBC's Front Page Challenge, brought her extensive experience as lone female member of corporate boards of directors.

The mystery guest was Darcy McKeough, second in command. As treasurer, he was a high-flyer, not a penny-pincher. His major cabinet experience was with Municipal Affairs and Energy, where he'd been a big spender. Asking McKeough to practice restraint, Stephen Lewis said, was like asking Evel Knievel (a daredevil stuntman of the day) to park your car. Nor was McKeough a champion of "small is beautiful," except where unions were concerned. "The size of the postal workers' union is more of a problem than the size of Massey-Ferguson or Argus Corporation," he told a royal commission into corporate concentration later that decade.

What McKeough knew of social policy, he knew as a squire. The son of a Chatham businessman who sold plumbing supplies, customized luxury cars and held major shares in Union Gas, he was raised in private schools and on his family's hobby farm. After retiring from politics, McKeough worked his way up to the top of Union Gas.

McKeough was the committee's macroeconomic theorist as well as its co-chair. His April 1975 budget, brought down shortly before his appointment to the committee, marked his conversion to monetarism. Blaming inflation on excess government spending, he slashed corporate and sales taxes by $607 million to put spending power in the hands of "consumers, where it belonged."

McKeough's bias toward using public money to subsidize free enterprise became legendary in 1978, when he got Ontario Hydro to pay

Denison Mines in Elliot Lake $7.4 billion for a long-term uranium contract. McKeough rejected a bid by Ontario Hydro planners to buy Denison out and keep the money in public coffers, and Denison walked away with $2.2 billion in profits and a $30 million subsidy to explore for competitive uranium in Saskatchewan. The deal came to an end in 1991, having been widely regarded as the greatest boondoggle in Ontario history. The committee did not review that decision in its search for examples of government waste.

Ontario Hydro's nuclear binge racked up seven billion dollars in debt in the late 1970s. Government cuts in wages and services were needed to supply the funds for this type of capital spending, McKeough told the Conference Board of Canada. A critical history of Ontario Hydro by Paul McKay, later a senior energy advisor to the NDP government, refers to McKeough's nuclear shopping spree as a "distortion" of government priorities that "literally robbed" money from health, education and social budgets to subsidize cheap industrial electricity. The mid-1970s was turn-around time for governments across Canada, says economist Isabella Bakker, as they shifted money from social services and transfer payments toward industrial incentives. The Henderson report heralded that change in Ontario.

The committee's report was tabled in the legislature on November 20, 1975. Called The Report of the Special Program Review, the graphic on the front cover said a thousand words. It was a dollar sign.

The committee made 180 recommendations to slash costs by $1.52 billion in year one and $2.14 billion in year two. The cuts weren't all savings from staff, salaries and programs. Costs for about 40 per cent of abandoned programs were passed on to municipalities, private charities and user fees from individual citizens. Five years before "privatization" made it into Webster's dictionary, the Henderson report said there was no need to expand government programs when "there appears to be scope for transferring back to the private sector some of the activities that are currently carried out by the government."

The report rang the alarm on government overspending. "The most urgent problem facing all governments today is not merely to exercise extraordinary vigilance in containing current spending," it claimed, "but to face up to the difficult job of cutting it back." The general public as well as politicians had to wake up to the costs of their unrealistic expectations of government. The fundamental problem with health costs, the report claimed, was that "the public has come to view the provision and maintenance of health services as a government responsibility."

Introducing the report to the legislature, McKeough welcomed "the new discipline that is sweeping through the public sector." The report, he said, "corresponds to my own view that outlays from the public purse are seen too often, by too many, as a costless remedy to every conceivable economic and social problem of the day." Henceforth, he said, the government's prime responsibility was to promote private sector growth, more private consumption and higher personal incomes. "This can only be achieved through private sector economic expansion; it does not come about by expanding the size of the civil service nor by multiplying social services faster than we are willing to be taxed to pay for them."

McKeough promised to honour the Henderson report by freezing Ontario government programs, cutting back municipal grants, charging user fees for some health services, and rejecting all shared-cost programs with Ottawa.

Despite McKeough's threat to rally taxpayers against politicians who opposed his cuts, there was little on which to base a mass-based tax revolt in 1975. The rate of government staff expansion had already been cut in half after 1970, thanks to the COGP. Across Canada, the 1975 tax load (the portion of gross economic product paid out in taxes) was four points above that in the tax-hating United States but nine points below Austria and 18 points behind Sweden, where no tax revolts were brewing. Canada's marginal tax rate (the proportion of taxes taken out of wages) was six points below the U.S., 20 points below Austria, and 28 points below Sweden. Tax revolts, most commentators agree, aren't protests against high taxes but rather against poor government services and programs targeted to the poor. This may be why conservative tax rebels harp on the need to save on taxes by restricting government programs to the weak and defenceless. When the middle class has no stake in preserving programs, they are easier to eliminate.

There was no evidence of a taxpayer backlash at the time the report gained the government's approval. According to polls published by the Ontario Economic Council in 1977, only 2.9 per cent of the population had any sense of the size of Ontario's budget, and few high-income earners thought they paid too much in provincial taxes. Five people out of six wanted more spending on housing, health, education, social programs and the environment. However, as many as 48 per cent, according to the Council's polls, thought the government spent too much on administration. "It may be that people dislike government in the abstract but are less critical when it comes to precise programs and areas of spending," the study concluded. It may also explain why conservatives make civil servants the butt of their attacks, not the social programs they deliver.

One out of three ain't bad

The Davis government lost no time getting to the slash-and-burn items on the McKeough-Henderson agenda. In December, 1975, McKeough froze salaries of senior staff and cut 1,000 workers from the government payroll. Highway jobs sanding and ploughing roads were farmed out to contractors. Health minister Frank Miller announced the closure of psychiatric hospitals in Timmins and Goderich, sold four health labs to the private sector, and closed over 2,000 hospital beds across the province. A scorched-earth strategy was underway.

In marked contrast to its slow uptake on CECBA only three years earlier, OPSEU was onto the challenge overnight. The day after the report came out, an emergency staff meeting was held in the union cafeteria. Then and there, the union launched a community-based campaign against the cuts. Claiming that 9,000 jobs were at stake, Darrow lashed out at the report as "the most reactionary document prepared in Ontario in the 1970s." It would lead to a society where the unfortunate would be abandoned, and where, he told the media, "large numbers of the mentally ill will be allowed to walk the streets and remain a danger to both society and themselves."

Darrow flirted briefly with strike action. If the government saw so little value in civil servants as to accept the report, he told *OPSEU News* in December, the union would "take the entire civil service out for a month or two to see how well the province could get along without us." This was an empty threat. It would simply save the government the trouble of laying workers off. And the members were far from ready for militant action.

The union didn't have much choice about building community-based coalitions, says Pete Slee, who headed the campaign. Many workers still believed they had their jobs for life, didn't appreciate the union being the bearer of bad news, and refused to believe their world was coming to an end. "It's just like the body shutting out pain in a trauma," Slee says. Local merchants reacted faster; they understood that shutdowns of institutions would destroy the local economy. "That's what saved our bacon," Slee says. The families of institutional residents also came forward.

OPSEU spearheaded a campaign that gave the government a fight for its money, probably the first persistent community-based coalition the government had faced, says Slee. On December 15, a month after the report was released, OPSEU joined a number of groups to lobby McKeough: the Ontario Anti-Poverty Coalition, the Ontario Welfare Council, the Social Planning Council, the Ontario Federation of Labour, social workers and churches.

Deep in the heart of small-town Tory Ontario, cutbacks were seen as heartless attacks on the economic and social well-being of the entire community. OPSEU's campaign gathered force quickly, and had little trouble attracting stellar citizens to its side.

In Timmins, the OPSEU local joined the labour council, which persuaded the city to form a committee to keep the psychiatric hospital open. The next month in Goderich, 700 citizens turned out to cheer mayor Deb Shewfelt, who threatened an injunction to bloc the closure. In Hamilton, the OPSEU local held a public meeting of 700 people and launched a petition drive that got 83,000 signatures in favour of keeping Chedoke hospital open. Names on the petition were read into the legislative record, two pages at a time, by Hamilton NDP MPP Ian Deans. Brian Charlton, the revenue worker who got in hot water in 1975 for running as an NDP candidate, owed his election in 1977 largely to his role in this protest. In Thunder Bay, a coalition of unions, seniors and tenants got city council to vote against any cutbacks. In Durham and Owen Sound, health minister Frank Miller was pelted with snowballs by demonstrators out to save their local hospitals. By the spring of 1976, the union was distributing 200,000 leaflets and 75,000 petition-postcards across the province.

The entire labour movement adopted the campaign. In April, the OFL hosted a press conference of all public sector unions against the cuts. A week later, the annual presentation of the OFL's brief to the cabinet attracted the largest labour demonstration ever at Queen's Park, the *Globe* reported. The OFL brief called the Henderson report "frightening" and "redneck." OPSEU's North Bay SWAT team set up agitprop theatre featuring a badly-beaten psychiatric worker and a band led by moosehorn player Jerry Liberty.

In Toronto, the union faced an uphill battle to save the Lakeshore Psychiatric Hospital. Workers saw the shutdown as inevitable, and local merchants weren't as dependent on one employer as those in small towns. A coalition with community health groups was broken up when the government offered money to agencies with community boards. "They got off our bandwagon and stuck their hands out," Slee says. The union resorted to scare tactics, he says, and leafletted Parkdale residents – accurately, as it turned out – warning that their neighbourhood would be overrun by discharged patients with no place to go once Lakeshore shut down. The campaign won job security measures for all but 20 of 220 Lakeshore workers, who transferred to other institutions within commuting distance.

The OPSEU campaign was strong enough to slow the pace of shutdowns and layoffs, and force the government into a series of running battles that lasted ten years. The campaign also forced the Davis government to cut the rhetoric of the Henderson report. Lean and mean economics didn't play in Ontario, where government services were seen as crucial to society's immune system, where non-profit services were a point of pride to society's humanity, where government jobs propped up local economies. Increasingly, cutbacks were presented as pragmatic "convenience" and a form of compassion, not conservative ideology. This was especially so in the dismantling of psychiatric hospitals and institutions for the mentally retarded, carried out in the name of social integration of the disadvantaged. Compared to the Socreds in B.C., with their arch-conservative reputation, Ontario was both "less confrontational and more relentless," warned social policy analyst Alan Moscovitch. "We should not be less vigilant of changes because they have been presented with less ballyhoo," he wrote. There was no holding back the overall blueprint for a downsized government. The 1977 election returned another minority Conservative government, but put the Liberals, not the New Democrats, in second place. The Liberals drove the government hard to honour its original commitments. They gave the government the votes it needed to carry out its program.

Few government reports have rivalled the impact of Henderson's. "The thrust of our policies in the last two budgets has been to reduce the growth in government spending and trim our bureaucracy in order to make room for private sector initiative and improved take-home pay," McKeough told the legislature late in 1976. "This is known as private affluence and public squalor," New Democrat Michael Cassidy heckled. To study pensions and inflation, the government retained Touche Ross, who helped found the Privatization Council, a driving force in the worldwide trend to privatization. They would be joined by Adam Zimmerman of Noranda and James Fleck. As with the COGP reports, consulting firms remained key players in the government's invisible civil service.

The government hewed to its cutback line. In his 1980 budget, treasurer Frank Miller bragged that he'd ground down government spending from 17.2 to 15.5 per cent of gross provincial product over five years. "That 1.7 percentage point reduction translates to $1.9 billion in the hands of the private sector," Miller said. "These are resources that might otherwise have been in the grip of government had we not the gumption to implement the restraint program and stick with it."

Direct government jobs were cut from 87,000 in 1975 to 80,000 in 1980. The provincial share of school financing dropped from 61 per cent in 1975 to 51 per cent in 1979. In 1974, social assistance brought a family to only 70.9 per cent of the poverty line. By 1978, that edged down to 66.8 per cent. Ontario social security spending went up 17.3 per cent from 1974 to 1983, compared to the national average of 54.1 per cent.

The restraint program also burrowed into the core value systems of government departments. "Restraint has become reality; it creates a pressure that permeates all decisions and has placed a new premium on value for money," a 1985 review of government managers claimed. "Doing more with less has become an entrenched feature of the system." The review noted a lack of imagination in designing government programs for long-term savings. A 1986 review of human resources came to a similar conclusion. Without naming the Henderson report directly, it blamed the lack of leadership among senior staff on its obsessions: "Since 1975 the focus in the Ontario Public Service has been on downsizing through short term tactical actions."

If personal taxes didn't go down to match declines in service, that's because of the tax revolution launched under cover of the mayhem created by the Henderson report. In 1975, according to figures released by the Fair Tax Commission in 1992, corporate taxes made up 22 per cent of government revenues and personal taxes 30 per cent. Ten years later, corporate taxes had sunk to 15 per cent of the government take, while personal taxes took up the slack with 42 per cent of the load.

Beep Beep

OPSEU is part campaign organization, part union. Campaigns are not add-ons to the main business of a union, handled by an extra department to give expression to the larger vision of union leaders, as is commonly the case with industrial unions. Campaigns are essential to the job security and working conditions of government employees. But campaigns rise and crash with the political tides, bounce from one crisis to another. That's why they came to be organized on a quasi-military basis, co-ordinated by a "special operations" department and marshalled through membership "divisions." The ongoing organizing and bargaining functions that give a union life on the shop and office floor, among members facing routine problems with mean bosses, are often left fighting for space, profile and resources.

Apart from this built-in tension inside the union, government workplaces are not easy for unions to sink roots in. Authority is often bureaucratic rather than personal, petty rather than tyrannical.

In some areas of the province, scrappy groups were ready to take on the bosses. The mid-seventies were the roughneck days, says Wayne Campbell of North Bay. "You flew by the seat of your pants. You ran with guts, and you filed grievances whether you thought you could win them or not. You just went in and you bullshitted the employer. Back then, the government couldn't get its act together, and you could beat them." With this style, workers felt they owned the union. "We knew that if the union concept was going to work, we had to make it work." By contrast, he says, campaigns of the 1980s were run by specialists who knew PR and lobbying.

More often, the bare essentials of union protocol had to be nursed along. Campaigns staffer Jim Onyschuk recalls opening one meeting with the traditional union welcome to "brothers and sisters." Someone immediately jumped up and said "I'm not your brother and this woman beside me is not your sister." Onyschuk started again. "Ladies and gentlemen, brothers and sisters," he said. "That broke the ice. People were very fearful of the direction they were going in, and there was a real struggling with philosophy," he recalls.

Old-style services and activities that were part of CSAO's "friendly society" origins did not disappear. Throughout 1975, *OPSEU News* advertised discounts on charter flights and clothing purchases from selected retailers. In 1976 and 1977, the union scored a public relations coup by donating $20,000 to help peewee hockey leagues, winning praise from Christie Blatchford at the *Globe* for giving something back to the community. "We want the community to be aware that we're not money-grabbing people," executive board member Ev Sammons told the Toronto *Sun*.

At Queen's Park, staff reps Ivor Oram and Lillian Stevens set up camp in the high-rise office towers. Their job was to build a union, not just service it. To gain a presence and bring a core of activists around them, "we had brownbag lunches, we had Kentucky Fried Chicken lunches, we had pizza lunches," says Oram. "We were throwing Kentucky Fried Chicken at them for the better part of three years." This union version of Salvation Army methods was the appetizer for speakers and movies on basic union themes. "We were the visible proof that the union was there," says Oram. "Everything we did established union recognition, and the battles were every day, every moment, and on every issue." Staff handled the first stages of workers' grievances with supervisors, usually left to workplace stewards. But OPSEU had to turn its big guns on junior managers, most of whom couldn't see the union as an equal in upholding jointly-negotiated workplace rules.

To prepare for the day when workers could take charge of their own union, staff reps flogged educationals for the BEEP program. BEEP was a brainchild of Jake Norman, who liked the sound of acronyms – BEEP stood for Branch Executive Education Program – especially ones that could be put on a T-shirt with a cartoon of a roadrunner. Launched in November, 1974, BEEP was designed to "develop grassroots leaders capable of meeting anything" in the course of building their union local.

❖

Organizing: hospitals and ambulance services

Organizing boomed, a mark of the union's success in how others saw it. Darrow hired two crack organizers, Pauline Seville and Ivor Oram, from the failing CLC drive among private sector office workers. In traditional government style, OPSEU set up a special organizing department instead of including organizing as a standard duty of all staff reps, as is common in many industrial unions. Thanks to its large, stable and concentrated base of civil servants, OPSEU could afford to hire organizing specialists and recruit in small workplaces that most unions ignored because they were so expensive to service.

The health-care system offered lots of opportunities to a new union specializing in the public service. OPSEU appealed to hospital workers, Oram says, because it was new, had a high profile in the media as a union that carried out campaigns for its members, and was seen as a non-striking organization suitable for the professionally-minded.

There was a hospital revolution in the late 1960s, as the province pumped in money for new equipment and specialties and as hospitals changed from custodial institutions to medical workshops. A host of expanded and new "para-professions" sprang up that didn't fit in traditional hospital hierarchies. Lab and radiation technologists lost out in the new medical order. "In place of the equality and personal control of the old laboratories, a hierarchy of responsibility with numerous gradations has emerged," Oswald Hall wrote in 1969 in a background study for a royal commission on the healing arts. The labs were run like assembly lines, the blood banks were cramped, there was no room for career advancement, high turnover was epidemic, and low morale was universal, Hall found. Low wages and low prestige made workers' blood boil, especially when they compared themselves to doctors. "There is no other kind of work in our society where the gap between those who provide the service and those who help is correspondingly wide," Hall wrote. However, the professional pecking order of hospitals rubbed off on all workers. According to Hall's interviews, technologists and paramedics wanted collective bargaining, but they didn't want a union.

In this, Hall was partly correct. Some technologists did want representation, and, after looking around, they approached the CSAO. The association was certified as bargaining agent for technologists at Peterborough Civic Hospital in October of 1969. Other contacts soon followed, as the association wooed the Ontario Society of Medical Technologists.

Technologists also looked at three unions: CUPE, the Service Employees International Union and the Office and Professional Employees International Union. Competition was intense, but CSAO appeared the most attractive. Bob Hebdon, who participated in some of the meetings, says SEIU and OPEIU were rejected because they were international unions, while the CUPE representative talked of strikes – not the message aspiring professionals wanted to hear. "I told them about the arbitration briefs I wrote," Hebdon says. "They loved it."

Hebdon says there were doubters on the CSAO board. They were convinced, he says, when he showed how the government had used data about the wages of hospital technologists to convince an arbitrator not to award a large wage increase to technologists employed by the provincial government. "It was in CSAO's self-interest, in the interest of our existing members, to organize hospital technologists."

CSAO was on its way to expansion, when the Ontario Labour Relations Board threw a spanner into the works, ruling that the union could not represent technologists at the Oshawa General Hospital because it was a privately chartered institution, and the association's letters patent restricted it to employees in the public sector. To get around this hurdle, Bowen went to Ottawa and incorporated CSAO National, a convenient legal fiction whose letters patent were much broader. After two years of battling at the labour board and in the courts, CSAO National won the right to represent medical technologists. Technologists in nine hospitals were certified. Having served its purpose, the 900 members were transferred to CSAO at the 1973 annual meeting, and CSAO National was quietly wound up.

In his first year at organizing, Ivor Oram says, "I just walked cold into a hospital. If I saw a person in a lab coat or with a test tube, I approached them." Before long, hospital paramedics organized themselves and sought out unions that could best represent them. OPSEU cleaned up. At many meetings, reps from CUPE and the Service Employees International Union spent their time attacking each other, leaving an open field for Oram to talk up OPSEU's topnotch research and campaigns staff. "We've got a computer," he'd often say to clinch his argument. "Even though our computer couldn't get addresses right, we always bragged about our computer," says Frank Eastham, who sometimes accompanied Oram.

Oram built on the success with technologists from the early 1970s. The union took out newspaper ads offering help to technologists and radiologists whose jobs were threatened. At two meetings in Toronto, about 700 prospective members from 26 hospitals showed up, and the organizing drive gained steam. Once again, the labour board intervened, ruling in a series of decisions that technologists and radiologists had to be organized into bargaining units of paramedical staff, including physiotherapists, occupational therapists, social workers and dozens of other occupations. The union took this in stride, adjusted its organizing, and signed up bigger and bigger units.

"We appealed to their semi-professional status," Oram says. He became a regular visitor to the conventions of the Ontario Society of Medical Technologists, the Ontario Psychological Association and other professional groups, turning contacts made there into more organizing.

The union pressed for centralized bargaining for all parameds. Similar ideas were being advanced by the nurses and other unions in the hospitals, and the combined pressure paid off late in the 1970s. In three years, OPSEU organized 36 paramed units on top of the nine it had from the early 1970s.

Oram met similar successes among ambulance officers. "If we had no other way into a hospital, we'd go in through the back door, literally, and find the ambulance drivers. They were usually in the dungeons of the hospitals, but they knew everybody: the physios, the lab techs, the radiologists." At the same time, the union began to organize drivers working for private businesses. These private ambulance services were often makeshift operations, run by hustling entrepreneurs looking for a sideline. One operated out of a funeral home, guaranteeing a profit no matter what happened to the patient. His employees had no uniforms, they wore the dark suits of funeral home workers. When a call came in, they jumped into the hearse or the ambulance, whichever was needed.

Though divided geographically, the workers were a homogeneous group. They faced the same problems of low pay, shift work, heavy lifting from unusual positions, and a lack of respect from their employers. In Burlington, Gord Armes had to paint the ambulance garage floor every four months, and wax it regularly in between paint jobs. In Fenelon Falls, ambulance officer Mark Lowell drywalled the house of the owner of the local ambulance service. In Port Colborne, the ambulance service was a sideline to the owner's BP gas station. Larry Butters pumped gas, changed tires, repaired cars, snowmobiles and motorcycles and wiped the grease off his hands when an emergency call came in.

Organizing private ambulance workers was "a very nasty business," Oram says. To exact retribution, one private owner had union activists shovel huge snowbanks back and forth across a driveway, and wash and wax the ambulances repeatedly. But the workers held firm. For them, unionization was a godsend. "If you wanted to keep your job, you had to do what the boss wanted," says Armes. "We used the union as a support to say we're not going to do things that aren't job-related." And it worked. Armes again: "We stood up to our boss then. He's gone and we're not, because we had the support of the union."

The ambulance organizing drive grew like topsy, and the union began to push the idea of one union representing all ambulance drivers in the province. It was a logical outgrowth of the hospitals. The prominence of new Ontario-wide occupational groupings also put extra pressure on OPSEU to decentralize and set up regional offices across the province. That became a very visible sign of a union that was getting closer to its members, Oram says.

OPSEU's community-based campaign style intersected with daily issues as a result of increased understanding about workplace health and safety in the late 1970s.

The double-barrelled term "health and safety" entered public consciousness as a related set of issues in the mid-1970s, following desperate protests from cancer-stricken uranium miners in Elliot Lake and asbestos handlers in Scarborough. Until then, safety was seen as an issue for industrial engineers, and health was something to see the doctor about. When Bob DeMatteo joined OPSEU's staff in 1976 and heard someone ask about civil service health and safety, he thought of paper cuts. OPSEU conducted an investigation into health and safety problems at Ontario institutions that year, but the study focussed on the increased likelihood of inmate violence in overcrowded and understaffed units. Stressors and toxins weren't understood, let alone seen as union issues.

In 1978, controversy around Bill 70 – Conservative legislation that granted workers the right to know what they were working with, the right to serve on workplace committees setting basic safety rules, and the right to refuse unsafe work – opened OPSEU's eyes to a broader range of issues. DeMatteo was put in charge of making sure government workers got the same rights as others. A seemingly innocent proposal, it cast OPSEU as the spoiler of a deal cooked up between the OFL and the Ministry of Labour to exclude government employees. Heavyweights in the labour movement pressured OPSEU to back off, lest the whole bill be withdrawn, DeMatteo says. "We had to do our own work, or the government and the OFL would have walked all over us," he says.

Once aroused, OPSEU mounted a full-scale campaign that became as much a learning experience for the union as for the politicians. DeMatteo sent out questionnaires to field members' health and safety complaints, researched a booklet on public service health and safety problems, and organized a letter-writing campaign to MPPs. At hearings of the legislative committee reviewing the bill, OPSEU members told horror stories of beatings by inmates in jails and institutions.

DeMatteo had taught in Saskatchewan with Robert Sass, who made Saskatchewan the leading jurisdiction in North America for health and safety, and was tuned into health and safety as a new type of union issue that empowered workers directly. Workers on the job were to have the power and information to set things right, not union officials from central office and not distant experts who wouldn't suffer the consequences of their mistakes. In 1977, he set up the union's first training courses graduating scores of evangelicals with healthy suspicions about their bosses' motives. Course material was co-authored by medical student Jamie Meuser, but both took pains to stress that this was a union issue, not a medical one. "Our message was that we have to treat the workplace, not the human being," DeMatteo says. That required local union activists who were self-reliant, and who pushed their union into new frontiers of life-and-death responsibility for working conditions.

Good-time Charlie

Charlie Darrow was easy to like and easy to underrate, says Pauline Seville, who headed the organizing department during his presidency. He wasn't much with words, and passed himself off as one more nice guy who just wanted to get along. "But he was a very wise leader," she says, who knew his shortcomings, and knew who could help make up for them.

Holding together a union that was galloping off in several directions at once was no easy chore, and his heavy drinking started to get the better of him by the time of his second term in 1976. Darrow picked Mary Coates as his vice-presidential running mate for the 1978 union elections, a move that cut him off from former allies. Coates, a switchboard operator from Ottawa, combined a tough-talking style with a fairly conservative brand of labour politics. She crossed Sean O'Flynn in his battles with Jake Norman, and had few allies among progressive women. She ran a tight ship when she was vice-president in charge of finance, and made herself a lot of enemies by rejecting expense claims from local activists. Word was sent to Darrow that he'd be challenged if he didn't drop

Coates. Darrow stuck by his decision.

Four candidates opposed Darrow at the 1978 convention. The race was wide open. Ron Haggett from Brockville Psychiatric split Darrow's base among institutional workers. Sean O'Flynn and Ted Theobald split their home-base college vote. Martin Sarra had some support among Toronto clerks. The four candidates agreed to throw their votes to whoever was front-runner on the first ballot. O'Flynn went head to head against Darrow, and beat him by six votes. O'Flynn, straitlaced to a fault, had no hospitality suite. Darrow did, and it's said that the seven people he needed to win were holding up his bar when the final vote was held. Coates was defeated by correctional worker Vic Cooper, who was expected to throw his votes to her to block Vic Williams, a Horseman detested by Coates. "What's the matter? Your foot nailed to the floor?" she yelled, when Cooper refused to walk to her side. He stayed in the race, and won.

Though each presidential candidate had his own style, no differences over issues polarized the delegates. O'Flynn, Haggett and Darrow were close friends and long-time allies in the struggle to democratize CSAO and OPSEU. Nevertheless, old hands say the election was one of OPSEU's dirtiest.

According to Darrow's widow, his second wife Barb Darrow, he wasn't unhappy to lose the election. "To hell with it. I'll take the summer off," he told her. He went back to work at Woodstock as a counsellor for the mentally disabled. Six months later, O'Flynn hired him on as a staff rep.

Darrow's defeat left a bitter aftertaste among many oldtimers, who resented some of the low blows against him and who missed the rough-and-ready style that flourished in his era. A lot of people tut-tutted Darrow for his drinking, a common occupational hazard in the hard-driving, out-of-a-suitcase life of a union leader, says Rusty Fawcett, a fellow veteran and comrade on the board in the early 1970s. "But no one helped him dry out. Nobody ever thought of that. They all either wanted to support him because they drank with him, or get rid of him. You don't kick a man when he's down."

Charlie Darrow died of cancer in 1982.

CHAPTER FIVE

Desperately Seeking Union

Sean O'Flynn's race for the presidency was photo-finish all the way. "It was the most makeshift campaign I was ever involved in," he says. "At the last moment, I even had to borrow someone's sports coat for a campaign photo, when someone yelled at me for wearing a leather jacket." But there was never any doubt, even when he donned the traditional OPSEU dark blue suit for meetings with ministers and premiers, that O'Flynn's trademark instincts were hell-bent for leather.

O'Flynn was hard to get to know. Painfully shy and private, he was known to staffers and activists for his restless and impatient energy. He had "those great bushy eyebrows that would sort of hood over and see the dark side of life," says his close friend and occasional OPSEU lawyer, Don Brown.

O'Flynn desperately wanted OPSEU to become a real union, his former assistant Pauline Seville says, "but after working with him closely for a year, I came to no additional insight." O'Flynn wasn't a people person, and didn't like small talk, says Ev Sammons, vice-president under O'Flynn. "He was on the rip all the time. His happiest time was when he was running to a picket line, his hair and scarf flying." He got up at five o'clock every morning, read the papers, listened to the early bird TV and radio news shows, and made his decisions for the day, notwithstanding what he had decided the night before, says another assistant, Peter Warrian. His "enduring charm and dangerous quality," for Warrian, was "to move from personal ethics to direct action, with nothing complicated by way of analysis, strategy or organization in between."

The idea that unionism was a calling came naturally to the Dublin-born O'Flynn, who grew up thinking he would be a missionary to Africa. He quit the seminary after two years. "I was too single-minded for that. Not that I could figure out what to be single-minded about," he says. At 20, he went down into the English coal mines, where workmates nicknamed him "the pope," a reference to the fact that he never cussed. "I just figured that if I couldn't stick it out in the mines, I couldn't stick it out anywhere. It was useful in developing the habit of determination." Five years was enough to prove that, and he came up from the depths when he won a miner's scholarship to Oxford's Catholic Workers College. He came to North America to study industrial relations in Buffalo, then in 1969 landed a job teaching in Canada's first labour studies program at Welland's Niagara College. Shortly after college faculty joined CSAO, he won a seat on CSAO's board.

His six years as OPSEU president (1978 to 1984) are in striking contrast with the years before. Strikes in the jails, the colleges, and at daycare centres punctuated his efforts to turn OPSEU into a fighting industrial-style union and bring it into the mainstream of organized labour.

O'Flynn's values and background gave him a vision of what OPSEU could become, but an equally frustrating sense of what it was not. As a labour educator, he says, he wanted workers "to run their union and to grow in the running of their union." In this version of a pilgrim's progress, individuals would learn to rely on their own skills and the strength of their fellow workers to stand up to the boss. To build a union with that kind of base and spirit, he tried to "get responsibility down there, get them to fight their own grievances, stand up to management, stand up for their rights." He got that model from the UAW. "That was a hard gospel to sell in a civil service union," he says, because the union was seen as a servicing organization, not a tool of empowerment.

Getting away from a service model of unionism was no easy matter when the great majority of OPSEU members didn't have the legal right to strike. Bargaining galvanized members for nothing more bracing than a trip to the arbitrator, not a direct confrontation with the employer.

"My threat," says chief negotiator Andy Todd, "was that instead of hitting you with the one kilo brief, I'm going to hit you with the five kilo brief."

The lack of direct union presence was felt right through the system. Local union leaders didn't get time off for union business, a standard feature of industrial union contracts. There were few formal union grievances at the workplace, only 53 in 1977. O'Flynn brought that up to 324 in 1979, and 1,408 in 1981, as word went out that he'd throw the full resources of the union behind any worker who took on the boss. But grievances didn't make the union part of workplace decision-making, says Don Brown, co-author of the standard text on arbitration. The grievance system was highly centralized and far from the scene of action, so managers could afford to be stubborn, pass the complaint on up, where "it'd be easier to have the Grievance Settlement Board put workers back than to make the judgment yourself," Brown says.

Despite the size and profile of OPSEU, O'Flynn couldn't cut a political deal the way other top labour leaders could. Premier Davis respected raw union muscle. He saw stable labour relations as the key to Ontario's ability to attract investment. He cultivated good relations with labour leaders in auto, mining and steel who could help him avoid a B.C.-style polarization that might scare business off. He had appointed former UAW lawyer Tim Armstrong as deputy minister of labour to keep channels of communication open and relations on track. O'Flynn chafed at that backroom relationship. Armstrong held union leaders back "so they weren't as aggressive, weren't as militant as they would be, because he was their inside man fighting on their behalf; but Tim was working for the Tories, not the labour movement," he says.

At any rate, OPSEU was not considered a player at these meetings. If O'Flynn threatened Davis with worker protests, Davis said he knew his employees better than O'Flynn. "Labour relations with their own employees was treated almost as a non-event," says Don Brown, privy to the thinking of the Tory inner circles. "Davis would flatter O'Flynn and treat him like a big poohbah, but it was much more important to keep Bob White and Cliff Pilkey on side." OPSEU was a "paper tiger," Brown says, "absolutely not a factor in the governing of the province."

An internal review in 1978 showed that 24 per cent of OPSEU locals were "certifiably dead," says John O'Grady, O'Flynn's longest-serving assistant. O'Flynn's boldness, says negotiator André Bekerman, was to create an image for OPSEU that "cast a shadow larger than the creature, and hope like crazy the substance would follow. That's the race he was in, to make the substance catch up with the shadow."

Ironically, seeing OPSEU for the union it was not, O'Flynn sometimes missed the union that it was. The headlines of his presidency mark the forced march to catch up to "real" unions, unions that struck the boss and were in the Canadian Labour Congress. But the vital story was the growth of a "social" union that linked workers' needs with the community, a set of campaigns that put OPSEU in the forefront of the labour movement.

Playing post office

OPSEU wanted to be a union when it grew up.

It wasn't enough to bargain for better wages. The old CSAO did that. So did nurses, teachers and doctors, who still remained, in their own eyes, different from and better than the kinds of workers who joined "unions." For key activists in OPSEU, growing up to be "union" meant moving with a faster crowd than professionals, picking sides in larger battles.

The CSAO had been part of two earlier associations: the Canadian Council of Provincial Employee Associations, formed in 1948, and its successor, the Canadian Federation of Government Employee Organizations (CFGEO, known as "C.F. George"), formed in 1960. Both groups were largely ineffectual. With classic understatement, *CSAO News* reported in 1971 that delegates to the annual meeting "were not overly impressed with the overall effectiveness of CFGEO's operations."

CUPE president Stan Little took the view that his union alone could represent provincial government employees within the Canadian Labour Congress. With Public Service Alliance of Canada president Claude Edwards, Little pressed provincial employee groups to join CUPE, sending his assistant Allan Millard to meet with Gemmell and Bowen. The approach was rebuffed.

In 1972, CSAO vice-president Sid Oxenham, also president of CFGEO, spearheaded an attempt to create a national union, tentatively named the Canadian Association of Provincial Employees. Oxenham received lukewarm support from CUPE and PSAC, who were willing to accept CAPE as an alternative to merger with CUPE. But the proposal foundered. Neither Gemmell and Bowen nor the dissident group of CSAO board members would support it, above all because it involved surrendering the association's autonomy and control over its funds to the new national body. Lacking any purpose, CFGEO died at the end of 1972.

In July, 1974, CSAO leaders applied to join the Canadian Labour Congress. Provincial government workers in B.C., Alberta and Newfoundland had joined the year before, and CSAO thought it could join the same way, all by itself and in its own name. Leaders of the Canadian Union of Public Employees weren't very happy about that. They thought provincial public employees belonged in CUPE. CLC president Donald MacDonald didn't care much what CUPE thought. An old miner from Cape Breton, he didn't forget that local police organized by CUPE broke up picket lines. He was glad to tweak CUPE's nose by letting in provincial employees, says John Fryer, then head of the B.C. Government Employees' Union.

But 1974 was a different year. CUPE had more delegates than any other union at the CLC convention that year, one of the stormiest in the CLC's history. If provincial employees were to be allowed in the CLC, CUPE leaders insisted, they had to join through a national organization. This was seen as a compromise that saved face for CUPE by denying recognition as stand-alone unions to provincial upstarts. That was so ordered in 1975. Six provincial organizations complied with the CLC directive and set up the National Union of Provincial Government Employees in 1976. OPSEU thought NUPGE was a waste of time and money, and refused to jump through the hoop. The CLC expelled OPSEU. O'Flynn and a handful of OPSEU members and staff went to the 1976 CLC convention in Quebec City and handed out leaflets at the escalators, pleading that OPSEU shouldn't be forced to "buy a pig in a poke." But the CLC porkchoppers held firm. OPSEU could only join the CLC through a national organization.

Getting the boot from the CLC weighed heavily on many OPSEU leaders. It kept OPSEU out of labour councils and provincial federations that could help lobby the provincial government. It was also hard on the ego to be denied full union recognition by both the employer and fellow unionists.

One of O'Flynn's first orders of business was to appoint Bill Kuehnbaum, a Sudbury college teacher and board member, to find the least offensive way of getting back into the CLC's good graces. Kuehnbaum and his committee met new CLC president Dennis McDermott. McDermott was an avid collector of union buttons, as was OPSEU committee member Russ Smith. The two popped in and out of the meeting to show off their best buttons and make swaps. But McDermott couldn't be buttonholed on easing the rules for OPSEU's re-entry. There was no way around joining NUPGE, McDermott said. Kuehnbaum's committee recommended in favour of a shotgun marriage.

"NUPGE was a sewer we had to crawl through to get into the CLC," Kuehnbaum says. But OPSEU insisted that its NUPGE admission fees be kept low, so that NUPGE would have no more funding than it had before. "We wanted to keep it just big enough to finance a post office box and a phone machine," one OPSEU negotiating team member recalls. Talks with NUPGE representatives were tense. The Ontario Liquor Boards Employees' Union had joined NUPGE at the start, and its representative didn't like being told to give up the Ontario vice-presidency to make room for OPSEU. In the midst of his harangue against OPSEU, the liquor board representative slipped off his chair. "It was just one of those physical events that totally described what was going to happen from then on to the OLBEU people," Kuehnbaum says. "He ended up on his ass on the floor, and everybody was laughing." OPSEU's board agreed to join NUPGE in 1979.

OPSEU lost no time taking its members' concerns to the Ontario Federation of Labour. The Fed's 1979 convention passed 17 of 19 resolutions submitted by OPSEU locals, and recommended going for political rights for civil servants and against privatization.

By 1981, OPSEU reconciled itself to building NUPGE as an effective force for national lobbying and strike support. Referred to in the media as "organized labour's largest lame duck," NUPGE also got a new lease on life under the leadership of John Fryer, who had brought the B.C. provincial civil servants to unionism. OPSEU was committed to the new NUPGE and its 210,000 members, O'Flynn said, because of "the high regard in which we hold" Fryer.

Affiliation to the CLC gave OPSEU all the buttons and paraphernalia of full union status. It was a "quantum leap" that plugged OPSEU activists into union orthodoxy and prevented any ideological backsliding into association ways, says John O'Grady. Since unionism is a state of mind as much as a set of bargaining structures, the biggest change was in the thinking of OPSEU activists. "Before, we were not workers. We were civil servants," says meat inspector Mike Burke. "That changed when we joined the house of labour."

Let it bleed

Support staff in community colleges got their first collective agreement in 1968. A decade later, they had their first strike. That adventure in unionism marked the end of an adventure in education.

When the colleges first opened, "everyone felt part of the excitement," says Barb Darrow, a secretary in Thunder Bay's Confederation College since 1970. "You didn't even have time to stop and think about things because it was all happening so fast. You just went flat out," she says. "We were part of a brave new venture and it was like a honeymoon," says Bev Allan, who joined Ottawa's Algonquin College for the start-up.

"It was a dream come true," says Larry Sauer, who started at the Kirkland Lake campus of Northern College as an electronics technician in 1969. In many smaller centres, the colleges had pride of place, were perched on the tops of hills overlooking the town, and the prestige shone on all employees. Support staff were full members of the college community, took part in frosh week, wore shirts and ties or dresses, got the summer off, just like faculty and administrators, Sauer remembers. Technicians didn't punch clocks, but put in all the hours that were needed, just like professionals. Supervision was minimal. "The camaraderie of the early days didn't lend itself to a union. We worked as a team. We didn't believe there was management. We believed that we were management," he says.

Bargaining was a night out on the town, Sauer says. The college support bargaining team, elected on a province-wide basis, gave equal representation to technicians, maintenance staff and clericals. Under that system, women, who made up two-thirds of the staff, elected one-third of the bargaining team. Technicians were the prima donnas on the team, Sauer says. They had issues. Janitors had "problems." Women had "complaints." Team secretary Barb Darrow "looked nice on our arms when we went out to dinner, but she wasn't someone who bargained," Sauer says. When she raised the needs of her group, she was seen as a whiner. "Almost the same way the management treated support staff as a group, the males treated the women's group that way," Sauer says.

In 1975, the first year that bargaining took place under the new Colleges Collective Bargaining Act that allowed for strikes, Sauer noticed a management bargaining chart that listed support staff as a "costing unit." The chart listed teachers and administrators as an asset. The chart fitted with the new era of cost-control brought on by the Henderson report. During the spending cuts, "We got put in our place," Sauer says. "The support staff became the blue-collar workers of the college." They were dressed down in 1976, when they were no longer required to wear shirts and ties or dresses. Support workers also lost their summer holidays. "All of a sudden, the agreement kept popping up," and managers began referring to it as the union agreement, not the college agreement, he says. "That was the beginning of the fight for survival."

The old-boy style of bargaining ended in 1977 when North York Seneca College clerk Susie Vallance led a successful campaign to reject the settlement proposed by the union team. That was "the first statement of defiance" by clerical workers, says Vallance. Women came into their own in 1978, when workers started electing their bargaining representatives by region rather than by occupational group, thereby allowing women to use their majority. Vallance, Allan, and four other newcomers made up the first team elected under new union rules. Sauer lost out in the change. Seen – accurately, he says – as a "highroller" who got carried away with his expense accounts, he was turfed off the bargaining team.

Management wanted to hold the line on wage increases, to extend the bargaining pattern set by federal wage controls, due to expire that year. Progress was made on workplace issues. The bargaining team chalked up more security for part-timers, more sick time, pioneering language on protection from VDT radiation. But the August 31 expiry date for the old contract was long past when managers dug in their heels on wages.

The union took a strike vote, pitched as a pressure tactic to force management to come up with more money, just like the year before. "It was pumped, I'll be the first to tell you," says Vallance. Workers wore union buttons on the job, talked down the management offer, got angrier, more confident. The strike vote carried by large margins.

After months of belittling the union's wage claims, management's last-minute offer to raise wages came too late. A strike "was going to happen, no matter what," says Vallance. "It had become a question of fairness and dignity. They'd treated us with contempt, and it got to the point where we said we're not going to take it. You had to be in the room to watch that mood. 'Fuck you, we're going on strike.' I knew personally I couldn't undo that."

O'Flynn also opposed accepting management's final offer. The last contract had been lousy, he says, and he was determined the workers wouldn't be pushed around again. In the colleges and in the union as a whole, there was "no sense of members having any power. We were new, we were grappling, we were just determined we were going to get some respect somewhere." The union didn't know anything about strikes. "It had this big confrontation that never happened" in 1974, but "people had lost this sense that they could do anything for themselves. That was one of the big problems of the union," O'Flynn says. He'd never been on strike himself, but what he knew was "my instincts, my guts." Now he can't remember how the offer got turned down. Vallance says that if O'Flynn did interfere, "we didn't know about it."

In mid-January, 1979, the union launched its first province-wide strike. In Toronto, the pounding sleet tore all the picket signs to tatters. In Sault Ste. Marie, it was 15 below zero on the picket lines, says Bob Hebdon, who directed the strike there, "but morale was lower." Strikers felt powerless. Police kept pickets well back from traffic. Students gunned their cars at pickets. Teachers, after gestures of solidarity the first day, crossed the lines and picked up enough of support workers' chores to keep the colleges running.

The union's lack of strike experience showed. The strike manual provided for strike pay after the third week, a rule that O'Flynn overturned on the spot in favour of quick payouts. Pickets were assigned eight-hour shifts, triple the time most unions require in the dead of winter. There were no plastic covers to protect picket signs from the weather. After 13 days, strikers came in from the cold with a few face-saving improvements to management's last offer.

The strike came to be seen as a set-up, a piece of theatre to show the union could take its members out. "It was a bullshit strike" that betrayed the members' trust, says Peter Slee, who helped direct picketing at Hamilton's Mohawk College. It brought dishonour to the union, says Bob Hebdon, wracked by guilt after selling a strike vote as a threat that wouldn't have to be honoured. "It was OPSEU's 1901 Yonge Street agenda," says Sauer, who made his political comeback as president of his own local the next year by beating out the chair of the bargaining team responsible for the strike.

To this day, those closest to the action deny any secret agenda to provoke a strike that simply let OPSEU strut its stuff. The strike may have been a mistake in judgment, but it was an honest mistake, they say.

Few differ over the strike's long-term impact. It was a "recognition strike" by clericals who had to break down their image as the little sister who never got management's attention, says André Bekerman, negotiator for the bargaining team through most of the 1980s. Support workers stopped seeing themselves in the shadow of teachers, says Bev Allan: "We got tired of being walked on." A new generation of college support leaders got their baptism in that strike, says Debbie Field, OPSEU's women's rights co-ordinator assigned by O'Flynn to scout out Norma Rae's in the college ranks. Hebdon sees the aftermath of the strike as "a success story of maturity and self-reliance." Support staff pushed the next OPSEU convention to set up a formal strike fund and a workable administrative policy to direct strikes. The strike had become an accepted tool in public service bargaining.

The next round of college support bargaining brought a dental plan and a 15 per cent wage increase. Then came OPSEU's first job evaluation scheme, an early, pre-pay equity experiment in letting workers and managers rate jobs in some objective way.

Bargaining successes haven't stopped the pining for the old days, however. Job evaluations were "the final blow," says Sauer. "We were widgets. They'd taken away the professionalism and team spirit many of us brought to the job." The union minimized the losses, he says, but the agenda was set by management's downgrading of the old college spirit. "The highest mark on a job spec is C, the symbol of mediocrity," he says.

Jailhouse rock

Jails are "an us-them place to work," says Frances Lankin, a correctional officer at Toronto's Don Jail in the mid-1970s, later a leading cabinet member in Ontario's NDP government. "There was us-them between the guards and the inmates, and there was us-them between the guards and management. Then there was us-them with the outside world."

This underworld of union solidarity didn't leave OPSEU much choice. Either it led the struggle for recognition of the jails' distinct society, or it faced the threat of separation, desertion to another union that would. The government tried to buck the inevitable, faced a wildcat strike, and jailed Sean O'Flynn for his pains.

Guards are "prisoners of their own jobs, surrounded by work and an umbrella of stress 24 hours a day," says Len Hupet, an officer in northwestern Ontario since 1970. They have to be tight, union or no. They have to back each other up without question, whenever inmates get rough. They have to stick together socially because of weird shift schedules and neighbours who look down on them for the company they keep. They have to hang tight through all the political changing of the guard as Corrections ministers wend their way up or out of cabinet. "We change ministers almost as often as you change socks," Hupet says. After the 1960s, they were left to their own devices by liberal policy makers who believed in rehabilitating prisoners but not jails or jail supervisors.

Though liberal prison reform gained support among the general public in those years, it didn't carry much weight in the ministry. When Hupet took his basic training at Guelph in 1970, he thought he was "getting into the army." The raw recruits slept in an old army barracks, marched on parade in grey khaki uniforms. Once on the job, they "mustered for duty" five minutes before each shift, and got "written up," without hearing or representation, when charged for misconduct.

Flanked on one side by a militaristic management that gave them few rights, they were flanked on the other by prisoners who seemed to be gaining more civil rights. Guards were caught in the squeeze, "the forgotten men of our jails," as a correctional officers' brief of 1972 put it. Guards were stressed out by the constant danger of a regime that gave prisoners too much leeway, 25 guard leaders presenting the brief claimed. The same year, three guards at one jail quit to protest punishment meted out to them after a scuffle with inmates. Their action sparked a mass resignation by fellow officers until the charges were withdrawn.

In 1975, 80 per cent of the Don Jail's officers threatened to wildcat unless two guards received an impartial hearing of charges laid against them by management. To head off the confrontation, Jake Norman negotiated a commission of inquiry into jail conditions.

The union's brief to the commission complained of prison overcrowding and pampering of dangerous criminals. "The inconsistent application of punishment and the constant reduction of punishment sentences has left the inmates with the impression that they can not only defy the correctional staff but also attack correctional officers with impunity," Corrections leader Vic Cooper complained in his report to the 1975 OPSEU convention.

A new breed of guards recruited in the mid-1970s kept these protests from degenerating into a backlash against prison reform. Oldtimers were mainly immigrants with service backgrounds in the British army or police. "You had to be multilingual to follow all the accents at the Don," says Lankin. New recruits like Lankin tended to be young university grads with ambitions to right some prison wrongs.

Kevin Wilson started at the Don in 1976 after working there part-time while he finished university. He started working with a core of guards committed to changing OPSEU from within, rather than grumbling about it or going off on their own. They had no problem finding issues to organize around. Turnover among correctional officers averaged 30 per cent a year. Union reformers fought for pay that matched other police officers', better shift schedules, early retirement, and new jails to relieve overcrowding. Until two new Toronto jails were built in 1977, the Don often jammed 1,000 prisoners into a holding tank built for 300.

By 1977, the new group within Corrections was pressing hard for recognition as a distinct wage bargaining group within the public service. That demand brought the guards smack against government policy on bargaining teams. Government strategists liked dealing with a small number of union bargaining teams. That saved negotiating time on separate agreements. Large teams also diluted the weight and militancy of minority groups with special problems not shared by other workers. In 1973, the government wanted to keep its civil service bargaining in five groups. The union countered with a proposal for 12 groups. Both sides compromised on eight. That put guards in the same category as institutional workers in psychiatric hospitals and centres for the developmentally handicapped. Institutional workers were mostly women. Their jobs were defined as custodial. Jail guards were mostly men, and defined their jobs as police work, which paid much better than custodial jobs. So there was little of what industrial relations specialists call "community of interest" within the institutional team. The guards resented being dragged down by institutional workers the government deemed low-income earners. Guards also felt the institutional workers weren't ready to put up a fight.

In the 1979 round of bargaining, guards put forward one issue. They wanted their own category. The union was open. At first, it looked as though government managers were, too. But in November, 1979, Kevin Wilson, chief bargaining spokesperson for the guards, told a tense meeting from across the province that the government wouldn't give them a separate bargaining team. Frances Lankin was first at the mikes. "We'll take it." She took a mike, and moved a strike. An angry roar endorsed her motion. The motion was put to all Ontario guards on November 29. "It was as easy as throwing a match on gasoline," Wilson says. Guards voted 77.5 per cent in favour of striking for their own, ninth, category. The deadline was set for December 3.

The government held firm. They didn't want to fall for another bluff, as in 1974, reasoning that if they caved in to correctional workers, other groups claiming a special identity would demand their own bargaining team. There was little sense that the jails were headed for a blow-up.

The night before the strike deadline, O'Flynn met at the Royal York Hotel with a government team led by Rollie Scott. Scott offered to submit the controversy to an arbitrator if the union cancelled the strike call. O'Flynn said it had gone too far for that, and walked out. Scott chased after him. "My god, man, do you know what you are doing? You'll go to jail," Scott said. "I know, but it's too late," O'Flynn replied. "His face was very tense," Scott says.

Picket lines went up the next day. The lines were solid, and spirits were high. There was little the government could do. It seemed ludicrous to threaten guards with jail terms for their illegal strike. The media was friendly. So were police, who liked the "Our cops are tops" buttons strikers wore. This was the height of the Iran hostage incident, and one placard addressed to the minister demanded: "Hey! Ayatollah Walker, Release hostage # 9." It was the season to be jolly. In Cobourg, guards sang a Christmas carol:

> OPSEU bells,
> OPSEU bells,
> OPSEU all the way;
> Oh, what fun when we get the ninth,
> We'll be back to work some day!
> OPSEU bells,
> OPSEU bells,
> OPSEU all the way;

Oh what fun it is to strike
For rights and equal pay.

On the second day of the strike, provincial mediator Harvey Ladd, leader of the world-famous Newfoundland loggers' strike of 1959, worked out a compromise. The controversy would be arbitrated, but the union would have its choice of arbitrators. There'd be no reprisals against strikers, save for a letter on their files noting they'd gone absent without leave.

Harry Arthurs, a leading professor of labour law, opened arbitration hearings immediately. Ross Dunsmore of Hicks Morley put the government's case. "Eight present categories not sancrosanct," he said, according to Arthurs' notes. But if guards got a separate category and a special deal, Dunsmore argued, "employer gets stuck entirely with the obligation of explaining to all employees."

OPSEU argued that correctional workers had a right to self-determination, but assured Arthurs that the union wouldn't go on a spree to set up any more new categories.

Arthurs kept his own counsel. "This strike results from uncontrolled grassroots agitation," he wrote to himself. A separate category would force the union to be more responsible, he noted on a margin. It wouldn't be able to blame arbitrators for its own lack of unity and priorities. Arthurs appreciated government fears about facing an infinite number of new bargaining teams. Like most arbitrators, he liked large bargaining units and looked upon small, tightly-knit groups of strategically-placed workers – in the kill room of a meat plant, or tire room of a rubber plant, for instance – as a thorn in the side of both union and management. But the guards were an exception to the rule, he thought. Their interests were submerged. They were not trying to form another union, just a separate category within the same union. And since there was no right to strike, Arthurs reasoned, the employer had no cause to fear a permanent strike threat, as might be the case in industry if each sub-group came up for settlement one at a time.

Arthurs asked O'Flynn if the union would accept an embargo on any further splintering of the bargaining system. O'Flynn said the union was prepared to pay the price. This was really no concession for O'Flynn, who disliked fragmented bargaining teams as much as the government, but it sounded good to be losing something.

Arthurs ruled in favour of a separate category for correctional officers, and imposed a ban on any new categories until 1982, unless both parties agreed to them. In the next bargaining round, guards held three brief meetings with management, and walked away with a 27 per cent wage increase.

The government got its pound of flesh from O'Flynn. He was charged with contempt of court for defying a November 30 injunction prohibiting the illegal strike. "It is my obligation as president of this union to do what is right and just in the interests of the members," he told the judge. "My duty to them is clear, as is my conscience. I therefore recommend that they proceed with their plans to strike."

The next day, Justice Douglas Carruthers called O'Flynn "irresponsible" and said he "seemed determined to rise above the law and take 3,000 law-abiding citizens with him." Carruthers sentenced O'Flynn to 35 days in jail.

O'Flynn served the mandatory two-thirds of his sentence in the Metro West jail. Friends say caging O'Flynn did something to his free spirit. He was bitter at guards who criticized him for accepting a deal that allowed a letter to be placed on their file stating they had gone absent without leave. O'Flynn found jail degrading and humiliating, says Don Brown, who visited him every day. He hated being herded around, denied laces in his shoes, a belt for his pants. O'Flynn had always been a painter. His early abstracts had flair and splash. After 1979, his paintings were filled with lines and confined spaces.

O'Flynn makes light of his time in jail now. "It made me appreciate life, liberty, good wine and all that, but that wore off," he says. "At least Davis became aware of my existence."

Union password

CLC membership and a burst of strikes marked OPSEU's coming of age as a union in the late 1970s. Similar markers weren't available to measure the union's progress during O'Flynn's last four years as president. O'Flynn had a hard time coping with that slowdown. He kept pushing and shoving to put OPSEU on the progressive edge of unionism. But, says one senior staffer fed up with O'Flynn's short attention span for the plodding details of union-building: "He wanted to be a union leader without doing all the patient work, just like a kid who wants to be a concert pianist but doesn't want to practise." His frustration led him to try out new approaches that provoked a major identity crisis within the union leadership.

O'Flynn had an instinct for drama, and was drawn to the sharp confrontational tactics of famed U.S. community organizer Saul Alinsky and of the American civil rights movement.

In 1981, Scarborough's Centennial College moved to lay off 47 maintenance workers and replace them with low-paid contract cleaners. In June, O'Flynn forced the issue. Together with two Centennial workers, plus OFL secretary-treasurer Terry Meagher and Toronto Labour Council president Wally Majesky, O'Flynn occupied the college president's office. After eight days, Minister of Colleges and Universities Bette Stephenson intervened, and the college agreed to save the jobs.

The same year, O'Flynn brought institutional care workers to the brink of illegal strike action. When bargaining showed no progress, O'Flynn told staff to talk up strike action. The caregivers, mostly women, were ready. They'd just seen their wages fall far behind correctional workers after they won their separate category through strike action. "We thought we deserved the recognition," says Phyllis Chapple, chief steward at the St. Thomas centre for the mentally handicapped. "Our job was just as important, but we were being persecuted because we were women." Jail guards had cells and bars to protect them from inmate assaults, but workers at institutions had to "just stand there and take it," she says. Staff in St. Thomas voted unanimously to strike, and had a strike trailer at the ready.

Staff had put their reputations on the line when they rallied members to take a militant stance. But at the last moment, O'Flynn called in staff reps and told them to quench the fires they'd kindled, that he wasn't about to go to jail again. "Here we were, ready to go, and all of a sudden he stuck a pin in the balloon," says Jim Tait.

Members didn't take kindly to the union's flipflop. In Smiths Falls, says Henry Brugma, workers at the massive centre for the developmentally handicapped were in a lynching mood when O'Flynn took the stage. Workers chanted "O'Flynn must go." There was almost a riot, Brugma says, but the meeting broke up without any resolution. "Sean didn't mind going to jail for Corrections, but didn't want to go back again for us," says Chapple.

The sense of betrayal, the sense that the union wouldn't be there in the crunch, lingered for years, even though the workers were always free to make up their own minds about striking. André Bekerman, the negotiator sent in to pick up the pieces the next year, says workers blotted out their own role in the decision not to strike, and "O'Flynn's weakening in terms of going to jail became a way out of dealing with that." Bekerman set out to rebuild the team on the basis of its own strength and agenda, not the heroics or non-heroics of one individual. For Bekerman, the leadership crisis demonstrated that "when you're in control of as powerful a machine as a union, you can't just agitate, you have to have something in mind, some plan, not just bitching."

In 1981, OPSEU established a $6 million strike fund in preparation for the day when all its members would enjoy the right to strike. The 1982 OPSEU convention highlighted "The right to strike: good enough for doctors; good enough for us," a contrast in legal rights the union frequently played up. As it turned out, the right to bargain at all became the central issue of the year, when Davis and Trudeau imposed wage controls on public service workers for the second time in a decade, and suspended the limited bargaining rights government workers had.

Fighting wage controls

Davis was a slow convert to having wage controls placed only on the public sector. In the 1981 election campaign, he said it would be unfair to single out public sector workers. For several months afterward, he resisted Trudeau's lead, refusing to take political heat for Trudeau's economic problems. But by the fall of 1982, as public sector workers became a convenient scapegoat for a recession that wouldn't lift, Davis came onside. He said he had no choice but to match Trudeau's controls on federal workers. In December, he used closure to force his controls bill through the legislature. The Inflation Restraint Act set a five per cent limit on public sector wage hikes negotiated that year.

OPSEU negotiators had an early sense that controls were coming. During the winter, government negotiators tipped the government's hand by demanding that all contracts be made for a maximum of one year, rolled back gains in long-term contracts negotiated previously, and also restricted bargaining on non-monetary issues. Union bargaining teams went after gains "as if this were our last chance," chief negotiator Andy Todd told the media. Office workers won a 13.6 per cent increase, their best showing ever, after a campaign that demanded a major catch-up for women trapped in the clerical ghetto.

Through the summer, OPSEU tried to hold Davis to his 1981 election pledge and his campaign theme to "Keep the Promise." Communications director John Ward warned that Davis was moving to controls, and "that will look pretty empty if he goes back on his word now." The media seemed sympathetic. When Davis tried to wriggle out of his campaign statement on the unfairness of singling out public sector workers by saying it was not a promise, simply an observation, one columnist suggested he should have campaigned on the theme "Keep the Observation."

When the Inflation Restraint Act was introduced in September, OPSEU staged a mass rally at Queen's Park. Fiery speakers and a crowd chanting "Bill Must Go" moved one demonstrator to put his lighter to a rented papier-mâché effigy of the premier. The premier in flames made good TV, and the union gladly paid to replace the rented effigy, Todd says.

Union activists also tried to bring the House down with a few madcap antics. On the final day of debate, December 15, OPSEU activists and staff filled the legislative gallery for the debate, tossed balloons in the air, and made loud sucking noises to spoof a cabinet minister rumoured to be a pothead. Efforts to remove unionists from the gallery provoked a confrontation with Queen's Park security staff that kept the TV cameras rolling. The union also demonstrated at constituency offices of key cabinet members. "What's a Tory promise worth?" demonstrators asked.

The members did not follow their leaders, however. A Windsor membership rally against controls attracted only 35 people. "It wasn't through lack of trying," says André Bekerman. "It's just that we came on too strong, and the membership wasn't there yet." An effort to "give the boss a charleyhorse" by tying up the government's internal mail and working-to-rule fizzled out.

The militants were extremely militant, as described by the *Canadian Annual Review* for 1982, "but at no time was there any sense of a massive ground swell of opposition among those subject to the bill similar to that which had faced the government to withdraw its teachers' strike bill in 1974."

The Tories had a solid majority from the 1981 election, their rightwing members were feeling their oats, and "we were pelting shit at the moon," says Peter Slee. When a government is prepared to take the punch, he says, a union has to recognize the difference between what it can and can't win. "Maybe we didn't give members a focus that could allow them to act," says Pauline Seville. "A lot of it was theatrical acting out." The union's shrill tactics offended many members, she says, and got in the way of serious organizing around concrete issues such as the rollback of clerical wages, which hurt the lowest-paid government workers.

Compared to many other unions, OPSEU at least put up a fight. At a time when industrial workers faced mass layoffs and wage cuts, five per cent raises looked pretty good. Union conventions went on the record for free collective bargaining, but CLC president Dennis McDermott said industrial workers weren't going on any general strike for public employees. "It is unlikely the Government will be shaken by verbal pyrotechnics," the *Globe's* labour columnist, Wilf List, wrote in his review of the national campaign to defeat controls.

In September, 1983, Davis modified his control order and extended it for another year. Under the new act, bargaining was allowed to resume, and the five per cent figure was redefined as a guideline rather than outright control on arbitrators. This shift anticipated a major supreme court win by OPSEU, not a rebellion from the ranks. The Supreme Court of Canada was about to hand down its judgment on an OPSEU complaint that the 1982 law's suspension of bargaining rights, together with the Ontario government's long-standing denial of the right to strike, violated workers' constitutional rights.

In October, a judge of the Ontario Supreme Court ruled that, under certain sections of Ontario's law, "the workers' freedom is more than merely infringed, it is emasculated." To celebrate the landmark decision, OPSEU sponsored a November rally of 1,500 at Roy Thomson Hall, with the NDP's new leader Bob Rae at the piano playing a medley on Tory misdeeds. O'Flynn boasted that "the sovereignty of the Legislature is a thing of history" as a result of the Charter of Rights. "Victory is a strange word to us workers. We have to get used to it. But victory has come and things will never be the same again for labour," he said. This grandstanding did not weigh on the Ontario government. It held that its latest revisions were not covered by the dated court ruling, which at any rate upheld the government's right to control wages.

OPSEU delayed bargaining until it settled on arbitrators who might take the five per cent guideline with a grain of salt. Government negotiators also stalled, claiming they had to wait for regulations that spelled out the limits of what they could offer. The two sides got down to bargaining early in 1984. OPSEU sent the guards up first, and broke through the five per cent ceiling with a 7.5 per cent wage increase. From then on, OPSEU made a mockery of controls. Arbitrated increases ranged from 5.3 to 7.75 per cent. This at a time when private sector unions were averaging 3.1 per cent raises and other public sector unions brought back awards averaging three per cent.

Despite this vindication of OPSEU's strategy and skill at arbitration, the delays took the bloom off the rose. Many members blamed the union, not the government, for their long wait before retroactive wage increases came due. Keeping members from a "take the money and run" approach takes education and discipline in the ranks, in its own way as taxing as the short and sweet confrontations of private-sector bargaining. For all the talk of educating OPSEU members to be "real" unionists, O'Flynn failed to mail out bargaining newsletters blaming the delays at arbitration on management and explaining the union's strategy.

Soul-searching

The lack of resonance in the ranks for OPSEU leaders' militant agenda led to a major period of soul-searching. In 1983, O'Flynn hired Peter Warrian as his chief of staff. Warrian was a former student leader of the 1960s who studied for the priesthood in the U.S. under the courageous Berrigan brothers before returning to Canada and secular life as research head for the United Steelworkers. Some say he was brought in to "steel" OPSEU, and give it the hard edge of an industrial union. Cynics say he was hired to establish connections for O'Flynn's expected leadership bid at the Ontario Federation of Labour.

In Warrian's eyes, OPSEU had a long way to go before it became a real union. Civil servants didn't have the same spunk as miners and steelworkers who had to confront harsh working conditions and discipline. Workers were more concerned about slights to their status from poor performance reviews than gut-wrenching workplace problems, he says. And OPSEU's structures compounded the problem. They were "designed for failure," Warrian says. OPSEU's top leadership and executive board looked after general policy issues. They weren't on the hook for bargaining. That lack of responsibility for a union's most important function produced an "ingrained culture that is politically irresponsible" and "fundamentally corrupting," he says. "All you get is pure politics" and feuding leadership candidates who make their careers out of attacking the union instead of the boss.

Warrian didn't have much luck getting staff on side. Orders for basic office equipment he needed were slowtracked. Someone stole his "little black book" containing key appointments and contacts. When he tried to act as chief of staff and direct employees, O'Flynn let him know who was boss. It was hard to be a working-class hero in OPSEU.

His first day on the job, Warrian was sent to New York to meet promoters of Saul Alinsky's community organizing methods. Alinsky, renowned for the flamboyant direct action and confrontation he advocated in his book *Rules for Radicals*, caught O'Flynn's imagination in the 1960s. He looked to Alinsky's followers for inspiration again in 1983, hoping they could help him build a union that gave workers power as well as service. In January, a month before Warrian started, the board decided to give Alinsky's methods a try.

The Alinsky seminars for OPSEU staff and leaders were a primal scream in the union's history, a traumatic encounter of the human potential movement with unionism. Alinsky trainers set out to humiliate and strip down seminar participants, just to make the point about how much people will endure from authority figures. People turned on by this teaching technique come to understand that power goes to those who take it, not to the meek who merely ask not to be abused. They learn to break the rules, not follow them, to expose relations of domination, not submit to them.

Opinion is sharply divided about the experience. "It's some of the best training I ever went through," says Susie Vallance, then a leading member of the executive board, now in charge of employment equity at Seneca College. Seminar leaders preached the same values as the women's movement, she says. They taught OPSEU to throw constitutions out the window, do away with titles, keep meetings to a minimum, and focus on leadership skills that organize workers to take power over their lives. "I came out higher than a kite," says Pete Slee, a staffer who'd handled media for several major OPSEU campaigns. He learned that slick, centralized media campaigns just proved the union couldn't build anything, and had to pay to be noticed. The right way is to work with the local membership to take on the boss every day. "Fighting fires doesn't build a union," he says. "All it does is put out fires." Likewise, grievances don't build a union, unless a core turns the grievance into an issue people will fight for. The Alinsky methods are "an ideology you have to buy," Slee says, because it has to be constantly maintained against the grain of a society that touts service, not empowerment.

Other activists found the teachings bizarre. At a picket line protesting the closure of an institution for the developmentally handicapped, a fresh Alinsky devotee suggested lying down in front of an oncoming truck. "What if the driver hasn't taken the Alinsky course?" board member Art Lane asked. The seminars helped focus the need for a guiding strategy and set of values, but the approach was "false and manipulative," says senior staffer Pauline Seville. "They were desperately looking for a formula that would turn OPSEU into a militant union. They were just looking for a magic formula," she says.

An inspired O'Flynn launched a new steward training system called PASS – for Power and Action through Steward Skills – and a new union publication called *PASSword*. Courses featured training in "power" and the means of challenging and building it. The publication came to feature "power tools" for stewards, usually legal precedents that could be used when filing grievances. Ironically, this legalistic focus was at odds with Alinsky methods of direct action. At any rate, the grievance procedure in the public service is so technical that stewards rarely take grievances to the level where knowledge of precedents is relevant.

Many activists hoped the union's drive to organize workers outside the civil service would give OPSEU a union grounding. New blood, brought in after intense organizing drives and faced with tough bargaining under the Ontario Labour Relations Act, might turn the organization around, it was thought.

Though OPSEU (and CSAO before it) had organized workers outside the civil service since the mid-1960s, a strategic turn to what was called "the OLRA sector" was a hallmark of O'Flynn's presidency.

The expansion of medical technologist units into other paramed classifications in the mid-1970s brought increasing contact with social workers, psychologists and other occupations, which developed naturally into organizing in a host of related areas, including children's aid societies, associations for the mentally retarded, school boards and child treatment centres. Again, OPSEU's experience in representing semi-professional employees was telling. The workers wanted professional recognition, better pay and better treatment. They wanted to be paid for the extra hours they put in. And they were feeling threatened by the funding pressure that resulted from the Henderson report. Workers at the Ottawa Children's Aid Society were a good example. When they were organized in 1975, they complained of lack of training, high turnover among staff, poor working conditions, management favouritism in awarding promotions and pay that lagged far behind workers in other CASs. To respond effectively to OPSEU's growing popularity, a strategy of organizing in a series of related sectors was adopted. Again, this fitted well with the experience of the union in central bargaining.

In 1978, OPSEU began a drive to organize the Art Gallery of Ontario. CUPE had tried before and failed, so OPSEU organizers knew in advance that management would offer stiff resistance. The union developed close relations with avant-garde artists. A small core at the Gallery met secretly for months before launching a two-week card-signing blitz. Managers went all-out to block the drive. The Gallery board, drawn largely from the financial and social elite, saw the union drive as a vulgar effort to make money off art and a betrayal of the friendly personal relations between volunteers and staff. "What they couldn't accomplish in their steel mill because of the United Steelworkers, they tried to accomplish in their hobby," says Pauline Seville, who headed the drive. "It was like the infidels had stormed the barricades at Rosedale."

The union successfully filed 13 unfair labour practices against management, and had management grilled by the government's Public Accounts Committee for wasting $23,000 on anti-union manoeuvres. O'Flynn, an amateur painter himself, was excited by the drive, took out a membership in the Gallery, and peppered directors at board meetings.

In the ambulance sector, union staff had tried unsuccessfully to strike a deal with the Ontario Ambulance Operators' Association to adopt a system of central bargaining similar to the one in the hospitals.

Halton-Mississauga ambulance workers struck for six weeks in the summer of 1979, attempting to win wage parity with ambulance officers employed directly by the provincial government. The strike won a significant wage increase, but fell short of its goal. But it taught important lessons about solidarity. When managers at York Regional ambulance service asked OPSEU ambulance officers to respond to calls in Mississauga, ambulances started running out of gas, and officers lost their way. Unfortunately, some other ambulance services not represented by OPSEU were used to answer calls.

Ambulance officers and the union concluded that coordinated bargaining was the only way to win further changes in their wages and working conditions. It was not until the mid-1980s, when the union mobilized its legal expertise in support of a small band of determined strikers at McKechnie ambulance in Collingwood, that a way was found to create central bargaining for ambulance officers.

By 1984, when O'Flynn stepped down as president, "OLRA members," those organized under laws governing private sector workers, made up 16 per cent of OPSEU's membership. In the next decade, it more than doubled. Since 1991, the union has defined that strategic constituency as the "Broader Public Service."

Taming of the screws

While the union was looking for ways to get more power at the workplace and bargaining table, OPSEU was becoming one of the most dynamic forces for social change in the province. A new brand of social unionism developed almost unwittingly during Sean O'Flynn's years as president. It didn't follow the industrial model. Socially-conscious industrial unions fought for medicare, pensions and the NDP, all several steps removed from the issues workers faced at the workplace. OPSEU's social unionism focused on social legislation with immediate playback in the workplace. It started to bridge those divisions, entrenched by the Committee on Government Productivity in the 1960s, that separated government policy, community need, and public sector work.

Social action had to be welded to hard wage bargaining, says André Bekerman, assigned to the correctional bargaining team after 1982. The way to a government's heart lies through its stomach, he says. "You don't move employers by eloquent arguments and appeals to the heartstrings. You move them by grabbing where it hurts. You drive wages down their throat," he claims. According to Bekerman's ABCs of industrial psychology: "As long as they can get away with paying you badly, they'll pay no attention to other problems you've got, because in their minds if you're a low-paid worker you can't be worth much, and your problems can't be that important. Once they start paying you well, then you must be worth a lot and it becomes worthwhile to listen to the rest of your problems. We went after wages to get their attention. Then it took union leadership to move on to social issues."

In the late 1970s, when guards were pushing for their own category, they wore the insulting term for their job, "screws," on their chest. "Jail guards make better screws," their T-shirts proclaimed. By 1984, they turned OPSEU into the leading jail guards' union across North America in the fight for prisoners' rights.

The Corrections division went into the 1982 round of bargaining to set a new agenda, Bekerman says. The team based its demands and strategy on members' response to questionnaires sent out to all locals. Overcrowding topped the list. Jails were packed to the rafters, housing double the number of inmates they were built for. Guards had a double caseload to watch over. And they had more multi-problem customers, many of them recent discharges from downsized psychiatric hospitals.

The division looked for allies. In 1983, it joined forces with the John Howard Society, the Elizabeth Fry Society and the Salvation Army to form the Ontario Council for Community Alternatives to Prison. To keep peace within the coalition, guards held back on calls for more jails, while reformers bit their tongues about closing all jails immediately. The council fought for expanded halfway houses, where prisoners, such as those who couldn't pay fines for alcohol abuse, could get treatment. It also worked to extend probation and parole systems that let people find their feet in the community, under supervision.

Executive board member and guard leader Kevin Wilson burned the midnight oil with a guard going to law school. They studied how U.S. prison reformers in 40 states used their constitution to launch cases against cruel and unusual punishment to force action against overcrowding. Wilson thought Canada's new Charter of Rights and Freedoms offered a chance to do the same. In January 1984, OPSEU hired Ian Scott to launch a lawsuit charging that overcrowding violated prisoners' constitutional rights.

The case hit a raw nerve. In 1983, Ombudsman Donald Morand had denounced the Ministry of Corrections, which, he said, "unreasonably omitted to take sufficient action to alleviate the extreme overcrowding." Corrections deputy minister George Podrebarac admitted as much in a private memo where he pleaded with cabinet for more funds. He described jails as "outdated and critically overcrowded," and warned that "without the benefit of the proposed bedspace creation, the overcrowding situation in Ontario's correction facilities is expected to reach explosive proportions."

Barrie jail guard and local union president Larry Folz had already gone public. "If you take an animal and cage it and taunt it, they become very agitated. They start to act like animals. Somebody had to know, and that's why I went to the papers," says Folz. A 21-year veteran with corrections, Folz was suspended for breaking the oath of secrecy. His grievance was won by a fluke. When the reporter he had talked to was found to be in Europe and unable to testify at the grievance hearing, Folz was reinstated.

By 1984, the government couldn't keep a lid on the problem. At the Don, where three to a cell was standard, a riot broke out. Three guards were injured. Seven jurors on the Public Institutions Inspection panel toured Ontario prisons, and denounced the inhumanity and the dangers of overcrowding. Liberal MPP Robert McKessock completed a study that accused the Corrections Ministry of having a "holding tank mentality." The superintendent of the Whitby Jail – built for 62, but routinely holding 102 – admitted to the local press: "We are definitely overcrowded on occasion and it has to create tensions and frustrations." Even Corrections minister Nick Leluk conceded: "We do have some high counts within some of our institutions with which we are not entirely pleased."

At the court hearing, Scott put the government on trial. He called an internationally-recognized penal expert, Dr. Sean McConville, who described Toronto's jails as among the worst he'd seen in the western world. Scott produced eyewitness accounts from guards and inmates. He provided government documents that backed the union's case. One set of documents, says Wilson, was "a smoking gun," proof that the government knew about the problem and did nothing about it. That set of documents was identified as coming from a "Mr. X."

The government tried to quash the case, claiming it was beyond the Divisional Court's jurisdiction. Judges rejected the government argument. Six months later, after all the documents had been reported in the press, the attorney general's office found a new approach. It went before Judge J. Rosenberg in August to declare all the government documents stolen material, used in violation of cabinet confidentiality, of copyright law, and of a worker's responsibility to the employer. Even the public service manual of standards and procedures, available in government libraries, was included in the blanket request for suppression of all background material.

The government wanted the originals back to identify the union's leak, Mr. X, who could be identified by tell-tale numbers on the documents. Scott's firm was caught by surprise. "We were in shock," says one senior lawyer working with Scott. "The government realized it was in a corner where they were the villains, so why not turn the tables." The firm had met and received documents from Mr. X without thinking through its obligations of confidentiality to its informant, nor the jeopardy that person was in. "The bells just didn't go off," Scott's colleague says.

Now the union was in the dock. Scott's lawyers appeared before Judge Rosenberg to counter the attorney general's demands. "It is important that people know they have a right in law to avoid being disciplined if they come across something that discloses impropriety or other misconduct," they argued. Rosenberg was unmoved. "Surreptitious delivery of confidential material cannot be sanctioned," he ruled. The material must be returned and the source identified.

Scott's firm appealed, claiming Rosenberg made seven errors in law, and failed to recognize a "public interest exception to the disclosure of public information." News editors were appalled. "Is the public better served by a complaisant public service, or one that sheds light from time to time on things government would rather were kept from public eyes?" asked the Ottawa *Citizen*. Rosenberg went an "extraordinary and unsupportable distance" by demanding the name of the informant, the *Globe* said, in wishing the union well.

In the face of Rosenberg's order, an alleged threat to blacklist the firm from all government contracts, and a "vacuum search warrant" to turn their offices upside down, Scott's firm turned over sealed documents to the court, pending an appeal from Rosenberg's order. One lawyer quit the firm to protest its decision. "They were saving their own ass," says Kevin Wilson, in their panic that the union's sources would be found out.

The union scurried to protect its source, while over at the ministry an OPP "thumbscrew squad" was closing in. The deadline for the union's hopeless court appeal was looming. And O'Flynn stepped down as union president, replaced at a fall convention by James Clancy.

"The government had a gun to our head," says Bekerman. Clancy offered to meet and draw up an out-of-court settlement on overcrowding. The government said it wanted the documents first. Clancy said the issues of substance had to be dealt with first. The other side blinked. "The Tory approach was not to slit throats and leave corpses around, but to stop just short and cut a deal," says Bekerman. A secret deal was arranged. Mr. X lost his job, but the government dropped criminal charges against him. The government agreed to put $150 million into new reform facilities, and to give guards a say in their design. The union agreed to drop its lawsuit. "And the government never found out who Mr. Y or Z (other union informants) were," says Wilson, now a senior policy advisor at Management Board.

Mr. X was subsequently hired by OPSEU, where he researched union proposals for new treatment facilities, until he could find his feet in a new area of work. His nerves shot by a year on tenterhooks, his career in a field he dedicated his life to in ruins, his marriage destroyed by the strain, he suffered a mental breakdown.

Social unionism is not just about the soft side of the labour movement that goes down easy with the public. It brought OPSEU in touch with the same kind of courage, will and sacrifice as was needed to build industrial unions.

Tree hugger

Civil servants are to be seen and not heard. That's been the case since 1947, when premier Drew introduced the oath of secrecy binding civil servants to keep everything they found out about government confidential. That oath, and laws passed in the 1960s and '70s against political action by individuals or their union, drastically limited civil servants' rights to free speech. OPSEU's fight for free speech, highlighted during the Free The Servants campaign of the mid-1970s, focused on the denial of political freedom, and on the right to work for or speak on behalf of a cause touching partisan politics.

In the early 1980s, the heyday of non-partisan public interest and environmental politics, free speech became more controversial. It touched on the rights and duties of civil servants to blow the whistle on wrongdoing. The right to speak on politics concerned tackling government from the outside. The right to speak on policy and practice was about fighting on the inside.

Don MacAlpine, a soft-spoken, shy forester with brooding brown eyes, worked for the Ministry of Natural Resources in Nipigon, centre of the logging industry in the northwest. After graduating in forestry, he joined the ministry in 1981, hoping to work in replanting and conservation. "I always thought there were enough people cutting trees," he says. His manager, George Merrick, was an outspoken critic of clearcutting, and knew MacAlpine's beliefs when he hired him.

The two were up against what MacAlpine calls "the old boys' network" in the ministry. "We were not allowed to give a realistic analysis, but only one that didn't stir controversy," he says. Hard figures on what was happening to the forest were hard to come by in the ministry, which relied on airplane scans updated by computers, with few on-the-ground surveys – the kind of "armchair forestry" that dominated government science following installation of the Committee on Government Productivity. After a one-week intensive ground survey of an area proposed for licensing to a major logging company, MacAlpine was convinced that the area couldn't sustain one quarter of the logging that was to be allowed. The license would violate the ministry policy of "sustained yield," he reported. That finding didn't sit well with senior ministry officials, who issued a memo to rush the permit through, so the logging company could use it as banking collateral. When MacAlpine raised his concerns with supervisors, he got nowhere.

In 1982, he provided his MPP, Jack Stokes, with ministry correspondence urging that the logging permit be rushed through. "There was no use going through channels. The pressures against me were coming through channels," MacAlpine says. "I was so disgusted, I didn't really care. Canada was supposed to be a free system and anything that was to be done should be done openly and freely and fairly," he says. He expected to get in some trouble, but didn't expect to get fired.

When Stokes released the material to the legislature, MacAlpine was hauled onto the carpet. Until then, MacAlpine hadn't contacted OPSEU. He saw the issue as a purely professional problem, not a workers' rights problem. In March, in full view of his fellow workers, he was fired for breaking his oath of secrecy and ordered to clear his desk. "That was designed to humiliate me and set an example for anyone else," he says. George Merrick was demoted. MacAlpine went to the Association of Professional Foresters for help and support, but the organization refused to pass judgment. "They couldn't do piss-all, but wouldn't admit it," says MacAlpine. Then he contacted the union.

In September, hearings began on his grievance charging unfair dismissal. Lawyer Alick Ryder turned it into a case for "whistleblowers' rights," the right to make information gathered at public expense about decisions harmful to the public available to the public. In November 1982, arbitrator Ted Jolliffe, former leader of the CCF when it had a shot at power in the 1940s, ruled that the government's decision was "not consistent with the principle of open government," and ordered MacAlpine reinstated with back pay. Jolliffe allowed that MacAlpine might have tried harder to go through channels, but ruled that a proper penalty was one week's suspension without pay.

Management appealed the arbitration decision, and refused to take MacAlpine back. In September, 1984, the arbitration decision was confirmed, and the government was ordered to cover back pay for the time MacAlpine lost on appeal. "I felt guilty getting paid for doing nothing," MacAlpine says. "It was kind of demeaning." MacAlpine became a union steward, and worked with OPSEU on a later campaign to establish proper logging plans for Ontario.

MacAlpine's case alerted the union to a new range of workers' and citizens' rights. "It showed the ability of the union to protect a very important function for civil servants, to be able to blow the whistle in cases of serious abuse and still keep their jobs," says Ryder. Shortly after the award came down, the OPSEU administration under James Clancy began a campaign to define whistleblowing as a crucial ingredient of activist democracy. The minority Liberal-NDP government of 1985 committed itself to "sunshine laws" that would open up government communications. The Ontario Law Reform Commission endorsed the union's position. Government workers should have the right to speak out on both general policy issues and specific cases of wrongdoing. Unfortunately, this was the only item of the reform accord signed by Liberals and New Democrats that was not carried out. It was left to the NDP government elected in 1990 to finally legislate political rights and whistleblowing rules.

Workers for social responsibility

Welfare workers, like the clients they serve, are paid to keep poverty out of sight and out of mind. The two groups are also expected to be on opposite sides of the government fence. Workers watch out for welfare abuse. Welfare recipients blame field workers for government abuse. In the 1980s, however, the two groups worked together to develop a fundamental critique of the Ontario welfare system. This was not mere whistleblowing against individual wrongdoing. This was workers and clients telling the government its entire system was wrongdoing.

Nick DiSalle started as a family benefits officer in Toronto's troubled Parkdale area in 1976. He was one of a score of "new hires" who came as liberal thinkers straight from a university campus.

Assigned to work with Italian cases, he was given three days' in-house training, three days in the field with an experienced worker, then left on his own. He thought his job was to help welfare recipients get back on their feet. "In fact, I was just checking to see if they were still poor and eligible. That was quite a shock to me," he says. With a caseload of 350, he spent four days a week in the field, handing out forms in 40 to 50 visits a day. One day a week, he stayed in the office to field calls from welfare recipients. "You never stopped hearing ringing bells for seven hours," he says.

For his first four months, DiSalle was a "good boy." His supervisor held up his record of visits and completed forms as an example for others at a training conference. By the end of the year, DiSalle was the "worst" worker in the office. He spent too much time trying to help individual clients cope with life and get off welfare.

There were four types of workers in government welfare offices then, DiSalle says. The "idealists" started as do-gooders. A do-gooder who got taken advantage of by a client became type two, a "cynic," proud not to be taken for a fool, and keen on policing welfare cheats. The "neutrals" just wanted to do a job and go home. The "shit disturbers" thought the welfare system was rotten, and turned to the union for protection when they went public with their complaints. DiSalle's local was built by this last group, many of whom went on to major leadership roles within the union.

In 1978, the disturbers demanded a separate local of welfare field workers instead of a composite local they shared with clerks. James Clancy became local president, and turned the local into a centre of agitation for welfare reform. In 1979, the local published a pamphlet called "People First," which detailed the crisis of a welfare system that trapped the poor in below-poverty level incomes and gave field workers no time to offer support. The workload complaint was bolstered by government consultants who recommended that workers serve no more than 200 cases. The local used the report to launch a drive to have wages reclassified in keeping with their heavy and difficult loads. In the ten years the grievance was on the boil the local was able to unify all "types" of field workers. With solid backing, "we lost the fear of discipline," says DiSalle. When managers told a staff meeting that they wouldn't meet with the union to resolve workload problems, a hundred workers left and joined Sean O'Flynn outside.

In the 1980s, the Ministry of Community and Social Services tried to implement a major recommendation of the Henderson report that would pass on provincial welfare expenditures to municipalities. Until then, municipalities took care of emergency and short-term cases, and the province picked up responsibility for people with long-term problems or chronic disabilities. Under the Henderson-inspired scheme known as "integration," municipalities were to take over a unified list of all welfare recipients.

Integration upset social assistance recipients, because municipalities paid less than the province and sometimes imposed humiliating means tests. Many municipalities didn't like the change, if only because they would get stuck with the whole bill for social assistance. Worse, they feared, generous municipalities would face an influx of welfare recipients fleeing "cheapskate" towns. In the name of integration and bringing welfare delivery closer to the local community, the scheme led to patchwork standards. Welfare recipients could feel pressure to migrate to cities unable to offer a support network. Last but not least, integration would result in a mass layoff of provincial welfare field workers.

Field workers didn't have the resources for a province-wide campaign. They were only one small unit within the giant ComSoc ministry. The union's ministry team wasn't a vehicle for them, as it had been for correctional workers. Clancy demanded that OPSEU fund "new-style divisions" (unlike the divisions that existed when OPSEU was founded) that allowed dispersed occupational groups to organize. This idea didn't fly with John O'Grady, O'Flynn's senior advisor. He saw "new-style divisions" as part of a drift toward "separate-deal unionism," at a time when OPSEU needed to pull together. He worried that OPSEU would turn into something like the Public Service Alliance of Canada, a federated union with little overall cohesion or vision. O'Grady's critics said he was just nervous about creating independent power bases directly linked to members.

The field workers got their division and some funding, however, and organized cavalcades to municipalities the province wanted in the integration project. They also organized Workers for Social Responsibility. Allied with welfare rights organizers who opposed integration, they wanted major increases in welfare payments, and caseloads on a scale that would allow field workers to support, not just report on, their clients. It was an early example of a new form of union action, coalitions between workers and client groups normally pitted against one another. Welfare field workers and recipients published a series of *Insider Reports* characterizing the welfare system as a vicious circle of enforced poverty and helplessness.

In 1988, major positions first put forward by Workers For Social Responsibility were accepted in the Thomson Report, a landmark study that called for a major overhaul of social assistance programs to encourage independence. The report also called for genuine "integration" of welfare services, via provincial funding of universal programs. That recommendation, first promoted by OPSEU, was eventually addressed by the NDP government in 1993.

Women's rights: Don't call me Lady

Once upon a time, the Ontario government used to discriminate against women, the co-ordinator for Women Crown Employees' Equality Programs admitted in her 1975 report. Until 1964, for instance, supervisors could specify if they wanted a male or female employee. Thankfully, those days were over. "It is apparent then, that most of the formal barriers to equal opportunity for women Crown employees were eliminated during the 1960s," the report claimed.

The report glossed over a few details. Like the mid-1970s average pay gap of $8,000 a year between men and women in the public service. Or the fact that only 36 of 698 middle-management trainees and five of 311 senior-management trainees were women at the time the cheery report was published.

The union, for its part, did not deal with many of these issues until quite late in the game. Before women came to the fore in the workplace, they had to come to the fore in their union. While the equality programs administrator was celebrating the long way women had come in government employment, women government workers were just starting to organize. Over the next decade, they developed a range of new union issues, structures and goals that changed the face of OPSEU.

In the bad old days, the CSAO opposed some instances of discrimination against women. It had a hand in the 1971 change of government policy that allowed women to take 12 weeks' unpaid leave after their second child. Until then, women with two children were expected to stay home for good. Now, women can get leave after "all visits of the stork," *CSAO News* reported. The next year, CSAO pushed a woman worker's grievance to judicial review to win her rights to job security after a period on maternity leave. CSAO also fought for pensions that gave women the same right as men to extend pension benefits to surviving spouses.

CSAO started pushing for equal pay for equal work during the 1960s. Though a far cry from today's concept of equal pay for work of equal value, the tradition led newly-formed OPSEU to turn down an invitation to co-sponsor a 1974 conference on affirmative action with the Women Crown Employees Office. The union denounced the program as tokenism, and raised the profile of its campaign to win equal pay for women cleaners, hairdressers and tailors in provincial institutions.

There is no indication that CSAO ever confronted sexual harassment of women by managers or co-workers. Women were left to handle that on their own. As late as 1970, female nurses in Ministry of Health chest clinics were sent home if they wore red nail polish, according to clinic staffer John Williamson. The rule in the clinics was that women were nurses and men were technicians. When the first woman broke ranks and took a job as a technician, her male co-workers swore up a storm to make her uncomfortable. "Teamsters couldn't do better than what they were dishing out," Williamson says. It didn't last for long. "I don't know what the fuck you're up to, but if it's for my benefit, you can bugger off," the woman told them her first day on the job.

As with the women's movement across North America, women began organizing within CSAO, and later OPSEU, to protest discrimination within the movement, not from outside. "Our focus was male domination of the union, not the workplace," says Debbie Field, the union's first woman staffer assigned to women's organizing. Sexism within the union was worse than in the workplace, says Susie Vallance, who says she was propositioned by a senior staffer when she came to speak to an executive board meeting about the problems of college support staff in 1978. "It was quite acceptable to prey on women," she says.

Women's issues were a new test for unions in the 1970s. They weren't just another set of issues to challenge the boss with. They forced unions to deal with what they were about. That may be why women's issues were so often labelled "divisive." Harassment and belittling of women's needs are "part of our history, and the men better never ever forget what they did to us," says Bev Allan, a leader of college support staff. Dealing with women's needs also required special measures to help members become directly involved. "Women are too busy to be militant," says veteran North Bay clerk Heather Murray. "They're too busy doing three jobs, working at the office, looking after the house, raising the kids, and doing the shopping." On-site meetings, meetings at lunchbreaks, union-financed babysitting were all needed, she says.

Women's issues were treated as a bit of a joke throughout the early 1970s. A *CSAO News* note on women applying for the armed forces was headlined "Women's Lib Goes Wild." A report on "the hand that rocks the cradle" and "feminine presence" at the 1972 convention referred to "one lady" who said the union should cover babysitting expenses so women could take part in CSAO. Only four of CSAO's 28 board members were women, the "lady" complained. Her motion was defeated. That year, *CSAO News* reported that "CSAO strikes blow for women's lib" by persuading the government to address women as Ms. Employee files had so many wrong listings for Miss or Mrs. that the union convinced managers to "invoke the Union spirit of equality and simultaneously strike a blow for women's lib" and settle for Ms. The entranceway to CSAO conferences featured placards announcing "activities for ladies," says Ann Wells, a support staff member from Algonquin College in Ottawa. When she objected that some ladies had come as delegates, not just spouses accompanying their menfolk, the convention declared her an "honorary lady."

The new generation of 1970s women activists also had their difficulties with the handful of leading women who preceded them. There was a big difference between women activists and women's activists. The women who made it in the early days had learned to hold their own in a man's world. For them, sexism was "a way of the world," says Vallance, and they made a point of attacking any "special favours" for their sex. The new wave of women activists insisted on changes that encouraged all women to take part in the union. Sexism is the problem, participation is the solution, the saying went.

In the first phase of women's organizing, it meant a brand new approach that led to support groups and caucuses. Many women felt a need for support groups to help overcome socialization and social pressures that undermined confidence and self-esteem.

Pride in women's gifts did give some women a can-do sense of themselves. Ruth Lunel, a retired Oshawa revenue clerk renowned over the decades for her many volunteer efforts, always felt that women made better organizers than men. "If men can't run a household, how can they run a country?" she asks. Ann Wells, an early president of her local, took pride in her special eye for details that make meetings work. "Women recognize the underlying flaw in something that's happening that men have a tendency to just walk past, because they've always had this support role behind them that took care of all the little details," she says.

But most women needed a boost. They had to explain to husbands that they weren't put on earth to make them comfortable, and to their kids that mom was trying to build a better world for them to grow up in, says Helen MacNeil, long active among clerical workers. Men never had to deal with those nagging doubts, she says.

Sticking up for themselves was still new to many women activists of the 1960s and '70s. Pam Lee proofed high school exams at the Ministry of Education in the mid-1960s, when "everything had to be correct." If she let an error through, "Mr. Burroughs would say he was disappointed. I would feel so dreadful at that. He'd do it so gently, but I'd feel like I'd made the most appalling mistake in my life." Secretaries then were told that they didn't need as much money as men, and they believed it, says Heather Murray. "We were docile women. We accepted it. That was before the days of feminism and the women's movement. If a man told you that's the way it was, that's the way it was." Working as a clerk at the North Bay Psychiatric Hospital, Murray plugged equal pay for nurses, but that was special, she says. Nurses were professional. "We didn't have a lot of self-esteem," she says. It wasn't easy for women to confront their bosses, says Jill Morgan, a former secretary at St. Clair College in Windsor, now a union staffer. Raised to be polite and likeable and to do for others, not taught how to build support for themselves, "they have to be pushed really hard to grieve." She got over that in 1976, when she was insulted by a downgrading of her classification. "It was the day that changed my life," she says. "Before, I thought I was doing union work for others."

❈

A generation of women activists

In Toronto, women began meeting in a Region 5 women's caucus in 1975, spearheaded by a dinner meeting of women after a community college faculty division meeting. The caucus started as a support group for the first generation of women activists who wanted to rise together as women. Meeting in living rooms, they became fast friends who encouraged each other, listened through rough drafts of speeches, and heckled each other in preparation for the big day at convention. "Mainly it was empowering women, realizing that yes, you do have power, and yes, you can do anything you put your mind to, and yes, you have a lot of power if you work together," says former Ministry of Environment clerk Joyce Gulbis.

Unlike most union bodies, the caucus had no formal rules, structures or leaders. Invitations went out through the grapevine, and "we just got together," says Eileen Burrows, president of the faculty local at Centennial College. "Networking is just the way women relate to one another. As little girls that's what we did, and we just grew up doing things outside the structure because the structure didn't accommodate us," she says. "There was no money, no perks and no recognition, so the people who came out were truly committed, and we went away with these huge jobs and we did them," says George Brown teacher Susan Stylianos. "We operated as women, and other labels were secondary," says Vallance. "We had things to do and didn't have time to deal with politics. We were all so disenfranchised, there was no issue that divided us. And we didn't care who we offended."

Women organized a formal caucus in 1976, when Maxine Jones issued a call at the convention mikes for women to get together. The next year the caucus convinced the convention to endorse a new staff position in the union to co-ordinate equal opportunities. A first for any union in the country, the new staffer reported directly to the union president to ensure that women's needs were taken into account at all levels of the union. Charlie Darrow, with his wicked sense of humour, appointed a male, Neil Louttit, to the job. Louttit wrote OPSEU's first report exposing the female wage ghetto. He recommended that a woman be hired to replace him.

Debbie Field, a prominent socialist-feminist teaching at Sheridan College, applied for the job as the candidate of the Toronto women's caucus. Women are the most proletarian group in the union, and feminists know how to get them active, Field said in her job interview. O'Flynn went for it. OPSEU was very open that way, Field says. "It was such a new union that it didn't have a hardened bureaucracy. There was open space, a sense of a frontier union."

Field's term as equal ops co-ordinator was traumatic for her and the male staffers she confronted. Her first demand was a $12,000 a year pay cut so she could be equal to the workers she represented. "This drove the staff reps crazy," she says. "They knew the scorn I held for them as fat cats." Male staffers retaliated by posting Toronto *Sun* pinups on her office door.

The style of those days was aggressive. Gentle assertiveness came later. "We grabbed unionists by their lapels, and said you've got to do this or you're shit," says Field. They trained to take on hecklers and take over mikes at union gatherings, to overwhelm the opposition, to push their resolutions through, mainly because of the hostile reception they received when they first raised questions around sexual harassment. "The sexism just exploded. It was absolutely devastating," says Burrows. "'What do these bitches want?' It was really, really dreadful." The boot camp training paid off. "Once you kicked them in the balls, their hearts started to listen," says Bev Allan. Debates within the union got hot and heavy. To cool out one staffer who made a sexist remark at a staff meeting, staff rep Barb Marshall poured a jug of water over him. It was a time to struggle. In 1979, Heather Murray denounced OPSEU for hiring so few women staffers, and urged all women "to band together and fight this 'female tokenism.'"

That style didn't take account of the slow, wrenching and deeply personal changes men had to work through, says Debbie Field, now executive director of Foodshare, but for those braving the opposition "it was so hard the other way. There were so many catcalls." Though the women's caucus talked about the gentler style that women would bring to union discussions, women had to be hard to stand up to the hecklers, she says. "We thought it was a suit you could put on and take off," Field says. "It was an intensely hostile environment," says another major organizer of convention floor battles. "A foot away from me when I spoke against sexual harassment, this man with a beer belly was yelling at me 'Give me a break, you bitch.' You had to be really brave," she says. "We developed our own stereotypes of men, because those who spoke at conventions were Neanderthals," says Vallance, now in charge of employment equity programs at Seneca College. "We sure hadn't been exposed to other men. They stayed silent."

As equal ops co-ordinator, Field wrote a regular column for the union's newspaper that took as its slogan the turn-of-the-century cry of women garment workers: "Yes, it's bread we fight for, but we fight for roses too." Her columns dealt with a wide range of subjects, from health and safety, to electronic monitoring of clerical workers, to the need for union-sponsored daycare at all union meetings. Her best article, she says, was on making it easier to be active. She plugged the need for union-financed child care at all union gatherings, for meetings timed to the needs of working women who had a second job as homemaker to rush home to. "The union had to be transformed by feminism in order to make unionism survive," she says.

"I was conducting a kamikaze raid on OPSEU to make it a tool of women instead of male dominance," Field says, but "my failure was that I remained at the level of ideology." That went over well at radical conferences, but it didn't do much to organize women around specific changes they needed to fight for, she says. When she set out to organize women's caucuses in every union location, she began in Sudbury, heartland of the militant proletariat. Field mailed out 2,000 notices for her meeting. Three women came. "I was totally devastated," she says.

The women's caucus made steady progress. In 1978, the convention agreed to support equal pay for work of equal value, and to pay childcare expenses for all union meetings. Women had already lobbied the executive board. Darrow stared at his fellow board members and said: "The time has come, and we're going to have to do this anyway," Eileen Burrows recalls. In 1979, in their third convention try, women convinced delegates to outlaw sexual harassment within the union. That year,

OPSEU also donated $10,000 to women strikers at Fleck's near London. Unknown to most OPSEU members, the factory owner was the same James Fleck who staffed the Committee on Government Productivity and the Henderson report.

But the pace of change in OPSEU was too slow for Field. After two years, she wrote what she calls a "terrible" farewell, announcing her intention to work in a steel mill and do something serious about smashing female job ghettoes. Some of her closest friends were so insulted by what they felt was her snub to office workers that they didn't talk to her for a year.

Field was replaced by Frances Lankin. Lankin was not a feminist when she was hired. She was opposed by the Toronto women's caucus. But she brought her experience as one of the first women recruited to the Don Jail.

"Being a token is a horrible way to be introduced to a job," she says, a reference to the 1976 affirmative action program that put three inexperienced women in an all-male jail. Her first day on the job, an inmate stripping down in front of her stared at her breasts and said: "I don't much like women working here, but you do have a couple of interesting points about you." With the quick response time that now helps her in legislative debates, she stared back at his crotch and said: "It's too bad you don't." Once she settled in, Lankin hung out with male guards in a pool hall. When a new guard asked what a woman was doing there, she approached him cue in hand and said "That's right. You got something to say about it, rookie?" In an occupation where seniority counted more than sex, that broke the ice, Lankin says. When other women joined the staff and faced a rough initiation from the male guards, she asked what was going on. Why are you giving other women such a hard time? "Well, Frances," one of them told her, "you're different, you're one of the guys." That's when it clicked for her that being an affirmative-action exception or one of the guys didn't make anything easier for other women.

Lankin's personal style helped her focus on the transition to the second phase of women's rights activity, based on more formal structuring of women's participation within the union. "Frances had a major skill at taking a divided crowd and bridging troubled waters. She was a fabulous facilitator and natural counsellor, who always came through with what held us together just when a situation was about to blow," says Susan Stylianos, Toronto's representative on the Provincial Women's Committee in the early 1980s.

For all the difficulties, the gains made by OPSEU women – a staffer dedicated to women's issues, child care subsidies, the ban on sexual harassment, and a formalized provincial women's committee – put OPSEU far out in front of other unions. Partly, that's because OPSEU had more women members than most unions. By 1979, 49.3 per cent of public sector union members were women, compared to 29.3 per cent in the private sector. OPSEU was also a very "meeting" kind of union. Unions with decentralized bargaining don't have many province-wide meetings to do business at. OPSEU activists are frequent flyers, with a score of bargaining and ministry team meetings that give women opportunities to exchange notes and phone numbers. And the leadership didn't set itself against women's rights activists. O'Flynn, Pauline Seville recalled, preferred working with women, finding them more prepared to work as a team than males.

❊

The Provincial Women's Committee

Success bred its own problems, and one of these was structures. As the Toronto women's caucus became one of the places to be, it was targeted by different factions in the union and made a springboard for union careers. There were "too many mandates, or womandates, whatever," says Joyce Gulbis. Pam Lee, then president of the Queen's Park Area Council of downtown Toronto locals, wasn't sure what to think. She didn't like the in-fighting and careerism, but "that was part of what we were trying to do, move women up in the organization."

The lure of convention victories and new union posts narrowed the feminist critique of how unions operated, says former Sheridan College teacher Linda Briskin, later a prominent scholar in the field of women's studies. For Briskin, the real challenge was about transforming the union from a service institution to a participatory one. That required feminist leadership politics, not just women leaders, making leaders accountable to their base, not just making sure they were the right mix of sexes, she says.

Briskin was responsible for *OPSEU News*' appearance as a cheap pulp tabloid from 1975 to 1977. When she had asked to write up her report of a CLC women's conference for *OPSEU News*, she was told that it would cost too much if all members demanded the same right. She convinced a convention that the paper should be produced from cheap pulp so all could participate.

The debate among women over the relationship between participation and accountability came to a head in the campaign to fund the women's committee established at the 1980 convention.

Most women's rights activists supported creation of an ongoing structure committed to women's issues and designed to bring women's perspectives to all structures of the union. The Provincial Women's Committee (PWC) was designed to funnel, not entrap, women's energies. To be effective, however, it needed money to pay for travel. To get money, it needed structure and status.

After the 1980 convention, organizing to fund the PWC began. Within a month, 50 women activists took a funding proposal to the executive board. A vote to provide $20,000 lost. A second vote to provide $14,000 lost. A third vote to provide $12,000 barely won. Maxine Jones, Debbie Julian and Ev Sammons voted against, as did Sean O'Flynn. A second row developed over whether the PWC should be independent and elected, as desired by most women's activists, or appointed by the executive board.

There's some debate over why women on the board opposed these motions. "They were for themselves and the perks they got from being on the board," says one women's caucus organizer. "They never supported other women unless they were malleable pieces of clay." Others say they were worried that these structures would segregate women into one safe slot within the union, keep them from taking leadership of locals and bargaining teams, disenfranchise untitled women who'd been free to drop in on less formal groups like the Toronto Women's Caucus, or turn the women's cause into another layer of union bureaucracy rather than free women up for advocacy. Once women gained union recognition of their needs, they brought the union onside to deal with discrimination they faced in the workplace and society.

Women put their stamp on OPSEU's evolution toward social unionism. It couldn't have been otherwise. There was a social and demographic revolution in the 1970s that hit the public sector with full force. For the first time, women became long-term wage-earners, interrupting their paid jobs only for brief periods to bear children. One of the fastest-breaking social revolutions in human history, it changed the reality of women, families, society and workplaces faster than it changed social institutions or the attitudes of men, politicians and managers. That meant there were no neat boundaries around what were personal, workplace and political issues. Harassment was an issue of personal relations, workplace power and human rights legislation. Child care was an issue of family relations, workplace accessibility and legislation. Paid maternity leave, won by OPSEU just prior to wage restraint laws in 1982, became a matter for union contracts and social legislation.

Abortion, not on its face a workplace or union issue, became more than what it began as, a personal moral issue, because it crystallized the place of free choice in women's lives. For feminists, the abortion controversy became the touchstone of OPSEU's willingness to stand its ground for a woman's right to make choices in her life. When Dr. Henry Morgentaler was named guest of honour for a women's luncheon at one conference, "we knew we had made it," says Bev Allan. "In true women's fashion, we did it on our lunch time. The men would never do something like that."

At the 1984 OPSEU convention, the women's caucus organized a breakfast to rally for the expected floor fight on abortion. Of 150 who attended, 147 voted to take on the fight. When the resolutions committee ruled that the issue shouldn't come up for debate, a revolt from the floor overruled the decision and put it back on the agenda. "We had the mikes stacked from one end of the hall to the other, spoke, moved closure, and it carried," says one women's organizer. "It was the real event in terms of exercising power. We controlled it. We forced it onto the floor when some of the brass opposed it. We even had a woman opposed to abortion move the motion on the grounds that women had to stand together on the right to choose. It was exhilarating, a real marker time." The motion supported women's right to choose, and instructed *OPSEU News* to carry three articles explaining the decision.

OPSEU also tried to use its resources to champion the cause of child care. In 1982, OPSEU took 11 daycare workers out on strike against Mini-Skools, an Alabama-based profit-making chain, and tried to turn the strike into what some critics call a "showboat expedition" for universal, non-profit child care.

The union's bargaining team pushed Toronto Mini-Skool franchisers to cough up the highest wage offer in the chain. It wasn't good enough, and workers voted to strike in three locations along the northern and western rim of Metro Toronto. To make sure innocent parents and kids didn't get caught in the crossfire between the union and employer, OPSEU financed an alternative daycare centre run by strikers. Fees from the centre topped up strike pay. Many workers made more on strike than they did at their regular job.

"There was nothing ineffective about the strike," says Peter Slee, who set up the alternative centre. "The fact of the matter was that there wasn't a chance to win. The owner was losing his shirt, but he was prepared to take the punch." Few strikers had an economic incentive to bargain an end to the strike, he says, and activists crusading for publicly-funded child care, who had a vested interest in keeping the political issue at a boil, had a say in bargaining-team strategy sessions. "It didn't flow from any reality. It was a political thing, and we got caught in it," Slee says. The union tried to make a cause célèbre out of lousy wages, when child-care policy was too big to deal with through one strike, says Pauline Seville. The view the public got wasn't good either. Picket lines, far from where most union supporters lived or worked, were modestly attended. Picket-line scuffles developed between strikers and parents who preferred taking their children to strikebound centres.

"The union was impaling itself," says Peter Warrian, assigned to settle it four days into his new job as chief of staff. The issue was "overpoliticized into a holy war for daycare across the province on behalf of 11 underpaid women on Dixie Road." The final settlement was humiliating. The union accepted a phased-in return of strikers that allowed the owner to keep strikebreakers on staff.

Sex in the office

A new sense of women's needs changed the way bargaining was done for office workers.

Until the mid-1970s, the office rule of thumb in the civil service was that men, who could write, were clerks, while women, who could type, were secretaries. When OPSEU and the government agreed to eight bargaining categories in 1975, clerks and office workers each got their own bargaining teams. The government could pay higher wages to clerks, who were breadwinners, without having to pass the raises on to secretaries, who were, in the language of the time, "working for pin money." Secretaries never had the battle jail guards had, to get their own team. No one wanted them. Their low wages dragged down anyone associated with them. "It was the Not In My Back Yard syndrome," says chief negotiator Andy Todd.

Job definitions and wage rates defied logic. The titles got longer as they got more out of whack with reality. Art Lane, for instance, was a "clerk 4, atypical" when he chaired a job evaluation team attempting to negotiate changes to the outdated classification system in 1976. He proposed new job evaluations to eliminate discrepancies in white-collar jobs. Union leaders opposed his idea, he said, for fear that new classifications would lead to red-circling of male wages. "Equal pay was a very radical concept then," he says, and adds that management shot down any notion that the union could have a say over job classifications.

But technology made any distinction between clerks and office workers meaningless. When computers became standard and data entry was semi-automated, women filled all office and clerical jobs. Men went on to keyboarding in management. Regardless of skill level, however, women with job titles that were once filled by men still made more than women with job titles that had always been assigned to women. Pay grievances formed a backlog that spilled over into scores of "special cases" during wage bargaining. It was a headache for managers. The Tories, looking for some way to respond to the demands of the women's movement, were finding the old system embarrassing.

In 1980, the government signalled that it was ready to re-open talks on a new classification system. O'Flynn turned thumbs down, claiming the union wouldn't have enough say, Todd claims. "O'Flynn was an all-or-nothing type, and he often got nothing," says Todd. "It's like being a kamikaze pilot. It's wonderfully effective, but after a while you run out of pilots." Some say that senior union officials, impressed by the take-charge style of male Corrections workers, weren't much interested in doing something for women who weren't prepared to take militant job action.

Talks about merging office and clerical groups didn't get underway until 1983, when the union raised about 100 special cases. The issue wasn't about equal pay with men, by then long departed. It was about equal pay among women. Divided, they could not focus on new benchmarks that could be compared to men's work and men's pay. The categories were merged in 1986.

There was a common "body language" to the issues women brought to OPSEU. Escaping a fate as a sex object meant dealing with sexual harassment and abortion. Child care and paid maternity leave meant dealing with reasonable accommodation to pregnancy and breast-feeding. Health and safety completed the circle of security, dignity and privacy in the face of technological harassment.

By the late 1970s, secretaries and clerks worked under the glaring eyes of video display terminals. These transformed white-collar workplaces almost overnight. The huge capital outlay for computerized equipment, relative to typewriters, meant they had to be operated continuously to pay for themselves, forcing women workers to be more specialized, more sedentary, more ghettoized than ever. There was no talking back to VDTs. Many clerical functions in government offices were subject to machine monitoring, computers that snitched on washroom breaks, errors and slow input.

Bob DeMatteo, OPSEU's health and safety specialist, began receiving random calls from secretaries worried about rashes, sore eyes, stiff arms, or the health of babies they were carrying.

Until then, "workplace health and safety had been focussed on the industrial sector, on problems that men suffered," says DeMatteo. "Women's work looked safe and sedentary, so when we started to look into problems women faced in the workplace, people laughed. We focussed on VDTs because they showed the problems of women's powerlessness most glaringly. They were working under quotas. They were mechanically monitored. Many had to raise their hands and ask their employer's permission to go to the bathroom. I started reading studies from the United States and Scandinavia that showed the physical problems from radiation and from overuse of finger and wrist muscles."

DeMatteo encouraged workers to use the union to back up their right to refuse unsafe work. The result was a precedent-setting string of arbitration victories. Dorothy Moran, a secretary at George Brown College, refused to work on her VDT, which she blamed for rashes on her face and neck. "It was the first work refusal by an office worker in the country," says DeMatteo. When Moran's manager suspended her, "we were down there with gumboots," he says. The Ministry of Labour inspector gave George Brown's VDTs a clean bill of health, but the union insisted on the letter of the law, which gave workers the right to refuse what they reasonably considered unsafe work. In the next college-support collective agreement, workers won an automatic right to transfer out of VDT work stations without loss of pay.

VDTs touched a nerve among people concerned about radiation and the recently exposed role of government and company scientists in covering up the damage done by uranium and asbestos. Trust your "gut instincts," because government experts lie "without exception," leading U.S. investigative journalist Paul Brodeur told an OPSEU rally for clerks in 1981. The Ontario government claimed that VDTs gave off less radiation than a partner's kiss or hug. "Are they trying to reassure public servants, or scare them into abstinence?" he asked.

The gut instincts of pregnant women told them VDT radiation was unsafe. In 1980, shortly after she became pregnant, civil service VDT operator Helen Barrs read a Toronto *Sun* article, "Pregnant Belles Can Refuse VDT Use," reporting the victory of the telephone workers' union. She got a note from her doctor asking her manager to transfer her to other work while she was pregnant.

To humour her and give her peace of mind, her manager gave her a transfer to a lower-paid job. He was doing her a "favour," since there was no scientific evidence of any danger to her health.

Barrs grieved, and the battle was on to prove the health and safety effects of VDTs. The government called in its expert witnesses, who testified that VDTs were as safe as televisions and microwave ovens. The arbitrator wasn't impressed. DDT, birth control pills, and thalidomide had all been pronounced safe by scientists. The public could be excused for noting that scientists lined up for whoever paid. Barrs' right to reject the views of scientists was part of her right to refuse work she considered unsafe, the arbitrator said. The burden of proof shouldn't fall on workers to provide body counts documenting their fears, he ruled in 1981. The decision established for the first time in Ontario that believing VDTs can cause birth defects is a reasonable ground for a pregnant woman to refuse to work in front of a VDT screen. O'Flynn was jubilant.

In 1982, DeMatteo convinced O'Flynn that publicizing office health and safety problems could help in bargaining. That gave him fuller access to union resources than normally go to health and safety issues. DeMatteo and Lankin toured the province speaking to "brownbag lunch meetings" on job security and safety during technological change. "Health issues grabbed our members' attention more, because it was more real," DeMatteo says. "Workers started wearing union buttons saying 'the chips are down.'" On the eve of contract talks, DeMatteo released information on a government worker who developed cataracts from VDTs. The story was on the front page when bargaining began. For the first time, the contract gave the union rights to negotiate the effects of technological change, one of the first cracks in the monopoly over technology granted to management by CECBA.

In the course of his research on VDTs, DeMatteo stumbled across a 60 per cent miscarriage rate among women court workers at Toronto's old city hall. He laid a memo trap for government inspectors who refused to prosecute the government, and filed a complaint that became front page news. The union campaign won a "cadillac cleanup" at the old city hall, DeMatteo says, featuring ventilation to lower the density of electromagnetic radiation and radiation shields on all VDTs.

An OPSEU media barrage helped make VDTs one of the hot labour issues of the day. DeMatteo worked with the NDP's Richard Johnston to develop laws outlining a model safety code for VDTs. DeMatteo also wrote the standard text on VDTs, *Terminal Shock*, in 1984.

Love's labour lost

Militant unionism didn't come naturally to institutional care workers in psychiatric hospitals and centres for the developmentally handicapped. Their wages were low, about $6.40 an hour in the early 1980s, sure signs of the low status of the largely female workforce and the people they cared for. But they were scattered across small-town Ontario and divided between two giant ministries, Health and Community Services, that had hundreds of pressing causes. They lacked the esprit de corps and collective discipline of correctional workers, and their ability to create a high-profile crisis for one small, single-issue ministry.

As caregivers, they had a hard time detaching their emotions for their clients from their needs as workers. "There's a very personal element to the job," says Joyce Earl, a counsellor at the Rideau Regional Centre in Smiths Falls. Staff often referred to their clients, many of whom had to be diapered and fed into their advanced years, as their "babies," she says. "I have never seen anything like the love those workers have for their clients," says Hans van Beinum, who directed the world-class experiment in Quality of Working Life at Smiths Falls in 1984. "We were the wimps," says Viki Scott, who started at the St. Thomas centre in 1980. "When it came to fighting for ourselves instead of the kids, she says, "we didn't have a fighting bone in our bodies. Who puts a dollar sign on a hug?"

In the 1980s, the government gave the union a chance to build on that commitment. In 1981, Bill Davis won another legislative majority, and the power to finish the job set out by the Henderson report in 1975. In October, 1982, the Ministry of Community and Social Services (ComSoc) released its five-year plan dealing with institutions for the developmentally handicapped. The plan called for closing six smaller centres, and for a new non-institutional approach based on integrating the developmentally-handicapped into their communities.

Like most cutback programs in the liberal 1980s, the five-year plan was full of rhetoric against institutions and in favour of "normalizing" and "de-medicalizing" treatment methods. The rhetoric cut the union off from many of its most logical supporters, especially in the NDP, who would have risen up against cutbacks done in their own name.

Pictured as Neanderthals opposed to independent living so they could hold on to their jobs, unionists were thrown on the defensive. That's one reason why OPSEU never offered its full resources to the campaign against the closures, says Art Lane, who shouldered the load in eastern Ontario.

Rhetoric aside, the government proposed to close six smaller centres, not the large, impersonal institutions it claimed to criticize. ComSoc drew up its plans without consulting either the union or the financially-strapped voluntary associations that would be charged with the transition to community-based care. OPSEU leaked documents that explained this lapse. The cabinet submission for the plan referred to it as the "low-cost option." A senior official claimed it would save $71 million over five years.

"Let us talk about de-institutionalization as we find it, not as we dream about it," OPSEU campaigns department head Sean Usher pleaded in a 1983 brochure. The union supported the principle of de-institutionalization, but only if it were carried out in a way that guaranteed training and ongoing help for those living in smaller group homes, he said. Instead, the government planned to drop the handicapped on the streets and warehouse them in for-profit boarding houses. OPSEU's critique of the five-year plan was endorsed by Wolfe Wolfensberger, an internationally-recognized expert on developmental handicaps. "In life there are mistakes – stupid mistakes and smart mistakes – and then there are perversions that are no mistakes." He considered the five-year plan a perversion.

The most active campaigns were in small cities with no tradition of labour solidarity and alliances. Support was built on hometown loyalties and networks; and OPSEU had to develop campaign techniques that were intensely political, without being partisan, and that reached out to the widest number of citizens. These became the basis of the "Making

It Public" campaigns OPSEU marshalled in 1985 and 1990, when the union was credited with contributing to the election upsets that cost first Frank Miller, then David Peterson, their premierships.

The Bluewater Centre in Goderich was the first slated for closure. The campaign climaxed with "Save Bluewater Week," when the town turned out for a torchlight parade to the arena, where the mayor read a proclamation opposing the shutdown. OPSEU had invited ComSoc minister Frank Drea – commonly referred to on union buttons as "Drea is a four-letter word" – to debate. An empty chair on the podium dramatized his refusal to attend. Since townspeople couldn't see Drea in person, the union showed a filmclip of him defending government policy. The film showed a sobriety-challenged Drea, fumbling to find his notes and poking his face to make sure it was there, and made it difficult for the people of Goderich to take government policy seriously. Ultimately, the Bluewater Centre sent 72 of its 146 residents to larger institutions. The rest had to fend for themselves. Bluewater was later re-opened as a young offenders' institution, which rehired most of its former employees.

In St. Thomas, the campaign to save the START centre peaked in 1983 with a series on the community cable TV station, a display at the Simcoe fall fair and an anti-closure petition that gathered 10,000 signatures, says former START worker Viki Scott. The strong showing delayed the closure until 1985.

The community of Cobourg rallied against closure of D'Arcy Place, a small centre that people felt already fitted the bill for home-like surroundings. A deputation of 50 workers cheered the town council vote against the closure. The Cobourg *Daily Star* ran editorials urging that it stay open. Retirees from D'Arcy also formed a lobby group. In March, 1984, the *Star* reported, a caucus of eastern Ontario MPPs tried to convince premier Davis to stop the closure.

By 1984, a union tag team of James Clancy, Art Lane and Rainford Jackson dogged Frank Drea wherever he went to promote his five-year plan. OPSEU sponsored coalitions with parents of residents worried about the fate of their children, and with police chiefs and associations for the mentally retarded concerned about the lack of preparation for community living. A conference at York University tried to build a coalition out of these alliances, but the coalition was hard to sustain. The government promised funds to associations that came onside. Some parents dropped out of activity when the government gave priority to placements for their children. Lane completed the research for a court injunction, filed by parents with children in Oshawa's Durham Centre, to block the centre's closure. His research tracing the whereabouts of people removed from smaller institutions exposed the realities of de-institutionalization. Sixty-five per cent were transferred to larger institutions, one was sent to Penetang, a centre for the criminally insane, and two died. The research was never used, Lane says, because the parents who signed on to the suit dropped out when places were found for their children.

Neither the union nor the government grappled with the human rights of the developmentally handicapped. That was brought to the fore by Rideau Regional Centre resident Justin Clark, and the staff who supported him. Clark was born in 1962 with cerebral palsy, and was sent to Smiths Falls in 1964. Since he couldn't speak, he was classed as subnormal and unteachable until 1974, when Karen McLachlan, fresh from the new community college training system, tried communicating with a Bliss Board. The board had 400 symbols, and Clark "soaked it up like a sponge. His favourite question was 'Why?'" says Melanie Panitch, who teaches the mentally disabled at Humber College and is writing a history of the case. In 1980, the Centre planned to let Clark take a holiday with his counsellor, Norm Pellerin, part of an effort to phase him into the community. A worried staffer got in touch with Clark's parents, who denied permission for the leave. Managers at Smiths Falls fell in behind Clark's parents, a powerful family in Ottawa circles who took steps to have him declared mentally incompetent. Pellerin contacted the Advocacy Resource Centre for the Handicapped (ARCH), which supplied a lawyer to make the case for Clark's rights.

The heart-wrenching court case made history for the rights of the disabled. The outcome hinged entirely on Clark's competence, a matter defined in the 1937 act by the ability to handle money. ARCH had hoped to get away from either-or questions and lay out a spectrum of rights that went with varying levels of need, but this was ruled out. The government was stuck. If it argued against Clark's release by admitting that community facilities weren't available to meet his needs, it risked undermining its own rationale for de-institutionalization. Though Centre staff were divided, Clark's major witnesses were the staff who worked with him. The judge ruled that Clark was competent. Nine months later, when facilities had been readied for him in Ottawa, he became a free man.

Davis's majority government also hastened de-institutionalization of psychiatric patients. Davis had already cut back severely on the availability of psychiatric beds during the 1970s, reducing beds by 15 per cent while admissions rose by nine per cent between 1975 and 1980. The outpatient load for psychiatric hospitals increased by 140 per cent from the beginning of the decade, according to statistics gathered for the union-sponsored publication *Madness*. In the 1980s, the Conservatives singled out North Bay for closure. OPSEU's local there was one of its strongest, and "we knew that if North Bay was closed, the rest would fall like dominoes," says Heather Murray, a leader of the local and union representative on the health ministry's employee relations committee.

To block the closure, the local worked with community groups and former residents to set up outpatient clinics and alternative treatment programs. The local fought for a Native clinic, after a worker found that a Cree, who spoke no English, was being held simply because he gave his name as "Wolf" – a reference to his clan that had been mistaken for howling madness. That made the case for more culturally-sensitive approaches. Leaders of the local were not above encouraging the fears of residents of North Bay's fashionable district, worried that patients might be released in their area. "I had a man in charge of the Not In My Backyard committee, and I used to phone and crank him up once a week," says Murray. The government backed off, and the hospital was saved.

Cutbacks not only threatened jobs of institutional care workers. They were a threat to their daily safety. As early as 1975, an OPSEU anti-CECBA committee toured the province to show that understaffing was responsible for an increase of assaults on staff. In 1978, a criminally insane patient broke out of the North Bay hospital, and attacked two staffers who came looking for him, smashing both in the head with a plank. While they were still in intensive care, hourly updates on their condition were wired to the OPSEU convention, where the life-and-death reality faced by institutional workers was seared into delegates' memories. One of the assaulted workers, Bob Guillemette, died from head injuries.

At first, the threat of closures made workers nervous about raising demands for improved wages and working conditions, says Jim Paul, a leader of the OPSEU local at a facility for the developmentally handicapped near Edgar. But closures and cutbacks intensified the hazards of work and made them impossible to ignore. As borderline residents were discharged, the ratio of residents with profound behavioural problems and violent tendencies increased. There were no increases of staff, or staff training to deal with violence, or procedures to keep it in check. Especially on night shifts, staff were required to work their wards alone, far from help in the event of emergencies. Management refused to discuss the problem, since staffing levels were their sole prerogative under CECBA.

In 1982, OPSEU staff negotiator André Bekerman convinced the institutional care bargaining team to discuss the rising assault rate during wage talks. Government negotiators said that discussion belonged elsewhere, under working conditions. The team walked out and called a press conference featuring recent assault victims from every region in the province. That year, institutional care workers got a major wage increase, second only to Corrections.

Health and safety legislation was not geared to the needs of institutional workers. Laws regulated dangerous chemicals and machines, but not communicable diseases from bodily fluids and excrement that institutional workers often handled. Hepatitis reached epidemic proportions among staff. At the Southwest Regional Centre near London, Mary Lou Rutton refused to work in the wards when she got pregnant, worried that she might pick up hepatitis. Ministry of Labour inspectors ruled that the Health and Safety Act protected workers, not fetuses, and disallowed her refusal. Bob DeMatteo released the ruling to the NDP. After a week's ridicule in the legislature and media, the ministry reversed its verdict.

Around 1983, institutional workers started to identify stress as a workplace hazard. It was hard to talk about, says Thunder Bay worker Jan Holowka, because admitting stress was taken as a sign of personal weakness and "going crazy." Women relied on doctor's prescriptions for "mothers' little helper," valium, and kept the problem to themselves. High-flying executives suffered from stress and ulcers, the wisdom of the time had it, not working stiffs free from the pressure of decisions.

Gary Lenehan, president of the local at the hospital for the criminally insane near Midland, brought the issue to the attention of the union and of mental health researchers. When many of his workmates suffered heart attacks, Lenehan started checking, and found that no worker had ever retired from the hospital. They'd all died before reaching 65 – of 91 attendants hired in 1959, 46 had died by 1979, mostly from heart attacks and suicides. He started reading up on stress, about the rush of "fight or flight" adrenalin that cavemen got when they ran into a bear, and started to think about how that was repressed in a hospital for the criminally insane, where workers had to hold back their feelings about prisoners who'd carved up their victims, who might pounce on guards at any moment, who could complain to managers if guards were too strict. He thought prison reformers had done a better job of increasing prisoners' rights than the union had with workers' rights.

Lenehan toured hospitals across Ontario, begging researchers to study the problem, but to no avail. He convinced local administrators to start a Quality of Working Life program, in the hope that increased workers' control could help counter the helplessness that caused stress to build up. He met with Bob DeMatteo, who got in touch with Jeanne Stellman, a pioneer of public and workplace health at Columbia University. Stellman designed a low-cost questionnaire and strategy for identifying problems and solutions.

The government knew it had a stress problem. It was sitting on a study that found the alcohol-abuse level throughout institutional staff among the worst for any group in the country. The study was kept quiet, lest the government's Employee Assistance Programs be exposed as useless, according to former OPSEU vice-president Ev Sammons, a strong supporter of EAP programs. O'Flynn got wind of the study, and decided it was time for the union to take up the issue. An effort to investigate the problem jointly with management fell through when the government denied union access to the workplace to conduct interviews. The union did the study on its own, distributing questionnaires through stewards, and picking up the results at trailers and hotels near worksites.

Stellman's analysis, the first of its kind using Canadian data, was published in 1986. Stellman found job dissatisfaction, burnout, high blood pressure and digestive-tract disorders to be "pandemic" among institutional workers.

In 1985, the organizing momentum built over five years peaked with a sustained bargaining drive that netted 15 per cent wage increases for institutional care workers. In 1988, the union won the right to sit down with local managers to develop tailor-made strategies to deal with a full range of health and safety problems.

※

CAAT on a hot tin roof

In 1984, community college teachers went on strike for working conditions that would foster quality education. After more than a decade's embittered bargaining over traditional union issues, the strike was a high-water point for the new style of social unionism.

Bargaining at the community colleges had never been marked by productive problem-solving. Until 1975, management, led by corporate lawyer Fred Hamilton, rested its case on a fundamentalist reading of the Crown Employees Collective Bargaining Act. It rejected any union demands that infringed on management rights to set working conditions affecting quality of education. Hamilton said he wouldn't let union-style bargaining creep into higher education. "They had a university argument," says OPSEU's head of bargaining Andy Todd, "but they didn't have a university. They had a very pale imitation of the university system of governance, with the highest management and supervision ratios anywhere, but they tried to hide behind that paper-thin veil to clothe themselves in the respectability they sought." By forcing bargaining onto the straight and narrow issue of wages, the colleges denied the professionalism of teachers, their ability to use their qualifications to define standards that have to be met. College management's fixation with management rights, Todd says, "was a recipe not just for hard bargaining, but for ideological warfare. And that's what we've had in the community colleges from day one."

College presidents liked this hard-line stance, says Bill Kuehnbaum, a Sudbury college teacher who served on many teams, because "they were kings in their own little world. If they wouldn't let the government-appointed Council of Regents interrupt their running their colleges, why would they let the union be a check on their authority? So, from day one, we've had an adversarial relationship beyond all reason."

For union staff, working with the college faculty bargaining team was the assignment from hell. Academics didn't recognize bargaining as a skill, says Todd, and couldn't grasp that negotiations were about power, not repartee; priorities, not abstract rights; settlement, not process. "For academics, negotiating is like the Oxford Debating Club, and the purpose is to make the other side look like jerks. My purpose is to come away with some money." Bob Hebdon researched for several teams in the 1970s and early '80s, then begged off. "Seniority has to be worth something," he says. Now a professor of industrial relations at Cornell University, Hebdon laughs at the way faculty bargainers got taken in by their mistaken sense of themselves and their opponents. During bargaining in 1972, Hamilton asked each team member to speak on the unique conditions of their campus, then pounced on the innocents by insisting that no bargaining formula could capture that diversity. "That's typical of what suckers they were," says Hebdon. Both sides spent two days wrangling over a definition of time off for "professional development," until a trades teacher suggested it be called "preventive maintenance."

For their part, college teachers thought OPSEU did a lousy job of understanding, representing and servicing them. Many believed that OPSEU broke the promise made by organizers that the college division would enjoy autonomy and specialized servicing. In 1975, leading college team members worked out a two-track strategy to make or break the union. One group led a drive to switch to another union. The other group worked to reform the union from within.

The decertification drive was a flop. "You can't get it off the ground. You're just like Cape Canaveral," Kingston-area staff rep Rusty Fawcett yelled at one breakaway leader. Many public service activists never took kindly to having the academics in their ranks. In 1977, the executive board almost passed a motion to assist CAAT members in their decertification drive.

Most CAAT leaders came from the academic, not trade, wings of the colleges. For many, the hard-nosed approach of management bargainers was painfully reminiscent of the put-downs they experienced when they fought for additional liberal arts courses. Liberal arts were treated like fingerpainting, says Mel Fogel, a leader of one CAAT team, now director of personnel at Toronto's Seneca College. "Your outrage gets expended in different ways. You don't want to see yourself as a failure, so you take it out in other ways," he says. Bargaining, Fogel says, "is like a graduate seminar. If I'm going to debate, I at least want someone who's academically inclined." Disappointment and disgust gave bargaining a bitter edge that spilled over into a sense of class war. At one 1970s bargaining session, the faculty team got up on a pre-arranged signal and exposed their T-shirts with the slogan "Smash the State."

Most faculty bargainers thought a strike was the only way to teach managers a lesson. They suffered a major setback in 1979, when teachers voted both "No" to accepting management's offer, and "No" to the bargaining team's request for a strike mandate.

Most college teachers, a 1974 survey found, were satisfied with their wages, but unhappy over their lack of professional rights to define the quality of education. About two-thirds of Toronto's Humber College teachers complained they had no influence in college decisions, and about half wanted more democratic structures, the survey showed. A group of socialist and feminist activists thought these issues could be used to build the union. "I wanted to stand for something, not just against," says Susan Stylianos, an adult education teacher at George Brown. The group was quickly dubbed as "soft" and "rightwingers" by the academic team's elected leaders. Bill Kuehnbaum, one of the "hardliners," says he saw quality of education as a "wimp issue" that got in the way of "meat-and-potato" issues. "The other group was way ahead of us," he says now.

But the quality of education group had a hard time mustering support. Unlike high school teachers, college instructors weren't "classroom conscious," says John Huot, a member of Humber College's executive and an early supporter of the quality of education group. College instructors were hired as specialists, not teachers, recruited from the working world, not teachers' colleges, encouraged to keep up their ties to their former professions, not to their new profession of teaching. In an effort to establish a common bond as teachers united around classroom and workload needs, Huot preached that "a teacher is a teacher is a teacher." At Oakville's Sheridan College, Linda Briskin thought the union should challenge college shortcomings by organizing an independent division around teaching concerns over growing class sizes, marking workloads, and reduced student contact. "We were disorganized by the structure of the colleges in terms of not creating arenas for professional concerns, and the union reproduced that," Briskin says.

Their efforts met with grief within the union. In 1981, a CAAT meeting elected a quality of education committee, but gave it no power or stature. Briskin asked the executive board to fund a survey on teaching hours, preparation time and professional development, for the sake of a province-wide campaign to organize around common teaching problems. Though quality of education was teacher talk for cutbacks, which OPSEU opposed, O'Flynn made a mockery of the request.

Until 1981, quality education suffered many snubs. In 1981, the axe came down. At Cambrian College in Sudbury, for instance, general arts requirements for technical degrees were dropped, and class sizes shot up. "For all practical purposes, the administration was saying that the college teachers were to no purpose trying to carry quality around on their back," says chemistry instructor Cam Hopkins. Cuts at Humber, says Huot, were most savage in areas where teachers had put their souls into innovative projects. Unlike university presidents faced with such levels of funding cutbacks, college presidents didn't utter a peep of protest. Even administrators were demoralized. A 1983 survey found high levels of stress related to crisis management styles, lack of innovative decision-making, over-politicized administration, and lack of participation in decision-making. The Skolnick report, which assessed colleges in the wake of the 1984 strike, singled out that round of cuts as the most significant cause of teachers' loss of faith in the system.

On the heels of these cuts, and of 1982 public-sector wage controls, the quality of education group rallied in 1983. The bargaining team was "structurally incapable" of providing a vehicle for teacher discontent, an open letter to college local union presidents declared. Teachers, it said, needed a special division to deal with these issues, to form coalitions with students, and to take their case to the public.

Seneca College militant Howard Doughty denounced these proposals as "Montessori unionism." Coalitions were a "grandiose exercise in self-infatuation," and a public campaign on quality of education was a "dumb idea" that would only serve to rile the public over high wages paid to teachers, he wrote. "We are trying to get a better contract," and that takes a strike mandate. "We can do this by building up our Locals and not by escaping into radical make-work projects," his own open letter claimed.

Ron Martin, a Sheridan College drama teacher, OPSEU executive board member from the Niagara region, and supporter of the quality of education approach, was on the bargaining team for the 1984 contract. He hoped to follow in the footsteps of Ryerson teachers, who negotiated a formula for workload that expressed quality of education concerns in bargaining language. Teachers liked that approach, and gave the team a strike mandate to fight for it. That was the issue, according to a doctoral study of the strike by Netto Kefentse, that turned teachers' desire for self-control and professional development into group solidarity, that gave them the confidence and legitimacy to go on strike on behalf of education, not just themselves. "Most teachers felt they could look after themselves. They felt comfortable supporting a strike because it was for others," says team vice-chair Georgina Hancock. As the strike loomed, the entire team seized on quality of education to keep the members happy and the public at bay, says Kuehnbaum.

Martin thought the government would meet the union halfway, but college managers refused to budge on workload. At 6:00 P.M. on October 16, 1984, the night before the strike deadline, management said there was no deal. "I practically fell out of my chair," says Martin. "I couldn't believe that after all these years they had finally drawn the line. The next morning, we were out on the bricks." In 22 colleges across the province, 7,600 teachers went on strike.

The strike was short and spirited. At George Brown College in downtown Toronto, students hired a bus to travel to other campuses and build support. Printing students brought artistic placards to the picket line hot off the press each day. "The spirit was just incredible," says the local strike co-ordinator, Susan Stylianos. "People came out of the woodwork that you'd never in your wildest dreams think would be active. They were good souls, and they were there when you needed them. I think that has something to do with why they became teachers."

Many brought their families to the picket line. One kid's placard – "Save the whales, and my daddy too" – won the heart of the media.

The strike was still solid in November, when OPSEU held its convention.

O'Flynn had given notice in the spring that he was moving on to become vice-president of the Ontario Federation of Labour, so the race for president was wide open. Vice-president Ev Sammons was considered likely to win. Widely seen as O'Flynn's successor and backed by many of O'Flynn's allies, she was also seen as the one to beat by those who found O'Flynn's administration too erratic, too ideological, too far removed from rank and file concerns. Art Lane, an institutional care worker in Brockville and Smiths Falls, blocked Sammons in her home-base in eastern Ontario and among institutional workers. Ron Martin had the edge in O'Flynn's old stomping grounds in the Niagara region and among college teachers. James Clancy was the dark horse, a welfare field worker from Toronto who had led the struggle against welfare integration and de-institutionalization and pulled together a populist coalition that backed his vision of "building up from the locals, reaching out to the community."

Sammons took the lead in the first ballot, with 300 votes against 200 for Clancy, 174 for Martin and 75 for Lane. Martin and Lane threw their support to Clancy, who edged out Sammons 346 to 340. Fred Upshaw, a psychiatric nurse from Whitby, had an easy win as vice-president. Announcing the results was honorary elections chair, Gren Jones, fired in 1970 for trying to turn CSAO into a union.

A few days later, the college bargaining teams met. The union side, furious at government ads belittling their cause, repeated all its original demands. Managers sat still for an hour. When no one broke the silence, they folded their papers, shut their briefcases and walked out of the room. An hour later, they attended a government press conference announcing a legislated end to the strike. Under the back-to-work law, an arbitrator was appointed to rule on wages, and professor Michael Skolnick, a former researcher for colleges minister Bette Stephenson, was asked to review college educational standards. OPSEU denounced the legislation as strikebreaking, and called the appointment of a wage arbitrator an evasion of the strike's central issue – workload. It called for a boycott of Skolnick's review. Within a year, teachers received a wage settlement that paid them for time lost while on strike, and a ringing endorsement of their cause by Skolnick. Within two years, they won a workload formula that met their demands around quality education.

But the strike didn't fade away that easily. A week before it ended, eight teachers at Northern College's Haileybury School of Mines drove across the picket line. The strikebreakers were led by Merv Lavigne, a teacher at the college and president of its alumni association. Haileybury School of Mines alumni were the old guard of the hardrock mining industry. They ran HSM "more like an industry than a college," the North Bay *Nugget* said, and resented their tie to community colleges, described by the industry tabloid *The Northern Miner* as a "haven for many industrial misfits, left-wing radicals, and academic malcontents devoid of the work ethic." Alumni president Lavigne led the drive for an independent school "directed by a small council from the mining industry," and free from "typical Mickey Mouse community college programs."

The day the strike began, a group of mine managers and teachers formed the Committee for Responsibility in Education. A week later, its leader, Merv Lavigne, told local media that "it's time the teachers started behaving like professional people instead of radical jerks." He wanted to cross the picket line and teach, but the Colleges Collective Bargaining Act, like most teacher labour legislation, prohibited strikebreaking. Lavigne said the law violated his constitutional rights. On October 2, he asked a judge to "decertify OPSEU as my bargaining agent."

Months after the strike was over, Lavigne's case was taken up by the National Citizens' Coalition, led by Colin Brown, the insurance agent who lost out when the union convinced the government to get a better deal elsewhere in 1974. The NCC launched a million-dollar Charter case on Lavigne's behalf. Under the NCC's direction, the issue was no longer Lavigne's right to cross a picket line or his right to get out of union dues. The NCC developed a shrewd court challenge that went to the heart of OPSEU's history.

The NCC lawsuit accepted OPSEU's right to collect union dues from all who benefitted from its collective agreements. But it charged OPSEU with taking Lavigne's money as forced tribute to a series of political causes he disagreed with. This infringed Lavigne's freedom of speech and association, the NCC charged. OPSEU had used Lavigne's dues to buy lunch for a conference of an anti-poverty group that protested the waste of public money on Toronto's Skydome. OPSEU had spent Lavigne's dues on a convention that supported women's right to choose abortion. OPSEU had spent Lavigne's dues on donations to striking British miners and for a delegation of Central American health-care workers to visit Canada. OPSEU had spent Lavigne's dues to send executive board members to an NDP banquet featuring Tommy Douglas. None of these expenses had anything to do with bargaining, the sole rationale for compulsory union dues, the NCC claimed.

Against the advice of senior CLC leaders, Clancy mounted a public defence that lambasted the NCC as "designated hitters for big business" and defined the court case as "the labour trial of the century." The case, the union said, turned the Charter of Rights on its head by denying the right of union conventions to use dues revenues to speak on social issues or work with community and labour groups that supported OPSEU causes. Lavigne and all other union members and non-members got their 5.4 cents worth – the actual per capita amount of dues spent on the campaigns cited by the NCC – from OPSEU's increased ability to build support for its bargaining goals. The issue was OPSEU's right and need to be a social union, and OPSEU's evolution toward social unionism as an expression of membership needs and wishes, not directives from dictatorial leaders, the union said.

In 1991, the Supreme Court of Canada threw out Lavigne's case, and ordered the NCC to pay OPSEU's court costs. The union had a history that was worth defending.

Notes on Sources

General

I have donated to the OPSEU library four boxes of photocopied materials and a box of audio tapes which include all the material used to write this history. They are accessible to all researchers.

Ontario is Canada's neediest province when it comes to histories. This is especially so for histories of government, perhaps because most people falsely see the province as having a stodgy and complacent past, with little innovation and few clues to Canadian realities worthy of attention.

I relied on a few general histories to get me started: J. Schull, *Ontario Since 1867*; C. Armstrong, *The Politics of Federalism: Ontario's Relations with the Federal Government, 1867-1942*; and J. Saywell, *The Office of Lieutenant Governor: A Study in Canadian Government and Politics*. There are good overviews of the Ontario political system that give little snippets about how the actual work of government was delivered: D. Bellamy et al, *The Provincial Political Systems: Comparative Essays*; and G. Bell, A. Pascoe, *The Ontario Government: Structure and Functions*. The surveys I used most were Fred Schindeler, *Responsible Government in Ontario* and Donald MacDonald, ed., *Government and Politics of Ontario*. There are occasional references to the Ontario civil service in S. Frankel, *Staff Relations in the Civil Service: The Canadian Experience*, H. Arthurs, *Collective Bargaining by Public Employees in Canada: Five Models*, J. Hodgetts, *Provincial Governments as Employers: A Survey of Public Personnel Administration in Canada's Provinces*, and T. Cole, *The Canadian Bureaucracy, Canadian Civil Servants and Other Public Employees*, all as lively as their titles suggest.

There is no shortage of original material to excuse the lack of detailed attention. The Provincial Archives of Ontario has about 30 boxes of files from the department of the provincial secretaries, who had responsibility for staff relations in the early days. There are also three volumes of scrapbooks of news clippings, a miscellaneous collection of pamphlets and handbooks related to the civil service, files on the Civil Service Association of Ontario, and records of the Civil Service Commission after 1919. As well, many of the premier's private papers have material on staff relations.

OPSEU also has a decent collection of records, including major CSAO and OPSEU publications, executive board minutes, and a fabulous file of clippings, leaflets and memorabilia on the post-1972 period kept by communications director John Ward.

On the borderline of original research are mounds of government documents. In the early years before self-congratulatory annual reports became standard, sessional papers printed enormous line-by-line details by supervisors and day-by-day reports from front-line workers in many departments. The Civil Service Commission printed an annual report for most years between 1919 and 1966.

After 1970, *Canadian News Facts* is an indispensable summary of major events in Ontario politics and government.

"Loyal she remains"

The best places to go for the basic facts of politics, constitutional relations and government functions in pre-World War I Ontario, when James Whitney was premier, are: C. Humphries, *"Honest Enough To Be Bold": The Life and Times of Sir James Pliny Whitney*, and the biography of his Liberal opponent, M. Prang's *N.W. Rowell: Ontario Nationalist*. The most insightful interpretation of the period, one of the all-time greats, is H. V. Nelles, *The Politics of Development: Forests, Mines and Hydro-Electric Power in Ontario, 1849-1941*. Constitutional relations are nicely explained in G. Stevenson's essay on "Federalism and the political economy of the Canadian state," in L. Panitch, ed., *The Canadian State: Political Economy and Political Power*. The political flavour of the times can be recaptured in fun-loving H. Charlesworth's *More Candid Chronicles* and snotty J. Willison's *Reminiscences Personal and Political*. The story of long-serving Charlie Fitch and the opening of Queen's Park is told in *Topic*, November-December, 1966, when poor old Fitch finally retired. Sessional papers, such as *Ontario Public Accounts, Sessional Papers*, No. 1, 1912, give line-by-line expenses for all politicians and departments.

I wrote about women workers in this period of Ontario in *Honest Womanhood: Feminism, Femininity and Class Consciousness among Toronto Working Women, 1896-1914*, before I knew anything about women civil servants. Records and reports on women are very spotty, but this section relies on sessional papers that cite names and salaries of women workers, and some random reports in the Toronto *Star* (November 4, 1906 and May, 1913). The harrowing story of Laura McCarthy comes from files of the provincial secretary. When I passed her story on to the Ontario Women's Directorate, they decided to include her in their poster celebrating 40 women pathbreakers, to be issued in 1994. The directorate will try to find out what happened to McCarthy after she left the government service.

The pomp and circumstance of turn-of-the-century Ontario are revealed in the 1895 *Report of the Commissioners appointed to inquire concerning the mode of appointing and remunerating certain provincial officials*, and Saywell (above). The best antidote for pork-barrel caricatures of old Ontario politics, and a good introduction to the complex Tory traditions of Ontario, is S. Noel, *Patrons, Clients and Brokers: Ontario Society and Politics, 1791-1896*. Noel's sobering comparison of abuses of patronage in olden and modern times is made in the summer, 1987 issue of *Journal of Canadian Studies*. Also good on the early civil service is J. Hodgetts, *Pioneer Public Service: An Administrative History of the United Canadas*. Civil service working conditions are defined in the March, 1878 "Act Respecting the Public Service of Ontario."

The full Garrow Resolution debate, so wrongly blamed for the denial of political rights to civil servants – even in the video on political rights, *To Serve In Silence*, which I helped produce for OPSEU in 1985 – can be found in *Journals of the Legislative Assembly*, March 17, 1897 and in provincial archives catalogues of legislative speeches recorded by journalists.

I spend a fair amount of time on the crackpots and anti-democrats who promoted efficient and technocratic approaches to government because I feel they are responsible for so many stereotypes about civil service history, and because their impact has been so damaging to the quality of workplace relations and public service. The agenda of progressive reform is exposed in C. Derber, *Power in the Highest Degree: Professionals and the Rise of a New Mandarin Order.* I take a few strips off the major leaders of progressive reform in Ontario in my University of Toronto Ph. D. thesis, *Labour and Reform in Toronto, 1896-1914.* Lykke de la Cour's forthcoming Ph. D. thesis for the University of Toronto on Ontario psychiatric institutions details the kinds of cruelty that went under the name of science.

It was important to review the civil service before 1900 to get a handle on Tory traditionalism, which dominated civil service history until at least the 1960s. My sense of how this complex and contradictory set of values worked was strongly influenced by Noel (above), and by two great books on English history: P. Corrigan, D. Sayer, *The Great Arch: English State Formation as Cultural Revolution*, and T. Nairn, *The Enchanted Glass: Britain and its Monarchy.*

The legislature's annual *Sessional Papers* are the best place to look for crusading reports by government staffers. Eric Tucker's *Administering Danger in the Workplace: The Law and Politics of Occupational Health and Safety Regulation in Ontario, 1850-1914* is an excellent account of health and safety inspection. I dealt with inspectors and other civil service reformers in a draft history of health and safety, available at the Canadian Centre for Occupational Health and Safety in Hamilton. An incredibly harsh attack on the Don Jail as "the worst jail on the continent" by provincial inspector Bruce Smith was carried in the *Star*, May 4, 1914. The investigation into politically-inspired firings is filed as an unprinted *Sessional Paper* No. 73, 1908 in the provincial secretary's papers.

There are almost no records on the formation of the CSAO, save for the founding statements, reproduced in Bursey's draft history. The War's impact on the cost of living can be traced in the federal government's

Labour Gazette, and even more closely in the 1929 *U.S. Handbook of Labour Statistics*. The war's psychological impact on Martha Davidson and others is recounted in D. Read, ed., *The Great War and Canadian Society: An Oral History*. The rise of wartime militancy within the CSAO is evidenced in provincial archives news clippings. The scoop on disgraced CSAO leader A. Grigg can be found in the outstanding and remarkably honest promotional history of the Lands and Forests ministry, R. Lambert and P. Pross' *Renewing Nature's Wealth: A Centennial History of the Public Management of Lands, Forests and Wildlife in Ontario, 1763-1967*. The CSAO's brief calling for a major wage increase is in the provincial archives, miscellaneous collections, 1919, "Civil service, Ontario." Whitleyism is discussed at length in most British labour histories, and J. Sheldrake, *The Origins Of Public Sector Industrial Relations*. The only evidence of this style of thinking in Ontario is the Mothers' Allowance Commission, *First Annual Report*, 1922.

The wartime obsession with efficiency, which strongly influenced efforts to control the civil service after the war, is obvious in *Report of the Ontario Commission on Unemployment, March, 1916* and in the contemporary documents reprinted in B. Wilson, ed., *Ontario and the First World War*. The law banning idleness was reported in *Star*, April 6, 1918. The impact on the federal civil service is detailed in J. Hodgetts et al, *The Biography of an Institution: The Civil Service Commission of Canada, 1908-1967*. The standard federal civil service exam was reprinted by *Star*, November 4, 1906.

J.M. McCutcheon's career is outlined in his obituaries, carried by the *Globe* and *Star* on November 27, 1950, and in *Public Service Bulletin*, August, 1918. His views are most easily found in G. Lowe's *Women in the Administrative Revolution: The Feminization of Clerical Work*. They can also be found in the original in annual reports of the Civil Service Commission. For a general review of this generation of scientific managers, see the excellent account by R. Whitaker, "Scientific Management Theory as Political Ideology," in the Autumn, 1979 issue of *Studies in Political Economy: A Socialist Review*. The importance of "internal labour markets" receives its due attention in C. Heron, *Working in Steel: The Early Years in Canada, 1883-1935.*

Pensions, the first landmark of scientific management in the civil service, receive full treatment in McCutcheon's annual reports. The political context of the debate is presented in E. Drury, *Farmer Premier: Memoirs of the Hon. E.C. Drury* and C. Johnston, *E.C. Drury: Agrarian Idealist.* The near-fisticuffs incident is described in W. Brown's 1979 M.A. thesis for Guelph University, *The Broadening Out Controversy: E.C. Drury, J.J. Morrison and the United Farmers of Ontario.*

Information on job classification schemes, and government workers' response, can be found in McCutcheon's *Report on the Classification of the Public Service of Ontario, 1920,* and in extensive newspaper reports and letters to the editor throughout May and June, 1919, all available in the provincial archives clippings collection. The result, nine years later, was published as "The Classification of the Ontario Public Service."

Job classification, like other strategies to introduce scientific management in the civil service, was defeated by plain ineptitude and traditionalism, which returned to full bloom when the Tories were re-elected in 1923. The Tory regime is described in Peter Oliver's two books: *Public and Private Persons: The Ontario Political Culture, 1914-1935,* and *G. Howard Ferguson: Ontario Tory.* McCutcheon's lowly standing, other than in his own mind, is revealed in H. Scarrow's study of provincial civil service commissioners in the May, 1957 issue of *The Journal of Politics.*

For examples of the low regard for rationality in Ontario politics at this time, despite all the pretence of efficiency, see *Report of Commission of Enquiry, Kapuskasing Colony, 1920,* Lambert and Pross (above), G.T. Hackett's 1969 Ph.D. thesis for the University of Toronto, *The History of Public Education for Mentally Retarded Children in the Province of Ontario, 1867-1964,* A. McLaren's chilling *Our Own Master Race: Eugenics in Canada, 1885-1945,* the 1929 and 1930 reports of Ontario's *Royal Commission on Public Welfare,* Paul Axelrod, *Making a Middle Class: Student Life in English Canada During the 1930s* and the 1941 *Final Report and Proceedings of the Select Committee of the Legislative Assembly: Administration of the*

Department of Lands and Forests. The comparison of public with private sector standards is based on a 1929 Department of Labour study, *Survey of Industrial Welfare in Ontario*. CSAO reactions to these trends can be found in Bursey (above) and the May, 1926 *Civil Service Review*. Dawson's comments on the lost opportunity to serve excellence and democracy come from his *The Civil Service of Canada*.

The details of Depression-era concessions can be found in Bursey (above) and correspondence files of premier Henry, boxes 134 and 145. Working conditions for civil servants are spelled out in the July, 1931 order-in-council "OPS Regulations, 1931." To put those concessions in perspective, see such standard statistical handbooks as M. Urquhart, ed., *Historical Statistics of Canada*, and F. Leacy, ed., *Historical Statistics of Canada*.

Mitch Hepburn, whose antics bring this chapter to a close, is the subject of two biographies, N. McKenty, *Mitch Hepburn* and J. Saywell, *Just Call Me Mitch: Biography of Premier Mitchell Hepburn*. There are also scattered issues of the *Civil Service News* and *Civil Service Review* in the late 1930s.

"Loyal, Modern, Efficient"

Mercifully, there is no biography of George Drew, who led the Tories to victory in 1943. There are good sketches of his career and portraits of him in Roger Graham's biography of his successor, Leslie Frost, in E. Goodman, *Life of the Party: The memoirs of Eddie Goodman* and D. Creighton, *The Forked Road: Canada 1939-1957*.

The transformation of Toryism in 1942-1943, which gave the Progressive Conservative Party its modern name and winning political formula for the next 42 years, signalled a permanent shift to the left in Canadian politics. The Conservative makeover, shown in the Port Hope conference of 1942 and the 1943 election victory, is described in J. Granatstein, *The Politics of Survival: The Conservative Party of Canada, 1939-1945*, in Dave Millar's 1980 Ph.D. thesis for York University,

"Shapes of Power: The Ontario Labour Relations Board, 1944-1950," and in M. Brodie and J. Jenson, *Crisis, Challenge and Change: Party and Class in Canada*. The link between these changes and what became the Big Blue Machine is made clear in Keith Brownsey's paper to the Canadian Political Science Association annual meeting in 1990 on "The Family Compact: The Conservative Party of Ontario, 1935-1985." These changes responded to the profound radicalization of workers, which catapulted the CCF to prominence, themes discussed well in Gerry Caplan's *The Dilemma of Canadian Socialism: The CCF in Ontario*. Drew's commitments were made in a July 8, 1943 provincial radio broadcast, available as a pamphlet in the archives, and in his throne speech of February 22, 1944.

The JAC's terms of reference are laid out in the 1949 edition of *Handbook for Civil Servants*. The parallel federal experiment is discussed in S. Frankel, *Staff Relations in the Civil Service: The Canadian Experience*, and L. Barnes, *Consult and Advise: A History of the National Joint Council of the Public Service of Canada, 1944-1974*. Foster's private comment is in a June 22, 1944 letter to the deputy treasurer.

The development of a professional and technocratic civil service in Ottawa, so at odds with the hands-on and make-do style at Queen's Park, is discussed in D. Owram, *The Government Generation: Canadian Intellectuals and the State, 1900-1945*, in R. Bothwell, W. Kilbourn, *C.D. Howe*, Granatstein's *The Ottawa Men: The Civil Service Mandarins, 1935-1947*, and E. Reid, *Radical Mandarin: The Memoirs of Escott Reid*. The Saskatchewan CCF's creative use of an independent and professional civil service, requiring staff relations that encouraged unionization, is outlined in several essays in L. Lapierre, *Essays on the Left*, and in an extensive interview I did with former cabinet secretary George Cadbury and donated to the Sound Division of the Public Archives of Canada. The low level of civil service capacity in Drew's era is indicated in V. Lang, *The Service State Emerges in Ontario, 1945-1973*, K. Rea, *The Prosperous Years: The Economic History of Ontario*, and in D. Richmond, *The Economic Transformation of Ontario*. The dismal results in education are exposed in J. Porter's justly classic *The Vertical Mosaic: An Analysis of Social Class and Power in Canada*. The lack of strategic government planning and the low standing of Keynesian fiscal tools are discussed in separate essays by J. Jenson and D. Wolfe in the 1989 *Canadian Review of Sociology and Anthropology*, and in Wolfe's essay in M. Cross, G. Kealey, *Modern Canada: 1930-1980s*.

Daly's comments come from *Hansard*, April 7, 1948. Drew's flipflops on the merit system can be found in *Globe*, February 10, 1944. The pitiful weakness of the CSC is discussed in H. Scarrow, "Civil Service Commissioners in the Canadian provinces," in the May, 1957 *Journal of Politics*. The rant against "personnel" was carried by the *Telegram*, February 1, 1947. The comparison of civil service and teacher standing can be seen in P. Hennessy, *Schools in Jeopardy: Collective Bargaining in Education*.

The cold war hysteria that took over political debate around 1945 is most ably discussed in G. Caplan (above). The loyalty oath and political restrictions in the *Public Service Act, 1947* came out of that hysteria, as is clearly reflected in the legislative debates for October 27-30, 1947. Parallel U.S. moves in March, 1947 are briefly discussed in R. Jung, *Brighter than A Thousand Suns*.

Reports on rising CSAO militancy were widely covered in the press, especially *Star*, October 10, 1947, September 11, 1948 and *Telegram*, February 1, 1947. The botched effort to have civil servants sing along with the government is reported in a mimeo of *Highlights*, December 19, 1947. The crackdown on coffee breaks takes up an entire file, "cafeteria," in the provincial secretary's papers for 1948. Workplace rules for clockwatchers are laid out in the *Handbook for Civil Servants, 1949* and the Civil Service Commission's annual report for the year ending March, 1949. A brochure introducing CSAO to civil servants, *Twenty One*, urged members to break from the "Let George Do It" mentality, a cute but direct swipe at the premier; see provincial archives, MU 2137, 1945, #2, "CSAO."

The kinder and gentler Frost era is discussed in R. Graham, *Old Man Ontario: Leslie M. Frost*, in senior Frost minister T. Kennedy's *Tom*

Kennedy's Story, D. MacDonald, *The Happy Warrior: Political Memoirs*, and is neatly summarized in J. Schull (above). Frost happy face bromides on the economy are cited in D. Richmond (above). The action-line toryism of important Frost ministers is detailed in P. Oliver, *Unlikely Tory: The Life and Politics of Allan Grossman*. The unexpectedly warm relations between Frost and Communist Party legislators is mentioned in N. Penner, *Canadian Communism: The Stalin Years and Beyond*. In an interview with the author, Penner says that Alex Macleod (uncle of Shirley Maclaine and Warren Beatty and an inspiration for Beatty's film *Reds*) wrote premier Robarts' famous centennial year "two Canadas" speech on French-English relations, and also persuaded the premier to call Highway 401 the Macdonald-Cartier in honour of early representatives of "progressive" Canadian capitalist politicians.

The bad start in relations between Frost and the CSAO is covered in *Civil Service News*, August, 1950, December-January, 1951, and is made clear in Frost's letter of July, 1950 to the CSAO president. The controversies were picked up in the Toronto *Star*, November 28, 1950. The bogus show of defiance is documented in Bursey (above), based on interviews with CSAO leaders. The push for the five-day week is documented in Frost's correspondence files under "cabinet communications (confidential) 1949," and in a memo to all ministers, August 25, 1949. Frost's hardball moves against the Teamsters are discussed in Scarrow (above) and Beverly Dalys, *No Longer a Two-Bit Union: History of the Ontario Liquor Boards Employees' Union*.

The love-in between Frost and the CSAO is indicated in Frost's speech to the legislature on March 9, 1951, and in Civil Service Commission annual reports for the years ending March 1950 and 1951, as well as *Star*, September 13, November 30, 1950, and *Globe*, October 20, 1950.

Statistics on the rapid rise of real wages, low rates of turnover and quick rates of promotion are summarized in W. Gordon, *Report of the Committee on the Organization of Government in Ontario, 1959*, especially the chapter on the Civil Service Commission. The commission's annual reports for years ending March, 1956, 1959, 1960 give further breakdowns. Commission annual reports from 1946 on also record numbers of war veterans.

My views on the sociology of government workplaces and communities were shaped by reading classic analyses of class consciousness by R. Dahrendorf, D. Lockwood, F. Parkin, D. Runciman and B. Moore. A study of equal insight, filled with Canadian data from this decade, is W. Wood's 1959 Ph.D. thesis for Princeton, *An Analysis of Office Unionism in Canadian Manufacturing Industry*. The dark side of government service levels, from the point of view of clients, is dealt with at length in MacDonald (above). The reminiscences of workers come from taped interviews with OPSEU members that are now stored at OPSEU's library. Unless otherwise noted, all future statements from OPSEU members come from this collection.

The most useful statistics on women workers are in Civil Service Commission annual reports for the year ending March, 1950, March 1954, and 1958. The 1956 report records the change allowing married women to work. Foster's comments on married women workers come from a May 17, 1950 memo filed in the provincial secretary's papers under "1950 civil service salaries." Ms. Sanderson's case is raised in a May 2, 1950 memo from Foster, and her past salary range was tracked through public accounts for each year mentioned. The CSAO actually went public with the view that men should be paid well enough so their wives wouldn't have to work. See *Star*, June 6, 1951. The rap poem on equal pay was published in *The Trillium*, March, 1956.

The economic transformation of Ontario under Frost is well summarized in D. Richmond (above) and J. Schull (above). Organizational changes in the civil service are discussed in Civil Service Commission annual reports for years ending March 1954, 1959, 1961. My description of Finkelman draws on Millar (above) and on transcripts of his interviews with Finkelman, which Millar kindly lent me. My interpretation of these changes was influenced by M. Edwards, *Contested Terrain: The Transformation of the Workplace in the Twentieth Century*. The assessment of the general labour scene and public opinion on labour matters comes from

W. Wood (above). Gordon's 1959 report (above) carried forward many views he held in 1946, when he chaired the *Royal Commission on Administrative Classifications in the Public Service*. A review became pressing after publication of the provincial auditor's reports for 1956-1957 and 1957-1958. Gordon's 1959 report was endorsed by the *Interim Report of the Select Committee of the House Appointed April, 1960 to examine into and to study the Administrative and Executive problems of the Government of Ontario*. Gordon didn't seem to realize the importance of his report when he wrote his autobiography *A Political Memoir*. Neither did Frost, whose comments are recounted in MacDonald (above).

CSAO's drive to something like union status is recounted in Bursey and Frankel (above), and in various issues of *The Trillium*, especially January, 1957, March-June, 1959. The CSAO's 1959 rally was splashed all over the Toronto dailies, especially *Star*, March 23 and 24, and *Globe*, March 23.

The tragicomic aspects of Ontario jails are discussed in W. Mann, *Society Behind Bars: A Sociological Scrutiny of Guelph Reformatory*, V. Sears, *Hello Sweetheart...Get Me Rewrite*, and S. Young, *Gordon Sinclair: A Life and Then Some*. The hairy incident at Don Jail was the subject of major media and legislative attention; see especially Legislative Debates for March 6, 20, 23, 1962.

Amendments to the Public Service Act in 1962-1963 are reported in the Civil Service Commission annual report for the year ending December, 1962, and in the Employee Relations Branch's 1964 edition of *Working Together for Ontario*. The way politicians understood these changes is made clear in the Legislative Debates of April 9, 1962, February 14, March 7, and April 2, 1963.

Accidental Union

For an introduction to the Robarts era, see A. McDougall, *Robarts: His Life and Government*, and J. Manthorpe, *The Power and the Tories*.

As a new employee, Lane would have been issued the brochures

Working Together for Ontario: Handbook for Employees, issued by the Civil Service Commission, and the CSAO's *Welcome to the Ontario Public Service*. Lane's reminiscences on the treatment of psychiatric patients are confirmed by M. Shulman, *Member of the Legislature*, H. Simmons, *Unbalanced: Mental Health Policy in Ontario, 1930-1989*, and Dr. C. Roberts, "A Report on Ontario Mental Health Services," February, 1963, which is in the miscellaneous file at the Ministry of Health library.

Demographics, the baby boom, and the structure of public sector workplaces made the government workforce ripe for unionization across the country during the 1960s. See for instance, J. Boivin's essay in M. Gunderson, ed., *Collective Bargaining in the Essential and Public Service Sectors*, S. Goldenberg, *Collective Bargaining in the Provincial Public Services*, J. Rose's essay in M. Thompson, G. Swimmer, *Conflict or Compromise*, the Institute of Public Administration of Canada, *Collective Bargaining in the Public Service*, and J. Hodgetts and O. Dwivedi (above).

Information on grievances and the government stance toward relationships with CSAO is available in annual reports of the CSC. The CSAO's push for major wage hikes in the mid-1960s, and the involvement of David Lewis, can be documented in board of directors' minutes for January 25-26, 1965, and in regular Activity reports issued to CSAO activists that year. These were donated to me by former OPSEU vice-president Ev Sammons, the only files on her 40-year career that she hadn't burned the week before I called her for an interview. North Bay protests are covered in *CSAO News*, November, 1966, *Globe*, November 2, 1966, and board of directors' minutes for October 31-November 1, 1966. Other protests are covered in *CSAO News*, April, 1967, and board of directors' minutes for February and August, 1966 and March, 1967. Bowen's plea for modest and achievable bargaining goals was part of his report to the annual general meeting of 1966.

The implications of granting union status to workers at the former Guelph agricultural college once it became part of the university system are discussed in board of directors' minutes for May, 1966. Strikes at Guelph were reported in board minutes for December, 1967 and *CSAO*

News, April 1968. The transfer of responsibility for the Don Jail was followed up by the board of directors in December, 1967 and July, 1968 and in *CSAO News*, December, 1967.

The Rand Formula on union security, with its balance of union rights and responsibilities tied more to industrial peace than justice, is discussed in detail in *All For One*, a book I helped prepare for OPSEU as part of its evidence presented to the Supreme Court defending union rights to political involvement in the Lavigne case, discussed in the last chapter. CSAO and government tactics related to dues checkoff can be traced in board of directors' minutes, every month from June, 1966 to July, 1969, and in *CSAO News*, August, November and December, 1967 and June and November, 1969.

W. Little's report, *Collective Bargaining in the Ontario Government Service: A Report of the Special Adviser His Honour Judge Walter Little*, was tabled May, 1969. The province stopped using moonlighting conciliators such as Little after the 1971 publication of J.C. McRuer, *Royal Commission Inquiry into Civil Rights*. Little's report was criticized by arbitrator and labour law professor H. Arthurs in his *Collective Bargaining by Public Employees in Canada: Five Models*. A more positive view of the seat-of-the-pants, commonsense justice dispensed by the likes of Little was suggested to me by Queen's University labour law professor, Don Carter.

Evidence on the breakneck speed toward a social service state under Robarts is presented in V. Lang, *The Service State Emerges in Ontario: 1945-73*, and in the tenth report of the Committee on Government Productivity (below). The irony of Trudeau's bedroom comment is noted by H. Armstrong in his review of statistics on the growth of the government workforce in L. Panitch's anthology on the state. V. Nelles notes the Tory touch of keeping quiet about the extent of these changes in his essay in M. Whittington, G. Williams ed., *Canadian Politics in the 1990s*.

This achievement in downplaying dramatic change stands out in contrast to Quebec, where the new "state middle class" created by expansion of government services inspired unparalleled militancy, most notably during the 1972 general strike. My assessment of the differences between

Ontario and Quebec is drawn from M. Behiels, *Prelude to Quebec's Quiet Revolution: Liberalism versus Neo-Nationalism, 1945-60*, P. Desbarats, *The State of Quebec: A Journalist's View of the Quebec Revolution*, H. Guindon, *Quebec Society: Tradition, Modernity and Nationhood*, F. Lesemann, *Services and Circuses: Community and the Welfare State*, R. Lévesque, *Memoirs*, H. Milner, *Politics in the New Quebec*, D. Posgate, K. McRoberts, *Quebec: Social Change and Political Crisis*, and G. Pelletier, *Years of Choice*. If nothing else, a comparison of the list of Quebec books with the paltry offerings on Ontario confirm the success of the Tories in achieving a really quiet revolution in affairs of state, and underlines the fact that in order to get the attention of academics, just like the media, it's necessary for workers to stir up a storm.Educational changes in the Robarts era are detailed in two books by W. Fleming: *Ontario's Educative Society: The Administrative Structure*, and *Education: Ontario's Preoccupation*, and in several essays in R. Stamp, H. Stevenson and J. Wilson, eds., *Canadian Education: A History*. The negative side of educational changes is exposed in B. Curtis, D. Livingstone, *Stacking the Deck: The Streaming of Working Class Kids in Ontario Schools*, and in the *Simcoe Reformer*, July 12, 1968.

Fiscal policy changes are documented in D. Richmond (above) and the 1967 government report, *The Ontario Committee on Taxation*. Changes in housing policy are summarized in J. Bacher's monumental *Keeping to the Marketplace: The Evolution of Canadian Housing Policy*. The experiment in Native self-rule is recounted in C. Williams, *Decades of Service: A History of the Ontario Ministry of Community and Social Services: 1930-1980*.

For community colleges, G.Sullivan provides an overview of the origins of community colleges in his 1983 thesis for the University of Toronto, *The development of vocational objectives in the public secondary school system of Ontario, 1960-1969*. S. Arvay's 1984 Ph. D. thesis for York University, *The role of intra-capitalist class conflict in the development of education in Ontario: 1955-1962*, brilliantly links distortions in Ontario's finance-dominated ruling elite to the low standing of vocational education. In terms of contemporary documents, my assessment of the origins of the CAATs relies on the February, 1963 *Report of the Select Committee on*

Manpower Training, and a series of academic reports, with titles as longwinded and banal as their contents: *Report of the Presidents of the Universities of Ontario to the Advisory Committee on University Affairs, Post-Secondary Education in Ontario, 1962-1970,* published in 1962, *The Structure of Post-Secondary Education in Ontario: Supplementary Report No.1 of the Committee of Presidents of Provincially-Assisted Universities and Colleges of Ontario*, printed in 1963, and *The City College, Supplementary Report No. 2*, published by the same committee in 1965.

Changes in prison policy get a positive spin in Oliver (above), while progress in policy, if not administration, for psychiatric hospitals is documented in Simmons (above). The progressive side of regional government in social welfare policy is hailed in D. Steele et al, *Report and Conclusions, Hamilton-Burlington-Wentworth Local Government Review*, released in 1969, and S. Fyfe, *Report of Findings and Recommendations, Waterloo Area Local Government Review*, released in 1970. Popular resistance to regional government is explained in Jacek's excellent article in MacDonald (above).

My critical view of the drive toward big and centralized government, which had the same negative impact on citizen involvement as related workplace changes had on employees, is influenced by N. Chomsky, *Language and Politics*, and his *American Power and the New Mandarins*; by M. Foucault, whose dense ideas are made somewhat decipherable in *Power/Knowledge: Selected interviews and other writings*; by N. Poulantzas, *State Power Socialism*; and by C. Offe's 1980 article in *Studies in Political Economy: A Socialist Review*.

Though little is known about the COGP, that problem is easily solved and well worth the time. Most of what's wrong with government and government labour relations can be traced to the ten reports of the COGP, published between 1970 and 1973. *Report No. 10* is a good sampler. The stunning critique of the COGP's approach, G. Szablowski's "The Public Bureaucracy and the Possibility of Citizen Involvement in the Government of Ontario," was an unpublished working paper of the COGP, released in November, 1971.

The pressures on premier Robarts to launch a corporate review of government operations are outlined in Oliver (above). Premier Davis' long-time associate, Ed Stewart, wrote *Cabinet Government in Ontario: A View from the Inside*, reminiscences which covered the COGP period. There are also topnotch essays on the COGP by H. Segal and G. Szablowski in MacDonald (above). Another insider, J. Fleck, wrote about his experiences in the spring, 1973 issue of *Canadian Public Administration*. K. Brownsey (above) links the COGP to the rise of machine politics and the Big Blue machine. J. Simeon of York University has written, but not published, the best account of the COGP and its failures, and I thank him for lending it to me. The role of Ernest Manning and his son Preston in promoting privatization at COGP meetings is detailed in M. Dobbin's *Preston Manning and the Reform Party*. Similar developments at the federal level are discussed in B. Doern's *Science and Politics in Canada*.

The CSAO's reaction is indicated in *CSAO News*, November, 1970 and February-March, 1972. Legislators debated the COGP recommendations on December 17, 1971, March 28, 1972, April 6, 1972, April 17, 1972, March 27, 1973 and April 3, 1973. Longterm impact on government operations can be gauged from the 1986 report for Liberal cabinet minister E. Caplan, *Managing Human Resources in the Ontario Public Service*, and in the 1985 Price Waterhouse report for the Ontario government, *A Study of Management and Accountability in the Government of Ontario*.

Aside from interviews I conducted on workplace changes during the COGP period, I relied on transcripts of interviews by Pat Bird, an OPSEU member who's writing a history of clerical workers, and notes from interviews by Christine Greco, who studied the subject when she was a student at McMaster University. The Ontario Law Reform Commission's 1973 *Report on Administration of Ontario Courts*, part 3, discusses organizational changes affecting support workers.

Darcy McKeough's botched foray into government labour relations was reported in *Globe*, April 27, 1971. Union responses can be documented in the spring, 1971 issue of *CSAO News*, and in board of director minutes for May 9 and 17, 1971.

CECBA, the most reactionary labour legislation in Ontario history until the NDP's social contract law of 1993, is discussed in Hodgetts and Dwivedi (above), *Star*, March 19 and May 18, 1972, and *CSAO News*, April and May, 1972. It was debated in the legislature on May 4, May 9, May 29 and May 30, 1972. *Canadian News Facts* reported developments in detail throughout October, 1972. Internal executive discussions are recorded in board of director minutes of March and May, 1972. John Ward of OPSEU staff lent me two binders of official documentation on CECBA.

Bowen's efforts to reorganize CSAO can be tracked in *CSAO News*, April, 1968 and January, 1970. See also board of director minutes for November, 1969. In 1972, labour journalist Marc Zwelling exposed Bowen's maneuvres in *Last Post*, which became an underground classic in the union. Jones' firing was reported in *Globe*, November 14, 1972.

The drive to organize community college faculty had a major impact on CSAO, which can be tracked in board of director minutes for March, 1967, February, 1968 and January, 1969, as well as in *CSAO News*, March-April, 1972 and September-October, 1972. The changed workplace conditions that prompted unionization are outlined in A. Porter, *Report of the Inquiry into the Operation of Conestoga College of Applied Arts and Technology*, released in 1974, and W. Stoddardt's 1974 article, "And Madly Administer the Community College," printed by the Ontario Council for Leadership in Educational Administration in 1974.

The wild ride of the Four Horsemen forced Bowen's resignation at the board of directors in March, 1972. The story was picked up by the *Star*, November 20, 1972. The staff strike was reported in *CSAO News*, May, 1973.

Raging Bull

The 1970s are the good old days of CSAO-OPSEU, and still evoke warm memories and vivid stories of great times doing great things. There's a huge fund of oral history about this special time, and I've relied on it extensively for this chapter. Folk memory can be checked against bureaucratic memory. The 1970s were when the union developed a professional staff of researchers and publicists, many of whom held onto minutes, memos, letters, clippings and briefs. John Ward, head of the communications department, has a huge file on this period, and I benefitted from it enormously. Unless otherwise indicated, all correspondence and documents referred to in this chapter come from this file.

Detailed notes on the CAAT meeting that set the tone for CSAO's belated militancy were taken by John Ward. Floyd Laughren's call to arms was issued in a legislative press release of March 6, 1974. The anti-CECBA brief featured at convention is in Ward's files. The board of directors approved the anti-CECBA campaign in February, 1974. Jake Norman's speech at the CSAO convention was carried in *Star*, November 25, 1974. Charles Darrow's career is outlined in *OPSEU News*, June, 1976, and in the *Star* obituary of February 15, 1982. *CSAO News* carried a brief biography of Ron Morse in May, 1973.

The government brochure denouncing CSAO militancy was discussed in the legislature November 1, 1974. Rollie Scott's memo to personnel directors, brownbagged to Ward, is dated August 1, 1974. Echoes of the yelling match between Darrow and Eric Winkler are in Winkler's November 19, 1974 letter to Darrow, and Darrow's December 16 bulletin to CSAO members.

Government amendments to CECBA were reported in *Star* and *Globe*, December 6, 1974. The separate legislation for college workers followed protests by teachers, covered in *CSAO News*, March, 1974. The legislative change is explained in *Life of the Party: The Memoirs of Eddie Goodman*. CSAO criticisms of the old arbitration system were outlined in a brief of January, 1973. For an overview of grievance issues and changes, see K. Swinton, "Grievance Arbitration in the Public Sector," in M. Thompson and G. Swimmer, *Conflict or Compromise*.

For the context of public sector bargaining demands in the mid-1970s, see J. Cousineau, R. Lacroix, *Wage Determination in the Major Collective Agreements in the Private and Public Sectors*, D. Foot, ed., *Public*

Employment and Compensation in Canada: Myths and Realities, M. Bucovetsky, ed., *Studies in Public Employment and Compensation in Canada*, and the Institute of Public Administration's 1973 *Collective Bargaining in the Public Service*. For an example of favourable media coverage of Chris Trower's handling of CSAO demands, see *Star* editorial, September 24, 1974. The impact of the AIB is discussed by L. Panitch and D. Schwarz in Thompson and Swimmer (above). OPSEU's early opposition to the AIB is made clear in *OPSEU News*, November, 1975.

The nation- and world-wide trend to government cutbacks in the mid-1970s can be seen from D. Wolfe's essay in Kealey and Cross (above), H. Chorney, P. Hansen, "The Falling Rate of Legitimation: The Problem of the Contemporary Capitalist State in Canada," *Studies in Political Economy*, Autumn, 1980, CSE State Group, *Cuts and Restructuring in Contemporary Britain*, and R. Mishra, *The Welfare State in Capitalist Society: Policies of Retrenchment and Maintenance in Europe, North America and Australia*. The proceedings of a 1975 Toronto industrial relations conference, edited by M. Gunderson as *Collective Bargaining in the Essential and Public Service Sectors*, give an inkling of the views of some key government bureaucrats.

The pressures on premier Davis to move toward cutbacks, and his responses, can be followed in *Canadian News Facts* from May to November, 1975. Information on most members of the McKeough-Henderson committee comes from *Who's Who*. Maxwell Henderson wrote an autobiography, *Plain Talk! Memoirs of an Auditor General*. The fits and fancies of McKeough on fiscal policy, analyzed by K. Bryden in MacDonald (above), can be checked in legislative debates for December 11, 1975 and November 23, 1976. Paul McKay puts his spending spree on nuclear power under the microscope in two excellent studies, *Electric Empire: The Inside Story of Ontario Hydro*, and *The Roman Empire: The Unauthorized Life and Times of Stephen Roman*. The report was debated in the legislature from October 28 to December 18, 1975.

My assessment of the report's significance leans on I. Bakker, "The Size and Scope of Government: Robin Hood sent packing," in Williams and Whittington (above), K. Banting, "The Welfare State and Inequality in the 1980s," in *Canadian Review of Sociology and Anthropology*, 1987, and N. Nevitte, R. Gibbins, "Neo-Conservatism: Canadian variations on an American Ideological Theme," in *Canadian Public Policy*, 1984. The relevance of the hysteria around public spending can be judged after reading B. Doern, A. Maslove, eds., *The Public Evaluation of Government Spending*. Ontario public opinion on these issues was analyzed for the Ontario Economic Council in D. Auld's *Fiscal Knowledge and Preferences in Ontario*.

OPSEU's reaction to the cuts was expressed in *OPSEU News*, December, 1975. Highlights of the anti-cutbacks movement were reported in *OPSEU News*, May and June, 1976. The different tacks taken in B.C. and Ontario are outlined in A. Muscovitch, "The Welfare State Since 1975," *Journal of Canadian Studies*, 1985. The impact of this generation of cuts on government staff can be seen in *Ontario Statistics, 1986*. The impact on government management style is reviewed in Canada Consulting Group, *Management and Accountability in the Government of Ontario, 1985* and Ontario Management Board of Cabinet, *Managing Human Resources in the Ontario Public Service*, released in March, 1986.

Union-sponsored chartered flights were advertised in *CSAO News*, June, 1975. Union-sponsored hockey tournaments were the subject of a glowing report in the Toronto *Sun*, November 21, 1976.

The transformation of working conditions in hospitals is discussed in O. Hall, *The Paramedical Occupations in Ontario*, Chemical Engineering Research Associates, *Private Clinical Laboratories in Ontario*, R. Fraser, *Selected Economic Aspects of the Health Care Sector in Ontario*, all background studies for the Ontario Committee on Healing Arts. Early union initiatives in the health and safety area are reported in *OPSEU News*, November, 1975 and June, 1976.

Desperately seeking Union

Sean O'Flynn stretched the union and its key staff and activists to the limit, and attracted many leaders who went on to make their own marks in senior management, government and labour circles into the next decade (though many have taken positions at odds with their earlier views). The union had a wide-open, even frontier, feel to it, and embraced a host of causes with great passion. The range of issues, backed by extensive historical documentation from third party sources, is conveniently available in a briefing book I prepared for the new Liberal government in 1985, *The Public Service Agenda: A Return To A Caring Society*. The energy inside OPSEU was so intense and sometimes factional that many outsiders came to refer to OPSEU as "the Lebanon of the labour movement." To guard against one-sided memories in the many interviews I relied on for the text of this chapter, I took care to confirm all reminiscences with either one written source or two oral sources.

Relations between CSAO and the CLC were discussed at the CSAO board of directors in July and August, 1973, and reported in *CSAO News*, December, 1974. OPSEU's evolution can be tracked in *OPSEU News*, June, 1976, December, 1979, and May, 1980.

The CAAT Support strike was covered extensively in *OPSEU News*, October, 1979. Early indications of unrest among correctional officers can be found in *CSAO News*, September-October and November, 1972. The strike was reported in detail in *OPSEU News*, December, 1979. Harry Arthurs kindly lent me his detailed notes on the arbitration hearing that resolved the strike.

Premier Davis' move toward wage controls was covered by *Star* and *Globe*, July 6, 1982 and by *Canadian News Facts* throughout the summer and fall. Davis spoke to the issues in the legislature on June 27, September 21 and December 15. OPSEU's bargaining gains that overcame controls legislation were reviewed in *OPSEU News*, July-September and October-December, 1984.

John Ward's files in the communications department contain all the documents and clippings related to the prison overcrowding campaign. The union's 1985 video, *To Serve in Silence*, contains lengthy interviews with correctional officer Larry Folz and forester Donald MacAlpine. Welfare fieldworkers documented their actions and views in a series of newsletters published by Workers for Social Responsibility in 1983 and 1984.

Conditions of women government workers in the mid-1970s are documented in *Report of the Executive Co-ordinator of Women's Programs on Status of Women Crown Employees in Ontario, 1974/5*, and in the Civil Service Commission's annual reports. Women's wages are evaluated in G. Bell, A. Pascoe, *The Ontario Government: Structure and Functions*, and M. Gunderson, "Decomposition of the Public-Private Sector Earnings Differentials," in Bucovetsky (above). Affirmative action for women was debated in the legislature from November 8, 1974 to July 15, 1975. The union's refusal to participate in token efforts to redress these problems is outlined in *OPSEU News*, January, 1976.

The union's early response to women's concerns is evident in *CSAO News*, February, 1971, April, 1971 and January, 1972. OPSEU's 1985 video, *A Rose Is Not Enough*, reviews early efforts of women to reform the union, and highlights the career of Corrie Barrett. Debbie Field wrote an insightful assessment of her tenure as equal opportunity officer, "The Dilemma facing Women's Committees," in L. Briskin and L. Yanz, *Union Sisters: Women in the Labour Movement*. I want to thank Linda Briskin for lending me her file of women's committee memos and minutes. She evaluated her learnings while active in OPSEU, in "Women, Unions and Leadership," in *Canadian Dimension*, January-February, 1990.

Highlights of the campaign against cutbacks at psychiatric hospitals are recorded in Tom Baker's April 12, 1984 memo to all stewards and staff, a copy of which is in the files I donated to OPSEU. In 1980, the union published *Ontario's Mental Health Care Breakdown*, and in 1982 it published the commissioned book-length report by John Marshall, *Madness: An Indictment of the Mental Health Care System in Ontario*. The campaign against closures of centres for the developmentally handicapped was reviewed by OPSEU's special operations director, Sean Usher, in his 1983 *De-Institutionalization: A Union Perspective*. Coalition efforts are recorded in *Report of York-OPSEU Conference January 27, 1984: Care of the Developmentally-Handicapped: Way of the Future?* Small-town coverage of the campaign was extensive; see, for example, *Cobourg Star*, March 28, 1984. The first investigation into occupational stress suffered by institutional care workers was reported in *OPSEU News*, June, 1976. An eloquent account of efforts to deal constructively with debilitating stress among correctional officers was given to me by Gary Lenehan when I edited *QWL Focus*, Spring, 1984.

The dysfunctional framework for community college bargaining is described by OPSEU staffer Katie FitzRandolph in "A bargaining structure that defies gravity," *Colleges Canada*, September, 1984. The 1974 survey that documented college teacher dissatisfaction with teaching conditions was published by J. Desroches in the *Canadian Journal of Higher Education*, 1978. Several studies document the depth of teacher concern for quality education and the evolution toward union action: D. Tripp, "Change in the Community College: An Impossible Dream?", *Ontario Council for Leadership in Educational Administration (OCLEA)*, fall, 1980; J. Wooley, "Occupational Stress Among Community College Administrators," University of Toronto Ph.D. thesis, 1983; and N. Kefental, "Teacher Professionalism and Public Sector Unionism in Toronto Community Colleges: An Analysis of Member Union Relations," University of Toronto Ph.D. thesis, 1988. The union's position was vindicated by Michael Skolnick's follow-up report for the government, *Survival or Excellence?*.

Extensive background on the Lavigne case can be found in the union booklet I edited, *All For One*.

INDEX

Abortion, 249-50, 253
Adams, George, 164
Advocacy Resource Centre for the Handicapped (ARCH), 259-60
Agriculture, Department of, 10, 14, 88, 124
AIB. *See* Anti-Inflation Board
Algonquin College, 208, 241
Alinsky, Saul (*Rules for Radicals*), 218, 224-25
Alinsky seminars, 224-25
Allan, Bev, 208, 211, 240, 244, 249
Ambulance sector: organizing of ambulance officers, 196-97; organizing of private services, 196-97; push for co-ordinated bargaining, 227. *See also* individual services
Anderson, Lieut.-Gen. William, 183
Anti-Inflation Board (AIB), 179, 181,182. *See also* Wage and price controls, 1975
Appointment, in public service, 5-7, 11, 42
Apps, Syl, 82
Arbitration board overseeing CECBA, 157-58
Arbitration: CAAT academic settlement, 1984, 269-70; changes brought about by, 128; re Corrections 1979, 216; five per cent guideline, 222; infrequent resort to in 1960s, 82; merit principle, 128; under 1975 wage and price controls, 181; under 1980s wage controls, 222-23; right to, 95; on whistleblowers' rights, 234-35. *See also* Grievances
ARCH. *See* Advocacy Resource Centre for the Handicapped
Armes, Gord, 197
Armstrong, Jack, 56, 82, 118
Armstrong, Tim, 161, 163, 169, 203
Art Gallery of Ontario: organizing drive, 226-27
Arthurs, Harry, 66, 96, 216, 217
Asbestos handlers, 198
Association of Professional Foresters, 234
Auld, Jimmy, 120, 164

Back-to-work legislation, 132; CAAT academic strike 1984, 269
Bakker, Isabella, 185
Bargaining. *See* Negotiations
Bargaining legislation: for civil servants and CAAT academic, 127
Bargaining rights: held by CSAO, not locals, 147; lack of, in CSAO, 41, 52; suspension of, 1982, 219; over technological change, 159; willingness of government to consider, 77
Barrs, Helen, 254-55
Basher, Col. Hedley, 73, 103
Bayly, Edward, 13
Beardall, F.G., 31, 39
Beaton, A.H., 11
Beatty, Dave, 162, 163, 164
Beck, Sir Adam, 32
BEEP. *See* Branch Executive Education Program
Bekerman, André, 160, 204, 211, 221, 232; bargaining strategy, 228; and institutional care debacle aftermath, 219; institutional care negotiations, 261
Big Blue Machine, 115-16
Bill 70, 1978 (on workers rights re health and safety): initial exclusion of OPSEU workers, 198; OPSEU campaign for inclusion, 198; on workers rights re health and safety, 198
Bill 105, 151. *See* CECBA
Bill 217 (on formalizing labour relations), 129, 130
Blackwell, Leslie, 44-45

296

Blatchford, Christie, 193
Bluewater Centre, 258
Bowen, Harold, 51, 84, 85, 86, 94, 126, 134, 205; and CAAT, 140; capitulation to CECBA, 144; changes to CSAO bylaws, 141; concern with union structure, 136; as CSAO president, 1953-57, 83; departure from CSAO, 145; incorporation of CSAO National, 195; Four Horsemen revolt against, 142-43; methods used to monopolize power, 136-37; November 1962 board meeting, 75; ousting, then re-instatement of, 143; push for collective bargaining, 70, 71; 143; response to 1971 budget, 129; role in evolution of CSAO towards unionism, 69; and strike threat, 1959, 72
Branch Executive Education Program (BEEP), 193
Brannan, Carl, 109-10
Brantford School for the Deaf, 146
Briskin, Linda, 166, 167, 248, 266, 267
British Columbia government workers union, 84
British-style civil service, 6, 27
Broader Public Service. *See* OLRA sector
Brockville Psychiatric Hospital, 78-79, 164
Brodeur, Paul, 254
Brown, Colin, 159, 160, 270
Brown, Don, 84, 162, 201, 203, 217
Brown, James, 11
Brownstone Inn, 178
Bruce, Grant, 162
Brugma, Henry, 219
Bryden, Ken, 74
Budgets, provincial: fiscal budgets, 98; 1944, 41; 1956-59, 65; 1971, 128-29; 1972, 131; 1980, 191
Bureaucracy. *See* Government bureaucracy
Bureaucratization of the workplace under COGP, 118-19

Burke, Mike, 207
Burkett, Kevin, 84-85, 135
Burrows, Eileen, 243, 244, 245
Business Council on National Issues, 182
Bylaw 66, 137

CAAT. *See* Colleges of Applied Arts and Technology
CAAT academic, 263-70; achieve right to strike, 162; CAAT/union staff antipathy, 265; characteristics of, 138-39, 266; characteristics of bargaining teams, 264; decertification attempt, 265; denunciation of CECBA, 150-51; first round of province-wide bargaining, 1972, 139; low morale after cutbacks, 267; 1972 negotiations, 265; 1974 survey, 266; 1983 bargaining team request for special division to handle teacher discontent, 267; 1984 negotiations, 267-68; 1984 strike, 263, 267-70; organizing of, 137-39; pre-1975 bargaining, 264; quality of education, 266-68; quality of education committee set up by OPSEU, 266-67; request OPSEU for funds for survey on teachers' problems, 267; resentment of OPSEU staff, 265; response to George Brown layoffs, 140; right to bargain, 159; right to strike, 158, 161, 162
CAAT support staff, 89, 138, 142, 240; 1978 strike vote, 209-10; 1979 strike, 209-12; achieve right to strike, 162; bargaining teams, 208-9; considered blue-collar workers, 209; contracting out work of, 132; first collective agreement, 1968, 208; right to bargain, 158; right to strike, 158, 161, 162
Cadbury, George, 40
Cambrian College, 138, 139, 267
Campaigns department: activities re "de-institutionalization," 257. *See also* "Making It Public"; Special Opera-

297

tions
Campbell, Wayne, 123, 151-52, 192
Canadian Annual Review: on 1982 wage controls, 221
Canadian Council of Provincial Employee Associations (CCPEA), 45, 205
Canadian Federation of Government Employee Organizations (CFGEO), 205
Canadian Labour Congress (CLC), 45, 91, 271; 1974 convention, 171, 206; 1974 and 1976 application of CSAO to join, 205-6; 1976 convention, 206; OPSEU affiliation with, 207; program of price and profit controls, 180
Canadian Mental Health Association study (*More for the Mind*), 103
Canadian Union of Public Employees (CUPE), 91, 195, 196; charges re making deal with U.S.-dominated unions, 171; CSAO rivalry with, 88; resistance to CSAO joining CLC, 205-6
Carr, Shirley, 171
Carruthers, Justice Douglas, 217
Carter, Don, 155, 162
Cassidy, Michael, 131, 157, 190
Casual workers, 123
CCF. *See* Co-operative Commonwealth Federation
CCM. *See* Committee of Concerned Members
CCPEA. *See* Canadian Council of Provincial Employee Associations
CECBA. *See* Crown Employees Collective Bargaining Act
Centennial College, 218, 243; occupation of president's office, 218
Centres for the developmentally handicapped: closings of, 256-57; working conditions in, 256. *See also* Healthcare sector; Institutional care; Institutional care workers; Psychiatric institutions

CFGEO. *See* Canadian Federation of Government Employees Organizations
Chapple, Phyllis, 218
Charlesworth, Hector, 10
Charlton, Brian, ii, 159, 189
Charter of Rights and Freedoms, 229; and Lavigne case, 270-71
Checkoff: membership dues, 52, 84, 90, 94, 125; for 1930s relief fund, 30. *See also* Union dues
Chedoke hospital, 189
Children's aid societies: organizing of, 226; Ottawa Children's Aid Society, 226
Civil servants: early days, 3-12, 26; nature of, in 1950s, 55-56; organize first association, 1911, 2, 12; public perception of, 59; work ethic in early days, 26. *See also* CSAO; OPSEU; various
Civil Service Appeal Board, 39
Civil Service Association of Ontario (CSAO). *See* CSAO
Civil Service Commission (CSC), 18, 65, 81; attempts to keep wages in line with classifications, 1944, 51; attitude to JAC, 38-39; complacency re male/female wage differentials, 1950, 62; CSAO call for equal representation on, 37; employee classification questionnaire, 1947, 42; lifting of discrimination against married women, 63; merit system applied to hiring, 42; responsibility for personnel policy shared with Management Board, 113; weakened under 1947 Public Service Act, 42
Civil service reform. *See* Committee on Government Productivity
Civil service reformers, early days, 8, 9, 17, 19
Civil Service Review, 27, 29, 33-34, 38; on George Drew, 37; on the JAC, 39
Civil service, department of the: creation

of , 1961, 66
Clancy, James, 258: elected as OPSEU president, 232, 269; as new welfare local president, 236; pushes for new divisions in OPSEU along occupational lines, 237-38; Lavigne case, 271
Clark, Dr. Judson, 24
Clark, Justin, 259-60
Class politics, 31
CLC. *See* Canadian Labour Congress
Clement, Merion, 135
Clockwatching, 47
Coates, Mary, 171, 199-200
Cobourg *Daily Star:* on D'Arcy Place closing, 258
Coffey, Ben, 141
COGP. *See* Committee on Government Productivity
"Collective Bargaining in the Ontario Public Service." *See* Little report
Collective bargaining: CSAO push for, 70, 71, 72; by occupation, 90; advent of, 142; right to, sought by teachers, 100. *See also* Negotiations
Colleges Act, 140
Colleges Collective Bargaining Act, 158, 209, 270
Colleges of Applied Arts and Technology, 89, 127, 137-40, 208-12, 263-70; adversarial relationship between management and staff, 264; attitude of university towards, 102; Council of Regents, 264; launching of, 100-2; legislation, 161-62; management style, 264; mandate of, 101-2; presidents of, 139, 267; quality of education loses ground, 267; right to bargain, 159; right to strike, 158, 161, 162. *See also* CAAT academic; CAAT support staff
Committee for Responsibility in Education, 270
Committee of Concerned Members (CCM), 174; charges against O'Flynn and supporters, 175

Committee on Government Productivity (COGP), 107-19, 130, 164, 183, 186, 228; appointment of, 96; "armchair forestry" following, 233; accomplishments of, 114; bureaucratization of the workplace, 118-19; contributing to businesslike efficiency in government, 109; contribution to diminished sense of worker autonomy, 119; contribution to end of expansion era, 131; effects on women workers, 124; failings of, 112-13, 114-15; formalization of methods for dealing with workplace problems, 120-25; government reorganization, 109; influence in the workplace, 117; layoffs as a consequence of, 148; members of, 110; ministry streamlining, 113-14; preparation for privatization, 112; Productivity Improvement Project, 110; public relations, 127; reclassifications of jobs, 118-19; report on human resources, 131; as stimulus for CSAO unionization, 116-17
Communists, 36, 44, 48, 49
Community and Social Services, Ministry of, 237, 256; five-year plan re health-care institutions, 256-61; implements "integration" scheme, 237-38
Community colleges. *See* Colleges of Applied Arts and Technology
Compulsory arbitration: Bill 217, 129
Compulsory retirement, 20, 44
Conestoga College, 139
Confederation College, 208
Confederation Life, 159
Conference Board of Canada, 185
Conscription in WW I, 17
Contracting out, 112; Centennial College maintenance workers, 218; of cleaning and maintenance jobs, 123; of highway jobs, 187; of work by CAAT support staff, 132
Cooper, Vic, 121, 200; report on prison

system to 1974 convention, 213
Coopers & Lybrand, 182
Co-operative Commonwealth Federation, 40; commitment to independence of civil service in Saskatchewan, 39; rising popularity during WW II, 36
Corporations Act, 173
Correctional officers, 73-74, 162, 212-17, 218; achievement of province-wide branch, 90; CSAO organizing of, 89; fight for prisoners' rights, 228-32; high turnover of, 214; 1972 brief, 213; 1974 wage offer, 167, 168; 1975 brief on jail conditions, 213; 1979 bargaining push for distinct category for jail guards, 214-15, 216-17, 228; 1979 illegal strike, 215-17; 1979 mediation, 216; 1982 negotiations, 228-29; 1982 settlement, 261; push for grievance rights, 74-75; at risk on the job, 213; strike song, 215-16; treatment of women staff, 246; working conditions, 121, 229
Corrections, Ministry of, 229, 230
Cost-of-living: allowances, 25; bonuses, 46, 52; to low-paid workers, 1942, 34; wage demands, 45, 46
Council for Leadership in Educational Administration study, 1974, 139
Court system: 1973 law reform study, 124-25
Craig, Bill, 119, 120-21
Cronyn, J.B., 110
Crown Employees Collective Bargaining Act (CECBA), ii, iii, iv, v, 130-31, 143, 162, 187, 255, 261, 264; amendments to, 158-59; amendments to re grievances and mileage allowance, 133; arbitration board, 157-58; catalyst in creating adversarial system, 147; CSAO brief demanding 24 changes, 153; CSAO campaign against, 152-58; Norman's opposition to, 150-51; passage of, 133-34; reception of, 132; repeal of, iii; threat of protest strike, 144; union brief on, 143; union protest during final reading, 144
Crown Transfers Act, 159, 164
CSAO (Civil Service Association of Ontario), 11; 1911 founding of, 12-13; aims of early organization, 13; 1920 annual meeting, 15; anti-strike attitude in early days, 15; 1927 charter, amendments to, 70; incorporation of, 1927, 28-29; 1933 annual meeting, 30; 1940s appeals for structured relationship with government based on equality, 37-38; cold war vs., waged by Drew government, 44-47; decision to hire full-time staffers, 45; first headquarters, 45; representation on department councils challenged, 47; 1950 referendum on joining Trades and Labour Congress, 51; Isabella Street headquarters, 52; motto ("Modern, Loyal, Efficient"), 52; 1952 annual meeting, 53; clubhouse on St. George St., 53; 1952 elections, 69; evolution towards unionization, 69, 81, 83-90, 116, 142; gaining recognition as representative of Ontario civil servants, 1955, 69; internal barriers to unionism, 53-58; 1956 annual meeting, 70; 1956 brief, 69; 1957 recruitment problem, 53; 1958 brief demanding formal bargaining, 71; internal disputes, 134, 141-42; exclusion of senior managers from membership in, 81; 1964 convention, 85; factors favouring unionization, 80; increasing militancy, 1960s, 85; fear of losing members to other unions as incentive to unionize, 87-88; registers as union, 1966, 88; as sole bargaining agent for civil servants, 92, 94; first collective agreement, 88; internal structure of, 135-36, 137; special relationship with government, 37, 92; consultants' recommendations on reorganization, late

1960s, 135; rejection of old role as social, service and self-help organization, 135-36; battle for control of, 141-45; efforts on behalf of women, 239; response to bureaucratization, 123; renewal after Bowen's departure, 147; 1974 convention, 157, 170; 1974 elections, 171; affiliation with other associations, 205; campaign against CECBA, 152-58; new-found militancy under Norman and Darrow, 148-55; reaction to Winkler brochure, 157; Free the Servants campaign, 152-58, 160, 170, 164; response to CECBA amendments, 159; 1974 attempt to join CLC, 205; change of name to Ontario Public Service Employees Union, 1975, 170

CSAO board of directors, 29, 70, 72, 75-76, 81, 84, 94, 135, 146, 195, 202; meetings on CECBA, 152, 154; resignation of, 51, 53; revolt vs. Bowen, 141-45

CSAO membership: exclusion of part-time and marginal workers from, 96; exclusion of professionals from, 95, 96

CSAO National, 195

CSAO News, 81; on CECBA, 144; on CFGEO annual meeting, 205; on COGP, 117; on Little report, 95; on women's issues, 239, 240, 241

CSAO-CSC relationship, 125

CSAO-CUPE rivalry, 91-93, 195, 205-6

CSC. *See* Civil Service Commission

Compulsory retirement, 44

CUPE-CSAO rivalry. *See* CSAO-CUPE rivalry

CUPE. *See* Canadian Union of Public Employees

Cutbacks, government, 181-82, 187-91; in college sector, 267; during the Depression, 30; in health sector, 187, 189; in institutional care, 256-57, 259-62; recommendations of Henderson report, 186-87; response of CSAO to Depression cutbacks, 30-31

D'Arcy Place, Cobourg: campaign to save the centre, 258

Daly, Charles, 42

Darrow, Barb, 208

Darrow, Charlie, 142, 174, 175, 176, 194, 199-200, 243, 245; named president, 154-55; dissatisfaction with CECBA amendments, 159; election as president, 1974, 171; electoral defeat, 1978, 200; general operations negotiations, 165-66; response to Henderson report, 188

Davidson, Dr. Martha, 14

Davis, William, 8, 99, 113, 160, 161, 217, 256, 258; and committee to review government expenditures, 182, 183; CECBA protest in North Bay, 151-52; election as Ontario Conservative leader, 1971, 115; endorsation of Gordon report, 68; importance of COGP to, 108; meeting with Gemmell over CSAO brief on CECBA, 153; relations with labour leaders, 203-4; and wage and price controls, 1975, 180; and wage controls, 1982-84, 219, 220, 222

Dawson, R.M., 27-28

Deans, Ian, 131, 189; on CECBA, 133-34

"De-institutionalization," 256-67, 259-60

DeMatteo, Bob, 198-99, 253, 254, 255, 255; publicizes Ministry of Labour ruling on Rutton case, 262; *Terminal Shock*, 155

Denison Mines, 185

Dennis, Lloyd, 99

Depression of the 1930s, 30-31; civil service job security during, 31-32; fringe benefits of civil servants during, 31; unemployment, 31

Derber, Carl (*Power in the Highest Degree*), 112

301

DiSalle, Nick, 235-36
District managers, 119
Dollar-a-year men, 39-40
Don Jail, 73, 74, 134, 213-14; wildcat strike, 1968, 89
Donahue, John (*The Privatization Decision*), 115
Donnelly, E.V., 15
Donut brigade, 144
Doughty, Howard, 267
Douglas, Tommy, 40
Drea, Frank, 258
Drew, George, 35, 36, 37, 38, 39, 45, 232; anti-welfare state attitude of, 48; attitude to concept of independent civil service administrators, 39-40; attitude to "malingerers," 46-47; election in 1945, 44; falling out with Finkelman, 66; loss of seat in 1948 election, 47; steps towards civil service reform, 42
Drury, Ernest C., 18, 20, 21, 26
Dunsmore, Ross, 216
Durham Centre, Oshawa: court injunction against closing of, 259
Dymond, Dr. Matthew, 86, 103

Earl, Joyce, 122, 256
Eastham, Frank, 154, 174, 175, 196
Economic and Planning Board, Saskatchewan, 40
Education, union, 135, 193; educational videos, 135. *See also* Branch Executive Education Programme
Education, Ministry of, 242
Education, public, 11; amalgamation of school boards, 1968, 99-100; as government showpiece, 99; grassroots resistance to government reforms in, 100; provincial share of financing, 191; reforms, 99; teachers seek collective-bargaining rights, 100. *See also* Colleges of Applied Arts and Technology; CAAT academic; CAAT support staff; individual colleges

Edwards, Claude, 205
Efficiency movement, 16-18, 21-22, 23, 26; U.S. influence on, 18
Elections, provincial: 1943, 36; 1945, 44; 1948, 47-48; 1959, 48; 1975, 183; 1977, 190; 1981, 220, 256; 1990, 235
Elizabeth Fry Society, 229
Elliot Lake, 198
Employee Assistance Programs, 263
"Enemy aliens," 17
Equal opportunities co-ordinator, 244
Equal pay for work of equal value, 12, 86. *See also* Women

Factory Act, prosecutions under, 11-12
Fair Tax Commission, 1992, 191
Farm colony for returned soldiers, 23
Fawcett, Rusty, 54-55, 125, 156, 200, 265
Field, Debbie, 211, 240, 243-44, 245, 246
Finkelman, Jacob, 66-67
Firefighters, 119
Five-day work week, implementation of, 1951, 51; debate, mid-1940s, 46
Fleck, James, 110, 116, 183, 190, 246
Fleck Manufacturing, 183-84: strike at, 184, 246
Fogel, Mel, 265
Folz, Larry, 229-30
Ford workers' strike, 1945, 90
Forest management practices, 24
Forestry workers, 56-58, 59, 118-19
Foster, Charles, 33, 39
Foster, Wilf, 83-84; compromise on Sanderson wage complaint, 62
"Four Horsemen of the Apocalyse," 141-42, 152, 174
Foucault, Michel: on new treatments in European asylums and jails, 107
Free the Servants campaign, 152-58, 160, 164, 165, 170, 177, 179; fight for freedom of speech, 233
Fringe benefits, 31
Frost, Leslie, 35, 41, 53, 65; civil service recruitment in time of, 54; conditions

of institutions during regime of, 59; directive to Walter Gordon, 68; fringe benefits for civil servants, 52; labour relations under, 48-49, 66; opposed to recognizing CSAO as a union, 52; paternalism of, 67; politics of, 48-49, 64; reaction to demands for formal bargaining, 71; relations with the CSAO, 50-51; response to 1956 CSAO brief, 69-70; response to 1959 strike threat, 72

Fryer, John, 205; as NUPGE leader, 207

Full-time staffers, first hiring of, 45

Fuller, Jim, i, 157, 178

Gallup poll on unionism, 1956, 67

Gardiner, Fred, 36, 49

Garrow Resolution, 1897, 7, 8, 76

Gemmell, George, 84, 85, 142, 143, 144, 145, 205; anti-CECBA campaign, 153-54; bargaining style of, 70; humiliation at North Bay, 137; meeting with Management Board over COGP, 148; resignation of, 154

General operational category: 1974 negotiations, 165-70; 1974 strike threat, 166-67, 177

George Brown College, 140, 243, 266, 268

Gillies, James, 114-15

Glee club, of civil service, 45

Globe and Mail, 86; on CECBA, 132; on CLC campaign vs. 1982 wage controls, 222; on institutional care workers, 86; on McKeough, 131-32; on OPSEU lawsuit on prison overcrowding, 231

Goodman, Eddie, 161

Gordon, Walter, 67; 1959 report of, 68

Goudge, Steve, 163

Government bureaucracy, 114; as a catalyst for unionization, 120

Government-civil service relations, 72; CSAO brief of 1956, 69; effect of decrease in numbers of industrial workers, 65; effect of growth of service sector, 65; effect of urbanization, 64-65; evolution from political to bureaucratic control, 77; government's hands-off approach, 75; government's hands-on policy, 43, 109. *See also* Labour relations; Management-worker relations

Government expansion and reform, 68, 97-112. *See also* Committee on Government Productivity

Government-labour relations, conference on, 183

Government managers, 1985 review of, 191

Government restraint. *See* Cutbacks, government

Government spending: under Drew, 1946, 41; 1977 Ontario Economic poll on, 187; as percentage of gross provincial product, 191. *See also* Henderson report

Greenland, Cyril, 103, 104, 105

Grievance Settlement Board, 162-64; CSAO right to appoint representatives to, 159

Grievances, 126, 193; Alinsky influence, 225; on equal pay for work of equal value, 252; first grievance committee, 1956, 70; formalization under COGP, 120; on health and safety effects of VDTs, 254-55; increase in number under O'Flynn, 203; informal avenues for complaint, 82-83; re job classification, 119; by MacAlpine for unfair dismissal, 234-35; no procedures for in CSAO, 27; procedure for, 66, 203, 225; right to grieve management decision re dismissal, appraisal and classification, under CECBA, 133; right to grieve mileage allowance, 133. *See also* Grievance Settlement Board

Grigg, Albert, 14

Grossman, Allan, 49, 50; as corrections minister, 103

303

Guelph Reformatory, 22; 1952 riot in, 103
Guelph University, 88
Guillemette, Bob, 261
Gulbis, Joyce, 243, 247

Haggart, Ron, 59
Haggett, Ron, 142, 146, 175, 200
Haileybury School of Mines. *See* Northern College
Hall, Emmett, 99
Hall, Oswald, 194
Hall-Dennis report, 99
Halton-Mississauga ambulance workers strike, 227
Hamilton, Fred, 127, 139, 264
Hamilton Recruiting League, 17
Hancock, George, 268
Haskett, Irwin, 74
Health, Ministry of, 25, 120, 239, 256
Health and safety, 197-99, 209, 261-63; Bill 70, 198; Health and Safety Act, 262; legislation, 261-62; right to refuse unsafe work, 254; Saskatchewan model, 198-99. *See also* Bill 70; VDTs
Health-care sector: organizing in, 194, 195-97; organizing outside civil service, 226; rival unions within, 195
"Healthy athletics," 13
Hearst, W.H., 17, 24, 26
Hebdon, Bob, 126, 142, 145, 149, 195, 210, 211; on CECBA, 134; as researcher for CAAT academic bargaining teams, 264-65; temporarily assigned as assistant general manager, 143
Henderson, Maxwell, 183
Henderson report on government spending ("Report of the Special Program Review"), 181-91, 209, 226, 256; impact of, 190; OPSEU response to, 187-89; recommendation re welfare expenditures (the "integration" scheme), 237

Henry, George, 30, 31, 32
Hepburn, Mitch, 32, 33, 35, 36, 48; anti-union stand, 35-36
Hicks, Robert, 92, 127, 130, 163
Hicks Morley Hamilton, 127, 216
Highway truck inspectors: work to rule, 1963, 85-86
Highways, Department of, 58, 80
Highways workers, 58, 61, 85, 118, 119, 120
Holowka, Jan, 122, 262
Homuth, Dorothy, 126
Hope Commission report, 41
Hopkins, Cam, 138, 139, 267
Hospitals. *See* Health-care sector; Institutional care; Institutional care workers; Psychiatric institutions; individual institutions
Howe, C.D., 40
Hudson, H.C., 34
Hughes, Laura, 11
Human resource management, 107, 111
Human resources, 1986 review of, 191
Humber College, 259, 266, 267
Huot, John, 266
Huron, Craig, 19
Hupet, Len, 212
Hurlburt, Robert, 184
Hydro workers, 132

Incorporation of CSAO, 28
Indian Development Branch, 100
Inflation Restraint Act (1982), 220, 222; OPSEU response to, 220-21; five per cent guidelines, 222
Institutional care, 78-80; coalitions against the Ministry of Community and Social Services' five-year plan, 258-59; cutbacks in, 189-90: dismantling of institutions in the name of social integration of the disadvantaged, 190; effect of COGP on, 121-23; five-year plan, 256-59; five-year plan, OPSEU campaign against, 257-59; 1975 health and safety investiga-

tion, 198; OPSEU attempt to discuss rising assault rate in 1982 negotiations, 261; reforms in, 103-5; segregation of male and female wards, 63; shameful conditions in institutions, 59. *See also* Heath-care sector; Institutional care workers; individual institutions

Institutional care workers: bargaining teams, 214; effects of cutbacks on worker safety, 261; female hospital workers' demands for equal pay for work of equal value, 86-87; 1966 demands of, 86; 1982 settlement, 261; 1985 settlement, 263; North Bay agitprop theatre, 189; sense of responsibility for patients, 256; signing up by UGWO of, 91-92; stress as workplace hazard, 262-63; threaten strike over parity with correctional officers, 218-19; war veterans, 80; win right to work with local managers to develop strategies to deal with health and safety issue, 263. *See also* Heath-care sector; Institutional care; individual institutions

Insurance benefits, 159

"Internal labour market," 19

IQ tests, 24

JAC. *See* Joint Advisory Council

Jackson, Rainford, 258

Jail guards. *See* Correctional workers

Jails: poor conditions in, 59, 121; riot at Guelph, 73-74. *See also* Correctional workers; Prison system; individual jails

James, C.C., 13

Job classification, 21-22, 27, 21-23, 24, 25, 42, 68, 252; hiring of U.S. consultants, 23; reclassifications under COGP, 118-19

Job evaluation, 252; first OPSEU scheme for, 211-12

John Howard Society, 229

Johnston, R.C., 52

Johnston, Richard, 255

Joint Advisory Council (JAC): creation of, 38-39, 74, 77; advisory status of, 43; first permanent secretary, 66; inadequacies of, 51; lack to power to implement decisions, 73; merely a "talkshop," 45; position of five-day work week, 46; recognizes CSAO as representative of Ontario civil servants, 1955, 69; replacement by Ontario Joint Council, 1963, 75

Jolliffe, Ted, 234

Jones, Grenville, 84, 134-35, 137, 140-41, 269; firing of, 141, 142

Jones, Maxine, 175, 243, 248

Julian, Debbie, 142, 248

Keatinge, T. Brendan, 74

Keatings, Jim, 83, 84, 140; firing of, 134, 141

Kefentse, Netto, 268

Kelso, J.J., 11

Kennedy, Betty, 184

Kenney, Lorne, 145

Kerhanovich, George, 80, 118

Kitchener Jail, 121

Koski, John, 139

Kuehnbaum, Bill, 138, 139, 206, 207, 264, 149

Lab workers. *See* Technologists

Labour, Bureau of, 13

Labour, Ministry of, 163, 198, 262

Labour board. *See* Ontario Labour Relations Board

Labour code, 1943, 66; 1975 changes to, 161

Labour legislation, 91. *See also* Ontario Labour Relations Act

Labour Relations Act. *See* Ontario Labour Relations Act

Labour relations, 67, 69; Bill 217, 129; formalization of, after 1969, 126-27; institutionalization and

305

professionalization of in 1960s, 65-66; pressure from rank and file, 1950s and 1960s, 68-69. *See also* Government-civil service relations; Management-worker relations; Ontario Labour Relations Act
Labour unrest, 36, 161
Ladd, Harvey, 216
Lakeshore Psychiatric Hospital: closure protest, 189-90
Lands and Forests, Department of, 3, 10, 14, 23-24, 33; management style in, 56-58; reorganization into Ministry of Natural Resources, 117-18. *See also* Logging
Lane, Art, 78, 79-80, 164, 224, 252, 257, 258, 259, 269
Lang, Neil, 57, 58, 118, 119, 120, 123
Lang, Vernon, 115
Lankin, Frances, ii, 212, 213, 214-15, 246-47, 255
Laughren, Floyd, ii, 138, 151
Lavigne, Merv: case against OPSEU as his bargaining agent, 270; over dues checkoff, 270-71
Last Post: on Jones firing, 142
Layoffs, resulting from COGP changes, 148; 1975, 187. *See also* Cutbacks, government
Leake, Albert, 11
Lee, Pam, 242, 247
Leluk, Nick, 230
Lenehan, Gary, 262
Lewis, David, 85
Lewis, Stephen, 113, 168, 179, 184; on CECBA, 132, 133-34; call for restraint in public spending, 183
Liberal party: on CECBA, 132
Liberty, Jerry, 189
List, Wilf, 222
Little, Stan, 205
Little, Judge Walter, 90; as special advisor on government-CSAO relations, 93-94. *See also* Little Commission on provincial bargaining policy

Little Commission on provincial bargaining policy, 90; report of, 126; academic analysis of report, 96; CSAO reaction to report, 95; government action on report, 96; recommendations of, 95
Living and Learning. See Hall-Dennis report
Logging, 113; MacAlpine's leak, 233-35; practices, 233-34
London Life, 159
Lord, Eric, 137-38
Louttit, Neil, 243
Loyal Orange Lodge, 10
Loyal Order of Foresters, 10
Lunel, Ruth, 241

MacAlpine, Don, 233-35
MacDonald, Donald (CCF), 48, 49, 68, 113
MacDonald, Donald (CLC president), 205
Macdonald, H.I., 109-10
Macdonnell, J.M., 36
Mace, Harold, 125
Macleod, A.A., 48
MacMurchy, Dr. Helen, 9
MacNeil, Helen, 242
Madness, 260
Mail and Empire, 32-33
Majesky, Wally, 218
"Making It Public," 258
Management Board, 153; creation of, 110; assigned technical control over civil service, 130; and CECBA, 153-54, 157-58; meeting with Gemmell and Morse over COGP, 148; responsibility for personnel policy shared with CSC, 113
Management-worker relations: arm's length, 56-57; in remote areas, 56
Mann, William: on Ontario jails, 103
Manning, Ernest, 112; as member of citizens' coalition, 159
Manpower programs: under George

Drew, 41
Manpower training, select committee on, 101-2
Marshall, Barb, 244
Martin, Ron, 138, 140; 1984 CAAT academic bargaining team, 268; runs for president of OPSEU, 269
Masons, 10
McCarthy, Laura, 4-5
McCarthyism, Canadian-style, 44
McConville, Sean, 230
McCutcheon, J.M., 18, 19, 20, 21, 22, 23, 24, 25, 27, 31
McDermott, Dennis, 206, 221-22
McKay, Paul: history of Ontario Hydro, 185
McKechnie ambulance service, Collingwood, 227
McKeough, Darcy, 105, 108, 113, 128-29, 130, 182, 184, 186, 188, 190; bias toward using public money to subsidize free enterprise, 184-85
McKeough-Henderson report. *See* Henderson report
McKessock, Robert, 230
McLachlan, Karen, 259
McManus, D.T., 33
McNaughton, Charles, 109, 128, 130, 132, 133, 147
McNeel, Dr. B.H., 103, 104
McRuer, J.C., 96
Meagher, Terry, 149, 218
Media. *See* Public relations
Mediation: Corrections, 216
Membership dues. *See* Union dues
Mercer Reformatory, 4
Merit system, 10, 18, 22, 23, 25, 27, 42, 68
Merrick, George, 233
Meuser, Jamie, 199
Michener, Roland, 44, 45, 46
Mileage allowances, 133, 179
Millard, Allan, 171, 205
Millard, Charlie, 171
Miller, Frank, 187, 189, 191, 258

Mini-Skools, strike at, 250-51
Minimum Wage Board, 16; minimum wage for women, proposed by CSAO, 16
Ministerial responsibility, 114
Minty, Mary, 4
Mohawk College, 211
Moran, Dorothy, 253-54
Morancy, Cec, 56, 82-83
Morand, Donald, 229
Morgan, Jill, 242
Morgentaler, Dr. Henry, 249
Morse, Ron, 148; resignation of, 154
Moscovitch, Alan, 190
Mowat, Sir Oliver, 1, 2, 7, 11
Mr. X: leak to OPSEU re prison overcrowding, 230-32
Municipal workers' strike, 132
Murray, Heather, 54, 60-61, 240, 242, 244, 260

National Citizens' Coalition, 160; Charter case (Lavigne) against OPSEU's right to use union dues for community and political campaigns, 160, 270-71; newspaper ads, 167; precursor of, 159-60. *See also* Brown, Colin
National Union of Provincial Government Employees, 206-7
Native people: right to administer welfare, 100
Natural Resources, Ministry of, 113, 117, 233
NDP (New Democratic Party): and Social Contract Act, ii; re CECBA, 131, 132, 133-34; 1990 election victory, 235; OPSEU support of, 228
Negotiations: bargaining strategy, 166, 228; CAAT academic 1972, 139; CAAT academic 1983, 267; CAAT support staff, 209-10; civil service, 1974, 178-79; Corrections 1979, 214-17; Corrections 1982, 228-29, 261; under early 1980s wage controls, 222-23; first working-conditions/labour

relations agreement, 178-79; general operational category, 1974, 165-70; government bargaining policy, 214; health and safety issues, 255; Inflation Restraint Act five per cent guideline, 222; institutional care workers' 1982 settlement, 261; institutional care workers' 1985 settlement, 263; limits on in CECBA, union opposition to, 143-44; from a management agenda, 127; militant wage negotiations of 1971, 128; new focus on male/female wage disparities, 251-52; 1959 wage talks, 72; pre-1975 style for CAAT academic, 264; wage controls of 1982-84, bargaining in advance of, 220; right to negotiate effects of technological change, 255; Ryerson settlement, 268. *See also* Bargaining legislation; Bargaining rights
"New Ontario," 2
Niagara College, 202
Niagara Parks Commission, 88
Nice, Fred, 58, 59, 61, 69; on bargaining rights, 76
Nixon, Robert, 132, 183
Noad, Frederick, 33
Noel, S.J.R., 7, 9
Norman, G.G. ("Jake"), 148, 149, 150, 151, 159, 165, 169, 173, 177; abolition of his position as general manager, 175; becomes general manager, 154-55; and commission of inquiry into jail conditions, 213; dissatisfaction with CECBA amendments, 159; first working-conditions negotiations, 178; and "Free the Servants" campaign, 152-58; at 1974 convention, 152, 173; progressive attitudes of, 176; resentment of, by members, 176; rivalry with O'Flynn, 173-76, 199; staff support of, 176
North Bay *Nugget,* 270
North Bay Psychiatric Hospital, 60-61, 87, 122, 136, 137, 151, 242; assaults on staff, 261; fight to save centre, 260
Northern College, Haileybury School of Mines, 270
Northern Miner, 270
Northwestern Regional Centre for the developmentally handicapped, 122
NUPGE. *See* National Union of Provincial Government Employees
Nurses, 87, 104, 204, 239, 242
Nurses' association, 91

Oath of secrecy, 44, 232, 234; Folz's revelations on prison conditions, 229-30; MacAlpine's revelations on logging practices, 233-34
OECA. *See* Ontario Educational Communications Authority
Office and Professional Employees International Union (OPEIU), 195
Office workers: in community colleges, 211; merger with clerical groups, 252-53; technology, impact on, 252; wage increase, 220; wage rollback, 221. *See also* VDTs
Official Seal of Ontario, 6, 10
Offler, John, 82
OFL. *See* Ontario Federation of Labour
O'Flynn, Sean, 151, 175, 176, 207, 223, 224, 225, 228, 247; CAAT support strike 1979, 210-11; change of union direction under, 202-3; conviction of, re 1979 Corrections strike, 212, 215, 217, 219; Corrections strike, 215, 217; election as first vice-president, 173; election as president, 171, 200-1; health and safety issues, 255; moving on to OFL, 269; occupation of Centennial College president's office, 218; position on government offer in 1978 CAAT support negotiations, 210; rejects CAAT academic request for survey funds, 267; retreat on institutional care strike threat, 1981, 219; rivalry with Norman, 173-76, 199; stand on talks with government on new job

classification system, 252; steps down as president, 227, 231-32; vision for OPSEU, 202-4; and wage controls 1982-84, 222, 123
O'Grady, John, 165, 166, 204, 207; opposition to structural change in divisions, 237
OHIP, 120
OISE. *See* Ontario Institute for Studies in Education
OJC. *See* Ontario Joint Council
OLRA. *See* Ontario Labour Relations Act
OLRA sector, 226; as percentage of OPSEU membership; defined as the "Broader Public Service," 227
Ontario Ambulance Operators' Association, 227
Ontario Anti-Poverty Coalition, 188
Ontario commission on government appointments, 1895, 6
Ontario Committee on Taxation, 98
Ontario Council for Community Alternatives to Prison, 229
Ontario Economic Council: 1972 report, 114; 1974 study, 115; 1977 poll on government spending, 187
Ontario Educational Communications Authority (OECA), 98
Ontario Federation of Community College Academic Associations, 138
Ontario Federation of Labour (OFL), 188, 218, 269; Bill 70, 198; brief on Henderson report, 189; 1979 convention, 207; press conference on government cutbacks, 189
Ontario Hospital for the Insane, 22
Ontario Housing Corporation, 114; setting up of, 98
Ontario Human Rights Commission, 87
Ontario Hydro, 32, 184-85; nuclear energy, 185
Ontario Hydro-Electric Power Commission, 8
Ontario Institute for Studies in Education (OISE), opening of, 99
Ontario Joint Council (OJC): increasing power of, 92; instability of, 77; setting up of, 75; "tea and crumpets affair," 126; weakness of, 85
Ontario Labour Relations Act (OLRA), 52, 87, 152, 226; 1971 changes, 160; problems caused by 1971 changes, 160-61
Ontario Labour Relations Board, 161; ruling against CSAO's right to represent workers in a private institution, 195; ruling on organizing of technologists and radiologists, 196
Ontario Law Reform Commission, 235
Ontario Liquor Boards Employees' Union, 207
Ontario Psychological Association, 196
Ontario Public Service Employees Union. *See* OPSEU
Ontario Society of Medical Technologists, 195, 196
Ontario Supreme Court: ruling on wage control law, 222
Ontario Welfare Council, 188
Onyschuk, Jim, 89, 149, 192-93
OPEIU. *See* Office and Professional Employees International Union
OPSEU conventions: 1975, 180; 1978, 200; 1982: highlights right to strike, 219; 1980, 248; 1984, 268-69
OPSEU executive board, 172, 175, 207, 223-24; agrees to join NUPGE, 207; first election of president by convention delegates (1974), 171; lobbies on women's issues, 245, 248-49; 1978 elections, 199-200; 1984 elections, 269; PWC funding proposal, 248; refuse to fund CAAT academic survey, 267
OPSEU News: on wage and price controls, 180; tabloid style (1975-77), 248; discounts offered in, 193; on abortion, 250
OPSEU staff. *See* Union staff

309

OPSEU: new name adopted (from Civil Service Association of Ontario to Ontario Public Service Employees Union), 170; incorporated status maintained, 173; new constitution, 170, 171-73; structure under new constitution, 172; new adversarial relationship with government, 178-79; evolution towards social unionism, 182, 188-90; response to Henderson report, 187-90; establishes community-based coalitions, 188; affiliation with union federations, 204-7; and NUPGE, 206-7; nature of special campaigns, 192; pressures to decentralize, 197; attempt to rejoin CLC, 206; achieves "union" stature with CLC membership, 207; 1980 convention, 248; declining militancy, early 1980s, 218-26; campaign re Bill 70, 198; 1982 convention focus on right to strike, 219; response to 1982-84 wage controls, 220-22; 1984 convention, 250, 268-69; Warrian's attempts to change internal structures, 223-24; structural change in divisions along occupational lines, 237-38
Oram, Ivor, 193, 194, 195-96, 197
Organization of Resources Committee, 17
Organizing: CSAO right to organize in public sector, 88; effect of labour code changes on, 160; in health-care sector, 194-97; late 1960s recruiting drive, 94; of correctional officers, 89; outside the civil service, 225-26; paramedics, 196
Orillia, hospital for retarded children, 59
Orillia Hospital for Idiots, 11
Oshawa General Hospital, 195
Ottawa *Citizen:* on OPSEU lawsuit over prison overcrowding, 231
Oxenham, Sid, 205
Oxford Regional Centre, 123

Panitch, Leo, 180
Panitch, Melanie, 259
Paramedics, 194, 195, 196, 226
Parks, provincial, 11, 114, 118
Part-time workers, 94, 139, 209
PASS. *See* Power and Action through Steward Skills
Paternalism, 9. *See also* Tory paternalism
Patronage, 5-7, 61
Paul, Jim, 261
Peden, Jim, 58
Pellerin, Norm, 259
Pensions, 13, 20, 54, 62, 95, 228; indexing of, 116, 162; raised by Frost, 51
Pentland, H.C.: writing on CSAO, 134
"People First," welfare pamphlet, 236
Personnel director, first appointment of, 66
Personnel: departments of, 68; government attitudes towards civil service workforce, 43; personnel council, 66
Peterborough Civic Hospital, 195
Peterson, David, 258
Phipps, R.W., 11
Planning/programming/budgeting system (PPBS), 110, 111, 112, 114
Podrebarac, George, 229
Policy and priorities committee, of government, 110
Political involvement of civil servants, prohibition of, 7-8, 44-45, 76-77, 156, 207. *See also* Public Service Act
Political rights of civil servants, 76-77
Pollock, Neil, 89, 141-42
Porter, John (*The Vertical Mosaic*): on elitism in education, 41, 101
Porter, Arthur: re Conestoga College, 139
Power and Action through Steward Skills, 225
PPBS. *See* Planning/programming/budgeting system
Presgrave, Ross, 83
Prison system, 73-74: effect of COGP on, 121; OPSEU lawsuit re over-

crowding, 229-32, 213, 214, 229-30; reform of, 11, 212-13. *See also* Corrections; Correctional officers; individual jails; Mr. X
Privatization, 112, 187, 190, 207
Privatization Council, 190
Professionals, exclusion of, from CSAO membership, 95
Provincial Institute of Trades, 89
Provincial elections. *See* Elections, provincial
Provincial Women's Committee (PWC), 248
PSAC. *See* Public Service Employees of Canada
PSGB. *See* Public Service Grievance Board
Psychiatric institutions, 59, 164; changes in methods of dealing with patients with introduction of drug therapy, 105; cutbacks, 259-61; effect of COGP reforms on, 121-23; introduction of female nurses on male wards, 104; introduction of "wonder drugs," 104; reforms in, 103; underfunding of, 60; working conditions in, 256. *See also* Health-care sector; Institutional care; Institutional care workers; individual institutions
Public Accounts Committee, 227
Public Institutions Inspection panel, 230
Public relations, 144, 153-54, 156-58, 189, 192, 193, 225
Public sector vs. private sector union internal structures, 136
Public Service Act, 18, 22, 156; changes re employer-employee relationship proposed by CSAO, 47; definition of political rights of civil servants, 76; 1878, 3; 1947, 44; 1947, weakening of CSC, 42; 1962 amendment banning political activity, 75-77; workplace-rules wording transferred to collective agreements, 178
Public Service Alliance of Canada (PSAC), 237, 205
Public Service Grievance Board (PSGB), 72, 162; CSAO brief on, 162
Public Service Labour Relations Tribunal: CSAO right to appoint representatives to, 159
PWC. *See* Provincial Women's Committee

Quality of education. *See* CAAT academic - quality of education
Quality of Working Life program, 256, 262
Quebec's Quiet Revolution, 98
Queen's Park Area Council, 247
Quetico Park, 118

Rae, Bob, 222
Rand, Judge Ivan, 90, 126
Rand Formula, 91, 92
Red Toryism, 106
Reform Insitutions, Minister of, 82
Reforms in civil service. *See* Government expansion and reform
Redick, D.L., poem by, 169
Regional government, 105-6; effects of, 106
Regional offices (OPSEU), setting up of, 197
Reisman, Simon, 113
Relief fund established by CSAO, 1931, 30
Renfrew jailhouse, 103
Renwick, James, 131
Request for Proposals (RFPs), 112
Retirement, 52; union staff, 143. *See also* Compulsory retirement; Pensions; Scientific retirement
Richards, George, 148, 177
Rideau Regional Centre, 259. *See also* Smiths Falls centre for the developmentally handicapped
Road crews, 119. *See also* Highways workers
Robarts, John, 95, 96, 101, 160; chair-

311

man-of-the-board style of, 109; as member of citizens' coalition, 159; cancellation of Indian Development Branch, 100; endorsation of Gordon report, 68; reluctance to set up COGP, 109; resignation of, 125
Rooney, Pat, 118
Rosenberg, Judge J., 230-31
Rowe, Garnet, 122-23, 137
Rowett, Mike, 144, 147, 176
Royal commission on labour disputes, 126
Rutton, Mary Lou, 262
Ryder, Alick, 234, 235
Ryerson settlement, 268

Salsberg, Joe, 44
Salvation Army, 229
Sammons, Ev, 122, 148-49, 193, 201, 248, 263; runs for president of OPSEU, 269
Sanderson, E.M., 62
Sargent, Eddie, 113
Sarra, Martin, 200
Sauer, Larry, 208, 209, 211
"Save Bluewater Week," 258
School for the Blind, 22
Schwarz, Donald, 180
Science Centre, opening of, 98
Scientific management, iii, 19, 21-28, 110, 127, 128
Scientific retirement, 20
Scott, J.R. ("Rollie"), 127, 130, 133, 154, 155, 157, 160, 161, 167, 168
Scott, Ian, 229, 230, 231
Scott, Viki, 256, 258
Seath, John, 11
Sebastian, Cam, 45
Segal, Hugh, 116
SEIU. *See* Service Employees International Union
Seneca College, 208, 245, 265, 267
Service Employees International Union (SEIU), 195, 196
Seville, Pauline, 177, 181, 194, 210, 221, 224, 247, 251; Art Gallery of Ontario organizing drive, 226-27
Sheridan College, 138, 248, 266, 268
Shewfelt, Deb, 189
Shulman, Morton, 109, 113
Sick days, 52
Sick leave, 116
Silinsky, Helen, 136, 149
Simonson, Tony, 74
Sinclair, Dr. S.B., 24-25
"Sixty Thousand Voices" (anti-CECBA song), 156
Skolnick, Michael, 269-70; report of, 267
Slee, Peter, 156, 176, 177, 180-82, 188, 189, 211, 221, 224, 250-51
Smith, Russ, 206
Smiths Falls centre for the developmentally handicapped, 122, 136-37, 219, 256, 259
Social assistance. *See* Welfare
Social contract, iii, v
Social Contract Act, ii, iv
Social Planning Council, 188
Social unionism, 182, 188-90, 204, 228, 232, 271; women's influence, 249
Sons of England, 10
Southwestern Regional Centre, 262
Sovereignty of elected officials, principle of, 95
Special Operations, 192
Speirs, Rosemary, 168
Squire, S.L., 26
St. Clair College, 242
St. Thomas psychiatric hospital, 33, 218, 219, 256; campaign to save centre, 258
START centre. *See* St. Thomas psychiatric hospital
Stellman, Jeanne, 262-63
Stephenson, Bette, 218
Stevens, Lillian, 193
Stewart, Ed, 108
Stoddart, William: on community colleges, 139
Stokes, Jack, 233-34

Storey, Roy, 54, 119, 166-67
Strike, right to, 94, 219; denial of, iii, 71, 95, 147, 153; high school teachers, 161; Supreme Court ruling on, 222
Strike fund, 219
Strike pay, 210
Strikebreakers, 270. *See also* Lavigne, Merv
Strikes: blanket prohibition of under CECBA, 132; CAAT academic 1984, 263; CAAT academic 1984, 268, 269; CAAT support staff 1979, 209-12; Corrections, 215-17; at Fleck Manufacturing, 184; general operational category strike vote, 1974, 166-68; Guelph University, 88-89; institutional care strike threat, 1981, 218-19; Mini-Skools, 250-51; by municipal workers in reaction to CECBA, 132; provincial rotating strikes threat, 1971; strike vote over AIB, 180-81; Windsor autoworkers' strike for a union shop, 1940s, 44. *See also* Back-to-work legislation
Stylianos, Susan, 243, 247, 266, 268
Super-ministries (Social Development, Resources and Justice), 111
Supreme Court of Canada: CSAO case on political activity prohibition, 159; OPSEU case on right to strike, 222; OPSEU case on suspension of bargaining rights for public sector, 222; ruling on Lavigne case, 271
Swan, Ken, 181
Szablowski, George, 115

Tait, Jim, 120, 142, 175, 219
Taxation, 65, 98, 186-87; corporate vs. personal, 191; provincial sales tax, 65
Teachers, public school, 43, 161, 162, 204; seek right to strike, 161
Teaching Profession Act, 1944, 43
Technologists, lab and radiation, 194-96, 226
Technology: bargaining rights over technological change, 159
Temple, Bill, 47
"Temps," 19, 62
Theobald, Ted, 200
Thomson report, 238
Thunder Bay Psychiatric Hospital, 57, 61, 121
Timmins Psychiatric Hospital, 189
Todd, Andy, 146, 150, 155, 157, 168, 171, 174, 176-77, 181, 203, 221, 251, 252; first working-conditions/labour relations negotiations, 1974, 178-79; gains made before wage controls, 220; and community colleges, 264
Tollgate operators, Burlington, 146
Toronto Board of Trade, 127; 1960s attempt by CSAO to join, 81
Toronto Labour Council, 28
Toronto *Star*, 4; on CECBA, 132; on CSAO growing militancy, 71; Trower interview, 168
Toronto *Sun*, 193; on VDTs, 254
Toronto *Telegram*, 43
Toronto Transit Commission, 8, 49
Tory paternalism, ii, 9-10, 11, 12, 25, 72; death of, 182; vs. scientific management, 128
Touche Ross, 190
Trades and Labour Congress, 45; CSAO referendum on joining, 51
Transport and Highways, departments of: merger, 117
Tree-planting, 123
Trilateral Commission, 182
The Trillium, 52, 72, 81; 1956 song about women workers in institutions, 63-64
Trower, Chris, 165-69, 177
Trudeau, Pierre, 179-81; Trudeaumania, 109; and wage controls on public sector, 219, 220
Tumpane, Frank, 74

UGWO. *See* United Government Workers of Ontario
Union dues, 45, 69, 90, 91; disputed by

313

Lavigne and National Citizens' Coalition, 270-71; effect on, of labour code changes, 169. *See also* Checkoff
Union militancy, growth in, 177
Union security, 88, 90-94; automatic membership and dues checkoff, 90-91; CSAO right to represent entire civil service, 91; of CSAO, as serving government interests, 92-93
Union staff: anti-Bowen faction, 142; motion re mandatory retirement at 65, 143; 1973 strike over CSAO board "witch-hunt," 145, 147; demand for job security, 143; relationship with Warrian, 224; seen as threat to membership control, 143, 176-77; unionize in 1969
Unionism, barriers to, 53-58
Unionization: factors favouring, 80
United Farmers of Ontario, 20, 21
United Government Workers of Ontario (UGWO), 91
Upshaw, Fred, 105, 155; election as OPSEU vice-president, 269
Uranium miners, 198
Usher, Sean, 257

Vacations, 37, 52
Vallance, Susie, 209, 210, 224, 240, 241, 243, 245, 209
van Beinum, Hans, 256
Varsity Stadium auction, 32
VDTs (video display terminals), 209, 253-55
Veterans, 23, 25, 53-55; hiring priority given to, 54, 80
Vezina, Mel, 57, 121
Video display terminals. *See* VDTs

Wage and price controls: 1975, 179-81; lifting of, in 1947, 45; 1975 strike vote over, 180-81
Wage controls in public sector, 1982-84, 219-23, 267; industrial unions' apathy towards, 221-22; rollback of clerical wages, 221. *See also* Inflation Restraint Act
Wage freezes, 1975, 187
Wages: provincial compared to federal civil service, 70; increase in from 1950 to 1960, 53-54; issue during WW I, 14; male/female disparity, 4, 14, 22, 238; 1919 brief on wages, 14-15; 1925 wage demands, 26; mid-1940s demands that wages be indexed to cost of living, 45; public compared to private sector, 126, 153, 222-23; struggle for increases after WW I, 15. *See also* Negotiations
Walshe, Shannon, 118
Ward, John, 148, 150, 171, 220
Warrian, Peter, 202, 223-24
Welfare capitalism, 26
Welfare expenditures: province's attempt to pass costs on to municipalities (the "integration" scheme), 237
Welfare recipients: policy encouraging independence, 238
Welfare reform, agitation for, 236-37
Welfare workers: government meets with OPSEU over workload complaints, 237; responsibilities of, 235-38; coalitions with clients, 238; different types of, 236; excessive workloads, 236-38; own division established, 237-38
Welfare: payments of, in relation to poverty line, 191
Wells, Ann, 241
Whistleblowers' rights, 233-35
Whitby Jail, 230
Whitby Psychiatric Hospital, 1960s reforms in, 104
Whitleyism, 16, 38-39
Whitney, James, 1, 2, 7, 10, 11, 13
Wildcat strikes, 36; by Hydro workers in reaction to CECBA, 132; by Don Jail guards, 1968, 89-90
Williams, Ross, 56
Williams, Vic, 121, 142, 173, 175, 200

Williamson, John, 239
Wilson, Kevin, 213, 214-15, 229, 230, 231, 232
Winkler, Eric, 148, 153, 154, 158, 166, 179, 184; brochure on inflation, 157
Withers, Ross, poem by, 169-70
Wolfensberger, Wolfe, 257
Women: activists, 241-50, 248; in CAAT support staff, 208-9; child care, 245, 249, 250-51, 253; disadvantages of, 241-42; discrimination against married women, 1950, 62-63; discrimination against within the union, 240, 241; early days in civil service, 3-5; effects of COGP on, 124; equal pay for work of equal value, 86-87, 239, 245, 252; exclusion from technical jobs, 239-40; exploitation of, 11; Fleck strike, 184, 246; government discrimination against, 238; harassment, 4-5, 249; health and safety issues, 253; high proportion of, in institutional care jobs, 256; as institutional care workers, 218; job security after maternity leave, 239; limited effect of wage and price controls on women secretaries, 180; low-paid ghettos, 251, 256; male/female wage disparities, 4, 14, 22, 62, 238; married women as "temps," 62; maternity leave, 239; nature of female civil service population in 1950s, 63; networking, 243; new staff position to deal with women's issues, 243; 1956 song about women workers in institutions, 63-64; 1972 motion on child care expenses at CSAO convention, 240; OPSEU position of equal opportunities coordinator, 211, 244; as organizers, 241; organizing of, 241; paid maternity leave, 249, 253; pension rights, 239; as a proportion of civil service, 4, 62, 247; Provincial Women's Committee, 248; report on female wage ghetto, 243; representation on CAAT bargaining teams, 208, 209; segregation of male and female wards in institutions, 63; sexism, 241, 244; sexual harassment, 239, 240, 244, 245, 247, 253; technology, impact on, 252; treatment of female jail guards, 246; under-representation in CSAO, 28; under-representation in management positions, 239; VDTs, 253-55
Women Crown Employees' Equality Programs, 238
Women's caucuses, 244, 245, 246, 249, 250; formal caucus formed, 1976, 243; Region 5, 242-43; Toronto Women's Caucus, 249
Women's issues, 240, 245, 247, 248, 249, 253
Women's movement, 240, 242
Work hours, 31, 46, 47; in civil service as compared to private sector, 31; five-day week, 52; 48-hour week, 37; flexibility, 116
Workers for Social Responsibility, 238
Working conditions: public vs. private, 26-27
Workmen's Compensation Board, 8, 18, 92-93
World War I, 14, 16-17
World War II, 30, 40; economic upturn in, 36; labour unrest, 36

York Regional ambulance service, 227
York University conference on government five-year plan for institutional care, 258

Zimmerman, Adam, 190